D1453544

CHANGING CULTURES

The Skolt Lapps Today

CHANGING CULTURES

General Editor: Jack Goody

The aim of the series is to show how specific non-industrial societies have developed and changed in response to the conditions of the modern world. Each volume will present a comprehensive analysis, drawing on recent fieldwork, of the contemporary organization of a particular society, but cast in a dynamic perspective that relates the present both to the past of the society and to the external forces that have impinged upon it. By concentrating on peoples that have been the subjects of earlier studies, some of these volumes will also reflect the developing interests and concerns of the social sciences.

Also in this series
The Nayars Today by Christopher J. Fuller.

The Skolt Lapps Today

TIM INGOLD
Lecturer, Department of Social Anthropology
University of Manchester

CAMBRIDGE UNIVERSITY PRESS
CAMBRIDGE
LONDON · NEW YORK · MELBOURNE

Published by the Syndics of the Cambridge University Press
The Pitt Building, Trumpington Street, Cambridge CB2 1RP
Bentley House, 200 Euston Road, London NW1 2DB
32 East 57th Street, New York, NY 10022, USA
296 Beaconsfield Parade, Middle Park, Melbourne 3206, Australia

Printed in Great Britain at the
University Printing House, Cambridge
(Harry Myers, University Printer)

Library of Congress Cataloguing in Publication Data
Ingold, Tim, 1948–
The Skolt Lapps today.

(Changing cultures)
Bibliography: p.
1. Lapps–Finland. I. Title.
DL971. L2153   947.1'7   76–8289
ISBN 0 521 21299 5
ISBN 0 521 29090 2 pbk.

9–14– 78

Contents

Illustrations and Tables

Tables

Foreword

The research on which this study is based was carried out principally between 1970 and 1973, supported by a studentship from the Social Science Research Council (UK) and a concurrent studentship from Churchill College, Cambridge. After an initial three months at Cambridge, I spent January–April 1971 as a visiting student at the Department of Social Anthropology, University of Bergen, Norway. Fieldwork, aided by a grant from the Emslie Horniman Anthropological Scholarship Fund, was carried out over a period of sixteen months between May 1971 and September 1972. During autumn 1972 I was again at the University of Bergen, returning to Cambridge for the period from January to August 1973. A scholarship from the Finnish Ministry of Education enabled me to spend the year 1973–4 writing up, and teaching, at the Department of Sociology, University of Helsinki, and to make two brief trips to the field in August–September 1973 and April 1974. Writing up was completed during 1974–5 whilst holding a post at the Department of Social Anthropology, University of Manchester. To all those bodies that have provided financial support I express my appreciation.

Acknowledgements are due to John Barnes and Fredrik Barth, who supervised my work at Cambridge and Bergen respectively, and to Ray Abrahams, who helped me with initial research proposals, for general academic guidance and pertinent criticism.

To all the anthropologists at Bergen and the sociologists at Helsinki, for the intellectual stimulus, kindness and hospitality which I received in both departments. In particular, to Arne Runeberg, for helping to make my year at Helsinki a profitable and enjoyable one.

In the field of Lappish studies, I owe acknowledgement to Bert Pelto (Connecticut), for initial encouragement to go into a field already charted by him; to Harald Eidheim (Tromsø), Vilhelm Aubert (Oslo), Erkki Asp (Turku) and Ludger Müller-Wille (Münster) for advice and assistance. I have greatly benefited from discussion with the authority on Skolt and Lapp Affairs in Finland, Karl Nickul; as well as with Pekka Sammallahti, Samuli Aikio and Mikko Korhonen, all of the University of Helsinki. I owe a special acknowledgement to Waling Gorter (Amsterdam), who was engaged in fieldwork just over the Norwegian border in Neiden during my own period in the field. Our collaboration during fieldwork was of mutual benefit, and enabled me to build up a more complete picture of

Foreword

Skolt relations over the international border than would otherwise have been possible.

Salme Korhonen, librarian at the Lapp Department of Rovaniemi City Library, has provided me with invaluable bibliographic assistance. I also benefited from access to the fine collections in the libraries of the Scott Polar Research Institute in Cambridge, and the Finnish Literary Society in Helsinki. I received archival assistance from Oulu Provincial Archives Department and the Land Registry at Rovaniemi. Markus Petsalo, priest of Lapland Orthodox parish, and Antero Niva, minister of Inari Lutheran parish, provided access to their parish registers for genealogical information.

A number of local officials provided me with help and information during fieldwork; including the former mayor of Inari Commune, Kullervo Tumme, health-visitors Jaana Koutonen and Paula Feodoroff, police-officer Lauri Kiiskinen, employment-officer Arvo Forsman, headmasters Martti Loimu (Sevettijärvi) and Pentti Riipa (Inari), and reindeer association secretaries Matti Sverloff (Näätämö) and Sulo Sarre (Vätsäri). Special thanks are due to building-inspector Mikko Rantala and his wife Elli.

At the provincial capital of Rovaniemi, I received help and encouragement from Oula Näkkäläjärvi of the Provincial Government, Yrjö Alaruikka of the Union of Reindeer Associations (Paliskuntain Yhdistys), and Pekka Sjögren of Lapland Radio.

To the Skolts and all the other local people I got to know during fieldwork I extend my deepest gratitude, particularly to my neighbours at Sevettijärvi and Rautaperäjärvi. For kindness and hospitality, special thanks go to the families of Pekka and Liisa Feodoroff, Olga Moshnikoff, Piera and Maria Porsanger, Mikko and the late Marena Gavriloff, and Anni and Pauli Kiviniemi.

Acknowledgement is due above all to my wife Anna, who acted for six months as co-fieldworker, helped to sort and file fieldnotes, typed up numerous drafts, and has been a source of continual insight and encouragement.

Notes on the text

Ethnographic present

The 'present' is taken as 1972, except where specific reference is made to
future developments. Where a precise datum line is required, for example in
defining age-population classes, the 'present' is fixed at New Year, 1972.

Proper names

The Skolt community at Sevettijärvi is unique, making it impossible to
mask its identity. Most place-names in the region can be readily found
from the map. I have therefore used real names for places throughout,
unless special mention is made to the contrary. Names are given in their
Finnish forms for places in Finland, and in their Norwegian forms for
places in Norway.

In order to protect the anonymity of individuals mentioned in the
text, they are not referred to by name. Where it is necessary to distinguish
a number of individuals, they are designated by capital letters.

Currency

Finnish money is reckoned in marks, abbreviated Fmk. There are 100
pennies in the mark. In 1972, the rate of exchange was approximately ten
marks to the pound sterling. In relation to Norwegian currency, one mark
was worth 1.60 crowns (Nkr).

Native terms

In order not to confuse a reader unfamiliar with the native languages, I
have kept Finnish terms to a minimum, and have avoided Skolt terms
altogether. Terms are presented in standard Finnish orthography, itali-
cized, and introduced with the abbreviation 'Fin.'. The plural is formed
by the suffix *-t*, and sometimes entails slight changes in preceding syllables.
Where quotations are given in original translation from Finnish sources,
they are marked 'trans'.

1 Introduction

The Skolts in historical perspective

It is not known when, or from where, the ancestors of the present Lappish population arrived in the projecting tongue of land bordered on the east by the White Sea, on the west by the Norwegian Sea, and on the north by the Barents Sea. Physical differences between the Lapps and later Scandinavian and Finnish colonists point to a long period of prior separation, whereas strong linguistic similarities between Lappish and Finnish bear witness to centuries of close contact. It seems probable that a population of hunters and fishermen gradually spread north and west from the Russian interior into Fennoscandia, following the movements of subarctic fauna as the ice-sheet from the last glaciation retreated slowly northwards. At the time of Finnish penetration, around the first century A.D., the indigenous population was sparsely scattered throughout all of Karelia and Finland except the south-west coastal periphery, as well as in the forests of northern Sweden and the Kola peninsula, and around the coasts north of the Arctic Circle from Lofoten to the White Sea. Only from around the twelfth century do records begin to designate this population by the term 'Lapp'. From this time onwards the retreat of Lappish settlement in Finland is historically documented, along with the extension of agricultural coloniz-ation from the south and west. In the sixteenth and seventeenth centuries, Lapps still inhabited the lake regions of central and eastern Finland, but by the nineteenth century they remained only in the northern extremity of the country, approximately above the 68° parallel. This retreat shows a striking correlation with the gradual elimination of wild reindeer stocks (Nickul 1970: 12-15).

As hunters and fishermen, the Lapps were loosely organized in small territorial bands (*siidat*[1]), whose constituent households moved seasonally between more or less dispersed dwelling or tent sites according to the availability of natural resources. Each *siita* was centred on a single village to which all its members returned for the slackest period in the productive cycle, between the New Year and early spring. Village sites were periodic-ally moved when surrounding grazing and firewood was exhausted. Among maritime groups the pattern of migration was linear, between summer fishing sites on the coast and autumn–winter hunting and fishing grounds inland. In the *siidat* of the interior forests, households dispersed radially from the winter village to exploit customary hunting and fishing grounds scattered throughout the territory. *Siita* borders were defined principally in relation to fishing waters and, though subject to negotiation, generally coincided with natural drainage boundaries.

The increasingly exploitative nature of contacts with settlers over the last six or seven centuries, at first indirectly through trade and taxation in hides and later directly through land appropriation, worked a transformation throughout these *siita* communities, generating widely divergent adaptations according to prevailing ecological conditions. In low-lying regions suitable for limited agriculture, Lapps responded to the increasing scarcity of game by establishing small farms, adopting a pattern of life superficially indistinguishable from that of their colonist neighbours. In the fertile inland river valleys and around the fjord coasts, farming was combined with a strong emphasis on fishing. On the higher, inland margins of the Scandinavian mountain chain, lying outside the limits of agriculture, the response was radically different. Lapps began to follow the migratory movements of the reindeer herds, which they sought not to hunt but to reproduce and accumulate as private property. As access to animals became conditional on ownership rather than territory, the *siita* broke free of territorial constraints and became a nomadic herding unit, whose migratory movements between forest winter pastures and mountain summer pastures became ever longer as the herds multiplied. This expansionary thrust, sometimes curtailed or redirected owing to international frontier restrictions, brought pastoralists into frequent conflict with the sedentary population, both indigenous and colonist alike. Many nomads became extremely wealthy, not only in reindeer but in hoards of gold and silver. The flamboyance of their dress and demeanour contrasted with the sobriety of the relatively poor sedentary farmers and fishermen, whom they regarded with some contempt. Although dating back no more than four centuries and embracing only a minority of the Lapp population, the distinctive style of life of these mountain reindeer pastoralists has earned them a central place in the popular conception of Lapp Culture.

Only those groups furthest removed from the incursions of colonists and pastoralists retained the original *siita* form until recent times. In the mid-nineteenth century, a territorial mosaic of *siita* units covered all but the southern coastal margin of the Kola peninsula, extending about as far west as the present border between Finland and the Soviet Union. Hunting still played an important part in the economy of these groups, although here too it was being replaced by a form of small-scale intensive pastoralism already practised by Lappish fishermen settled around the great Lake Inari to the west, where wild deer had become virtually extinct early in the century. The *siita* organization of the Kola Lapps to the east was modified through the immigration of Zyryan and Samoyed reindeer pastoralists from the Pechora river at the end of the nineteenth century, and after the revolution by collectivization measures. The more westerly groups remained more or less intact until disrupted by the effects of European hostilities in this century. Although no cultural discontinuity existed between these groups and their eastern neighbours, early travellers in the area described them as 'Skolts', apparently on account of a now extinct skin disease of that name to which they were supposedly prone.

It has been the fate of Skolt Lapp groups to inhabit a region lying on the pivot of the pendulum which, throughout European history, has marked the cultural and political divide between East and West. From the sixteenth century, the Skolt *siidat* represented the northern and western extremity of Tsarist influence. In 1532, the now legendary Saint Trifon founded an Orthodox monastery on the Petsamo river, whose religious and economic impact was felt throughout the region. The monks' efforts to convert the population to Christianity were at least superficially successful. Still today, the major cultural distinction between the Skolts and their western Lappish neighbours, apart from Russian dialectical influence, is their adherence to the Orthodox church rather than to Lutheranism or its more recent sectarian manifestations. However, the attempts of the monastery to usurp the Skolts' customary rights to land and fishing waters were curtailed

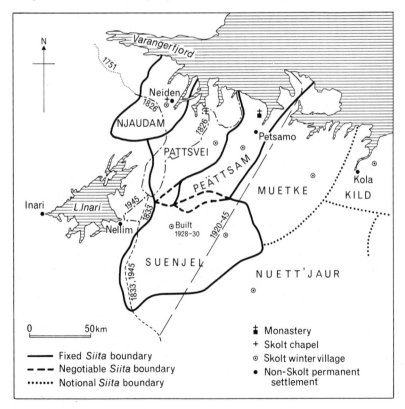

Fig. 1. The Skolt *siita* territories and settlement centres, in relation to international frontiers. Adapted from Tanner (1929: 226).

by a number of royal decrees issued between 1601 and 1775, including ·
one signed by Peter the Great and preserved by the Skolts into this century
(Mikkola 1941).

Seven *siidat* have been conventionally included under the Skolt caption,
of which five were maritime and two inland (fig. 1). The Russo-Finnish-
Norwegian frontier of 1826 bisected both Njaudam and Pattsvei *siidat*,
stunting former migratory movements. Further disruption among maritime
groups was caused by competition from wealthy nomadic Lapps extending
their migrations into Skolt territory, forcing the Skolts to abandon their
herds and settle as fishermen on the coast. The collapse of the coastal
exchange trade with the Russian *pomores,* following the revolution of
1917, cut off a vital source of supplies. What was left of the *siita* organization was thrown into chaos by the events of the First World War.

The situation after the war may be summarized as follows: of the
Skolt *siidat,* the coastal groups of Kild and Muetke, and the inland group
of Njuett' jaur, were left on the Soviet side of the frontier established by
the Treaty of Dorpat in 1920. Little is known of their present circumstances under Soviet rule. Of the remaining coastal groups, the few
surviving Skolts of Njaudam lived alongside Finnish immigrant colonists
in the Norwegian village of Neiden, and the inhabitants of Pattsvei and
Peättsam lay scattered and impoverished in permanent dwellings in the
region of Petsamo that was now ceded to Finland. Only one group avoided
complete disruption. This was the inland *siita* of Suenjel. The 1920
frontier had removed the eastern part of its territory, including the
winter village, but it remained otherwise intact on the Finnish side. A new
winter village was built with Finnish government assistance in 1928–30.
By the 1930s, conditions seemed set for a return to a more or less
traditional pattern of life in Suenjel, although contacts with neighbouring
groups, once frequent, were now either severed or curtailed. However
the men of the *siita,* already widely travelled through military service,
were also drawn into the development boom of Petsamo's inter-war
'golden era', as seasonal labourers in road construction, goods transpor-
tation, and nickel mining.

A detailed survey of the households, territorial divisions and migratory
movements of the Suenjel Skolts was made by Karl Nickul in 1938
(Nickul 1948). The *siita* then had a population of 229, constituting 38
households and representing seven patriclans. Most households maintained
dwellings in the new winter-village, whilst the *siita* territory was apportioned
into 'family areas' such that each household had a customary right to set
up cabins and exploit land and water resources within its allotted area.
Households would disperse from the winter-village for their fishing cabins
around the end of April, often moving between separate spring, summer
and autumn sites in different parts of their areas before returning to the
village for Christmas or the New Year. Patriclans, though they may once
have operated as exogamous units, no longer had any corporate functions.
Patrilineally inherited clan-names attested to descent from a common
ancestor, but most clans represented in Suenjel, including one of Karelian

origin, crosscut the boundaries of the *siita,* illustrating the possibility of territorial incorporation. The joint interests of the *siita* were represented by an assembly consisting of all male householders under an elected headman, which met annually in the winter-village. The assembly was the ultimate authority in all matters relating to the division or reallotment of areas, and acted as a tribunal for the settlement of internal disputes. Several authors have seen in the Lappish *siita* a perfect model of 'primitive communism' (e.g. Solem 1933, Tanner 1929); but with the loss of Suenjel after the Second World War, the extent to which this ideal measured up with practice can never be known.

Evacuation and resettlement

When the Winter War broke out between Finland and the Soviet Union in 1939–40, the Petsamo Skolts were evacuated to Tervola, in the south of Lapland province. They were able to return to their home territories for the short peace that followed, but found many of their dwellings destroyed. In 1944, the expulsion of the German army from Lapland necessitated a second and precipitate evacuation. This time the Skolts were moved far south to the environs of Kalajoki and Oulujoki in the region of Ostrobothnia (fig. 2). During this year-long evacuation period the Skolts suffered badly from malnutrition and disease (Nickul 1950).

On the conclusion of hostilities in 1945, Finland was obliged to cede the whole of Petsamo, including the *siita* territories of Suenjel, Pattsvei and Peättsam, to the Soviet Union. In view of their wartime allegiance to Finland and the uncertain future that might await them as Soviet citizens, the Skolts almost unanimously elected to remain in Finland. In 1945–6 they returned north to an area to the south-east of Lake Inari, not far from their former homeland, where they lived in old German barracks and makeshift cabins. Wage employment was readily available on postwar reconstruction sites and on a major Soviet hydroelectricity project over the border, but local conditions for reindeer management were poor.

The request of the Suenjel Skolts for a new territory in which their reindeer economy could be resumed was accepted by the Finnish government, and an area was designated for them in the sparsely inhabited region to the north and east of Lake Inari, adjoining the Norwegian frontier (fig. 2). With government finance, fifty-one permanent dwellings were constructed along a fifty-kilometre chain of lakes running through the area. Beside one of these lakes, Sevettijärvi, were built a school, church, and health clinic. It is by the name of this lake that the resettlement area has generally come to be known. In April 1949, the Suenjel Skolts moved to their new homes. Three Pattsvei families who had already set up in the area were also incorporated into the resettled community. The social organization of the Sevettijärvi community today, over two decades after the trauma of evacuation and resettlement, is the subject of this study.

A second, much smaller 'reservation' was designated for the remaining

5

Introduction

Skolts of Pattsvei and Peättsam origin, making up about a third of the total Skolt population, who stayed where they were in the south-east Inari region. Dwellings were built for them by the old Petsamo road between Ivalo and Nellim. These Skolts had long since abandoned the reindeer economy, and their post-war livelihood has been based on local wage employment supplemented by fishing.

Special legislation, enacted in 1955, granted Skolt householders title to the resettlement houses they occupied at the time, and to surrounding plots of land of up to three hectares in extent. The dwelling, together with its attached outbuildings and plot, technically constitutes the 'Skolt estate' (Fin. *kolttatila*). To prevent estates from passing out of Skolt hands, the law includes a fifty-year restriction on the mortgage or sale of property to outsiders. The accompanying ordinance specifies the borders of the Sevettijärvi and Nellim resettlement 'reservations', listing the privileges allowed to the Skolts within them: to collect firewood, to cut timber for building, to set up fishing cabins, to pasture livestock, and to gather hay, lichen and browse for their animals.

Prior to the fixing of the Norwegian–Finnish frontier in 1826, the greater part of the Sevettijärvi resettlement area had constituted autumn hunting and fishing grounds for the Skolts of the westernmost *siita,* Njaudam. Little evidence of their activities remains today; but Pattsvei Skolts resettled in the community still recognize distant kinship ties with the few descendants of Njaudam Skolts living over the border, and yearly services attended by both Finnish and Norwegian Skolts are held at the tiny 400-year-old Orthodox chapel in Neiden that once formed the hub of the *siita.*

During the second half of the nineteenth century a number of Lappish families established themselves in the area. Most were offshoots of local Inari Lapp clans, but a few mountain Lapp families also moved in from Norway and the Teno valley on account of frontier closures. Towards the end of the century Finnish colonists began to settle in the area along the historic trade route to Bugøyfjord in Norway. Their fortunes varied: some emigrated to North America, others died without heirs. The remainder have intermarried with the local Lappish population. Twelve households of mixed descent existed in the resettlement area when the Skolts arrived, all of them connected in a single network of kinship ties extending throughout the Inari region and over the Norwegian border to include Lapps and Finnish immigrants settled in the environs of Neiden and beyond. The network of social ties perpetuated by these 'old inhabitants' still remains largely disjoint from that of the Skolt community, both incorporating a greater time-depth and conceived within a framework of spatial and environmental parameters owing nothing to the subsequent geography of resettlement.

A total of 267 Skolts were resettled in the Sevettijärvi area. During the first decade after resettlement, the Skolt population grew rapidly owing to an increase in the birth-rate and a decrease in child mortality. Subse-

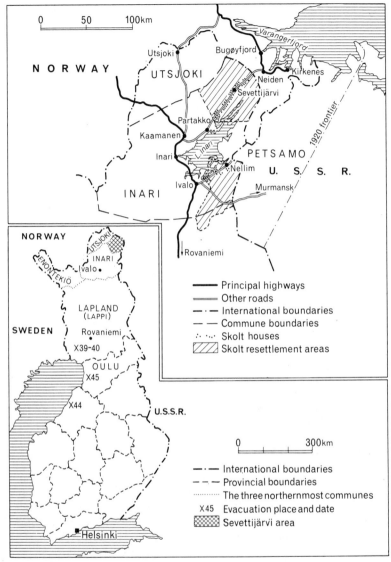

Fig. 2. Resettlement areas, administrative boundaries and highways.

quently, the rate of growth has fallen off drastically, largely on account of the loss of reproductive potential through emigration of unmarried females from the community. The present population, defined as those whose mother-tongue is Skolt and who were either born or resettled in the Sevettijärvi area, stands at 395, of whom 75 are either periodic migrants

7

Introduction

or permanent emigrants, and 20 absent in institutional care or homes of adoption (fig. 3). This leaves a permanent local Skolt population of 300; which may be compared with the resident non-Skolt population of 79, a third of whom are Finnish merchants and professionals who arrived in the post-resettlement period, together with their descendants.

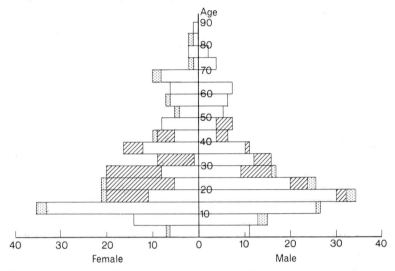

Fig. 3. Age/sex distribution of the Sevettijärvi Skolt population, defined as all those whose mother-tongue is Skolt and who were either resettled or born in the Sevettijärvi area, as of 1 January 1972. Age-classes: 0–4, 5–9, 10–14, . . . Speckled areas: Those in homes of adoption or institutional care outside the community. Shaded areas: Periodic migrants or permanent emigrants from the community.

Communications and administration

Resettlement transformed the status of the Skolt community in relation to the wider national society; from one of more or less autonomous self-sufficiency to one of almost total dependancy. The nationwide administrative structure of the modern Welfare State, formerly obscured by the continued operation of indigenous social institutions, was revealed in stark outline when the continuity of these institutions was undermined. Skolt fortunes are no longer guided by the *siita* assembly but by a remote bureaucracy, so converting the role of the headman from one of internal arbitration to one of brokerage with outside officials. Dependancy brought with it an awareness of isolation, and a resentment on the part of many Skolts towards the policy that had led them to settle in one of the most remote corners of the country; a policy that was felt to imply deliberate rejection by society at large.

The greatly improved communications of today, including post, telephone, radio and motor transport, have gone some way to relieve this sense of isolation, if not to reduce the scale of dependancy. By far the most significant development in this respect has been the integration of Sevettijärvi into the national, and international, road network. A dirt track covering the hundred-kilometre stretch from the main 'Arctic Highway' to Sevettijärvi village was completed in 1963. In 1969 it was reconstructed to allow normal motor traffic, and extended to the Norwegian frontier, connecting with the Norwegian road system at Neiden. Although it still lacks a hard surface and is extremely rough in parts, the road is used extensively by Finnish and Norwegian traffic, heavy lorries bound for Kirkenes, and the recent influx of car-borne tourists. For the Skolts it has meant that return journeys to local centres such as Ivalo and Inari, which could previously last up to a week by boat and sledge, can now be made in a single day by bus. Road construction has, in addition, provided them with a perennial source of casual wage employment, whilst by stimulating commercial activity in the region it has opened up new outlets for them both to market their produce and spend their earnings.

Before the coming of the road, Sevettijärvi lay on one of the busiest winter sledge-routes through north-east Finland, connecting Inari with the Norwegian trading post at Bugøyfjord. Today, the locus of exchange trade over the border has shifted to Neiden, only 43 km north-east along the new road extension from Sevettijärvi, and half-way to the town of Kirkenes with its vast iron-ore workings. Following the road in the other direction, south-west from Sevettijärvi: after threading its way through the Skolt community, it skirts the north-west shore of Lake Inari, past the neighbouring Lappish settlements of Partakko, to reach the main highway at Kaamanen. Thirty kilometres south from Kaamanen along the highway lies the village of Inari, an important and historic market and service centre for the surrounding Lappish districts. Local government and administration is concentrated in Ivalo, a further forty kilometres south from Inari. A pioneer town of Finnish colonization from the eighteenth century, owing its existence to a fertile river valley and the promise of gold in surrounding hills, Ivalo today represents the greatest concentration of population in the far north of the country. As an outpost of national commerce and industry in the Lappish backlands, it still retains a certain pioneer flavour. A three hundred kilometre stretch of highway connects Ivalo with Rovaniemi, the provincial capital of Lapland, lying just south of the Artic Circle and eight hundred kilometres north of Helsinki (fig. 2).

The housing, education, welfare, employment and land-use of the Skolts is subject to bureaucratic control at both communal and provincial levels of local government, as well as by regional branches of various State departments. Communal and provincial boundaries are shown on the map (fig. 2). The Skolt 'reservations' fall within Inari Commune, the largest in Finland in territorial extent, with a population of nearly seven thousand, of which the Skolts constitute no more than 7 per cent. The two depart-

9

ments of the national bureaucracy that are of greatest import for the Skolt community are the Forestry Authority and the State Roads Department (TVL). The first, which controls all but the 3 per cent of privately-owned land in the region, has its local base at Inari and is represented at Sevettijärvi by the Forest Warden: perhaps the most powerful individual in the community. The second, TVL, as the department responsible for road construction and maintenance, is by far the biggest employer of Skolt casual labour.

The natural environment

Most of the Sevettijärvi area is fairly low-lying, rising gradually towards the North from the basin of Lake Inari, with a water-level of 118 metres, to the tundra plateau which reaches a height of about 400 metres before dropping sharply to the sea on the coast of Varangerfjord. The landscape tends to follow a pattern of parallel grooves and ridges running from south-west to north-east in the direction of glacial movement. The greater part of the area, studded with lakes of all sizes, drains into the Näätämö river, which flows north-east across the Norwegian border and through Neiden into Varangerfjord, cutting a deep valley through the plateau. Only the southern part drains south into Lake Inari. The northern limit of coniferous pine forest crosses the area from south-west to north-east, very roughly following the 200-metre contour. Within the pine forest the land is rugged, strewn with glacial debris of rocks and boulders. Outside the forest limit much of the flatter land is swampy, but the higher fells have a smooth dry bed of glacial sand and gravel covered in sheltered spots with copses of mountain birch.

Lying on the border between maritime and continental climatic zones, the region is subject to highly changeable weather conditions. Temperatures range between the extremes of −40 °C in winter and + 35 °C in summer, but seasonal averages are moderated by frequent incursions of mild wet weather from the Norwegian Sea, which in winter may raise the temperature by some 30 °C within twenty-four hours. The averages for February and July stand at 13 °C either side of zero. The permanent snow-cover, established in early October, reaches an average maximum depth of 70 cm by the end of March, and disappears from all but the high fells in late May. Ice forms on the lakes during October–November and breaks up in June, not leaving the largest lakes until midsummer.

Owing to its position between latitudes 69° and 70° N, the area experiences marked seasonal variation in the length of daylight. From mid-May to mid-July there is continuous daylight, and from mid-November to mid-January the sun is not seen above the horizon. However, there is an hour or two of dusk on even the shortest midwinter days; and a full moon in clear weather can give ample light for outdoor visibility.

Introduction

Lapps and Skolts in the literature

In relation to their small numbers, the Lapps have been subjected to an exorbitant quantity of research. As an exotic and supposedly primitive culture lying at the back door of the great north-west European centres of learning, Lapps have presented an easy target; yet the complaint of many contemporary Lappish spokesmen, that the results of this research have neither been made available to, nor benefited, the subject population, is very largely justified. On the other hand, much recent and explicitly problem-orientated research has served only as a mouthpiece for the ideological claims of the Lappish minority movement, and lacks any objective or critical foundation.

Despite this proliferation of studies, the Lapps have attracted relatively little attention from competent social anthropologists. They are famous in the literature mainly for their bilateral kinship system (Pehrson 1954, 1957; Goodenough 1964) and for nomadic reindeer pastoralism (Whitaker 1955, 1956); but the concentration on mountain Lapp groups has tended to convey a somewhat distorted impression of the nature of Lapp society. An exception is Paine's (1957, 1965a) study of a remote coastal Lapp community in northern Norway. His subsequent study of a Norwegian mountain Lapp group has produced some promising insights into the nature of reindeer pastoralism (Paine 1965b, 1970, 1971a, 1972), which have influenced my own analysis (Ingold 1974b, n.d.b).

The history and social organization of the original Skolt *siidat* has been documented with great insight by the geologist Väinö Tanner (1929). A richly detailed and beautifully illustrated description of life in Suenjel is given by Karl Nickul (1948), who became involved with the community whilst making a cartographic survey of the area, and has since been among the most active spokesmen on Lapp affairs in Finland. The ethnographer T. I. Itkonen has compiled a volume of Skolt and Kola Lapp myths (1931), as well as a full-length phonetic dictionary (1958); whilst his encyclopaedic survey of Finnish Lapps (1948) is a source of abundant information on the Skolts.

After the war, the Skolts attracted less attention, as it was felt that any traditional ways worthy of study had been irretrievably lost. However, the Sevettijärvi Skolts were studied by the American anthropologist P. J. Pelto over a period of fieldwork in 1958-9. The resulting monograph (Pelto 1962) is marred by an anecdotal and irresponsible use of data; but since the orientation of the work is towards aspects of personality and culture rather than social organization, a critique of Pelto's conclusions lies outside the scope of this study. Whilst weak in analytic content, it furnishes an invaluable source of documentary information on the Skolt community during the early post-resettlement period, allowing a more confident reconstruction of the social and economic transformations of the last two decades than would otherwise have been possible.

Introduction

Less can be said for the massive series of investigations launched by the
Scandinavian International Biological Programme – Human Adaptability
Section (IBP/HA), of which the Skolts have been unwilling victims almost
yearly since 1966. As well as being suitably placed for a prestigious show of
East-West scientific co-operation, the Skolt community was picked on as a
unique cultural and genetic isolate supposedly doomed to extinction. The
programme reached its climax in July 1969, when a team of over eighty
investigators from nine countries, covered by a posse of press, radio and
television reporters, established themselves and their equipment in the
secondary school at Inari, and set about making systematic anthropo-
metric measurements and body tests on every man, woman and child from
the Sevettijärvi area, at the rate of about forty a day (Eriksson, Hughes and
Milan 1970, Lewin 1971). As an incentive, subjects were offered free
medical, dental and optical treatment. The ethnocentric attitude assumed
by the investigators towards their subjects was little short of appalling,
and overshadows any objective value their researches may have had. The
Skolts were felt to have a naturally irrational and child-like mentality,
and to be subject to phobias induced by primitive superstition. Their
obvious aversion to the investigators was considered a symptom of psychic
abnormality (Forsius and Seitamo 1970, Forsius 1973).

Linked to the programme was a sociological survey, one of a series of
acculturation studies designed by Asp and his colleagues at Turku University (Asp 1965, 1966, 1968, 1971), based on responses to lengthy
questionnaires administered to random samples of the Lapp population,
including Skolts. Such an approach, which automatically denies the relevance of social relations and takes little cognizance of the people's own
perception of their situation, can yield only forgone conclusions: ' The
Lapps seem to fear that the Lapp culture will be assimilated by the
Finnish culture ... However, the majority of Lapps seem to be quite happy
in their villages and content with life ' (Lewin and Eriksson 1970: 64).

Arrangement of material

This study is divided into three parts. The first part deals, in the broadest
terms, with ' economy ': the means by which Skolts gain a livelihood. The
first four chapters are devoted to reindeer management, an activity which
still structures the life of the community although the majority of Skolts
no longer derive their principal income from it. These are followed by
chapters on fishing and on the exploitation of other, subsidiary, natural
resources. The final chapters of the first part outline the principal sources
of money income: in local employment, welfare, and migration.

The subject-matter of the second part could again be glossed as ' society ':
the patterning of social relationships within the resettled community. After
outlining the overall spatial layout of the community and its social
correlates, the organization of the household is analysed from three

perspectives: the physical aspect in relation to the use of housing space, the developmental aspect of domestic group composition, and the economic aspect of the household as a unit of consumption. The special position of youth is taken up in a separate chapter. The two final chapters of this part examine the pattern of social relations within a typical neighbourhood and, in contrast, the position of the local elite in the ' central village ' of Sevettijärvi.

In the third part the perspective is inverted from internal to external, to examine the relationship of the community as a resettled minority, through its assembly and headman, with the bureaucracy and legislature of the State, with the machinery of party politics, and with the pan-Lappish minority movement. This leads, in conclusion, to a more general discussion of the ideology of culture, and the implications of viewing the Skolts from a wider perspective as constituting either a ' minority culture ' or a peripheral community.

In order to retain a sense of proportion, it is important to bear in mind the small numerical size of the community. The same population in a city would fill only one short street or occupy one tower block. The processes at work in the Skolt community are not unique; and in many respects it appears as a microcosm in which trends of fundamental significance are reflected in the careers of only a handful of individuals, or even of single characters. Statistical frequencies are therefore of little help in assessing what is, or is not, significant; and it is consequently hard to distinguish social forces from personal idiosyncracies. On the other hand, to be able to view a total community in ' close-up ' can be revealing, as I hope this study will demonstrate.

Part I The procurement of livelihood

2 Reindeer (1): Traditional pastoralism

Reindeer and men

The reindeer confounds any attempts to draw a definite dividing line between the categories of wild and domestic animals. Reindeer have been heavily exploited in Europe from Palaeolithic times, apparently with a degree of exclusiveness and selectivity sufficient to leave a record virtually indistinguishable from that which would have been obtained under pastoralism (Higgs and Jarman 1972, Sturdy 1975). On the other hand, there is little in inherited morphological or behavioural characteristics to distinguish the reindeer under contemporary pastoralism from its wild predecessor, and where the two populations still exist side by side, they easily intermix and interbreed. Human controls may have been applied in order to maintain or enlarge the deer population, but not to alter its characteristics from those for which it was originally valued. If anything, there has been an overall decrease in the size of the deer, illustrative of a general trend in the evolution of domesticated species. This may be viewed as an outcome of pastoralist efforts to concentrate deer on a limited range whilst maximizing herd growth by sheltering them from forces of natural selection that would otherwise tend to eliminate the smaller and weaker animals.

The taming of reindeer, that is, their socialization into a part-human environment, is of undateable antiquity. Deer were tamed for use as beasts of burden, providers of milk and decoys in connection with an economy based on the hunting of their wild counterparts. The advent of pastoralism may be defined by the extension and individualization of rights of ownership over live deer from the core of tame animals to cover whole herds. In Lapland, this can be dated initially to around the sixteenth century (Gjessing 1954: 16; Vorren 1973: 189–90), a time when existing wild deer stocks were coming under increasingly heavy pressure due to State colonization of the North, the expansion of trade and taxation, and the introduction of firearms. The intensification of pastoral controls, and the explicit formulation of rights over animals *vis-à-vis* others, represented a response to perceived scarcity.

The rapid transition to pastoralism was not marked by any technical advances over hunting. There have been no attempts until most recent times to alter inherited traits through artificial selection. The same skills and knowledge, used by hunters to trap deer through deceit, were used by pastoralists to bring them under closer control (Vorren 1965, Vorren and Manker 1962: 39–42). The basis for this control lay not in unnatural docility induced in the deer through genetic engineering or human socialization, but in the establishment of a symbiotic relationship of mutual advantage, leaving the reindeer a large measure of economic independence. Reindeer pastoralism thus has an inherent tendency to revert to a predatory form as the conditions of symbiosis are undermined (Hatt 1919: 129–9, Ingold 1974b).

The object of traditional pastoralism may be defined as the maximization of herd size through controlled reproductive increase. Reindeer pastoralists have been described as ' rudimentary capitalists' (Paine 1971a), to reflect the combination of an ideology of unlimited multiplication of individual holdings with the illiquidity, or lack of convertibility of the basic animal resource to other forms of wealth. This combination is unique to pastoralism, stemming from the reproductive capacity of animals, whereby wealth may be accumulated without the intermediary step of production for exchange normally involved in capital formation (Ingold n.d.b). Indeed, since animals represent both a store of wealth and a source of food and raw materials, the production of goods in consumable form as meat, hide and bone eats into, rather than augments, capital reserves.

It follows that the rate of slaughter is kept to a minimum. Deer are killed only to meet essential domestic consumption requirements as they arise, taking only those animals incapable of further increase. The pastoralist has to balance the needs of his family against those of his herd, the growth of the human population against the growth of the animal population. Under classic capitalism, in which producer and consumer are typically separate, production precedes and stimulates consumer demand, higher productivity allowing a greater level of capital investment. By contrast, under traditional pastoralism producer and consumer are typically identical, and higher productivity lowers the level of capital investment. Production is therefore consequent on, and limited by, consumption needs. In short, pastoralism may be defined by the combination of an ideology stressing the maximization of material wealth with a ' domestic mode of production' (Sahlins 1972).

Pastoralism, unlike agriculture, presaged a major increase in animal but not in human population density. As the application of traditional pastoralist values generates a herd in which mature animals predominate, the greater part of the augmented energy intake from pastures is expended in their maintenance and lost through respiration, leaving only a fractional increment contributing to growth and stored in tissues ultimately destined for human consumption. In other words, land is involved more in the support of wealth on the hoof than in the productive process. The pastoralist attempts to harness environmental resources exclusively on behalf of his animals, taking for himself only the material residue they fail to use up during their lifetimes. Thus, slaughter is anticipatory rather than predatory. This apparent altruism, seen in the provision of access to pastures, the protection from or elimination of carnivores and parasites, and the regulation of the pastoralist's own carnivorous requirements, forms the basis of the symbiotic bond through which deer are attached to their herders.

Unlike the hunting economy, in which predator and prey may have existed in approximate homeostasis, with each population exerting a controlling influence on the other (Paine 1971a), pastoralism is ecologically unstable. The exponential growth of herds following the designation of deer as reproductive capital with scarcity value altered the pressure on pasture resources from an abnormally low to an abnormally high level in the space of a few generations. Nevertheless, the rate of reproduction of the deer is sufficiently low to delay the immediate imposition of physical limitations to expansion. As long as the pastoralist has the possibility to appropriate fresh grazing areas, herd growth will appear to be limited in the first place by the reproductive potential of existing stock rather than by the carrying capacity of pastures. Thus, Lappish pastoralists continued to push out into new grounds as their herds increased, often bringing themselves into conflict with the settled inhabitants of the region. On the other hand, the growth of the deer population has been periodically checked by the ravages of predators and epidemics, as well as in the present century by two world wars during which deer were destroyed and slaughtered on a massive scale for emergency food supplies.

Expansion cannot, however, proceed indefinitely. Stock must inevitably be reduced at some point if the negative consequences of overgrazing are to be avoided. Nevertheless, when access to pastures is held in common, effective shares in the available grazing are proportional to herd size, so that a unilateral reduction would only weaken a man's competitive position relative to his herding neighbours. Herd growth consequently continues unchecked until the exhaustion of pastures forces herds to scatter, undermining the basis of traditional pastoralist controls. It is this situation of collapse that forms the background for developments in reindeer management among the Skolts and their neighbours over the last decade.

Pasture and life-cycle

The principle foods of the reindeer are lichens and beard-mosses in winter and early spring, and various grasses, marsh plants and the leaves of birch and willow in summer. In autumn, fungi are a favourite source of food (Isotalo 1971). Though relatively rich in digestible carbohydrates, winter lichen pasture is deficient in proteins and minerals, more being lost through excretion than can be taken up in the same time. At most, lichen suffices to maintain the deer without adding appreciably to growth. The condition of deer tends to deteriorate over winter, to the point that, by around March, they are no longer fit for slaughter. Spring can be a time of famine, when the formation of a hard snow crust prevents the deer from digging through to the pasture underneath.

During the short summer, lasting about four months, deer replenish their reserves of proteins, minerals and vitamins, and food is in relative abundance. They do not deliberately eat lichen in this season, and never touch it when dry. There is thus a very clear division between summer and winter food sources. Growth is effectively restricted to the summer season, so that by autumn deer are in prime condition for marketing. Fungi, the richest available source of digestible proteins, play an important role in fattening the deer in late summer, and are thus of considerable economic significance.

The carrying capacity of pastures is determined by the supply of lichen, on account of its low nutritive value and extremely slow rate of regeneration. Lichen grows fastest when cropped to medium height, more slowly when only lightly cropped, and very slowly when heavily cropped. Lichen that has been badly overgrazed, trampled, or destroyed by forest fire, can take some thirty undisturbed years to regenerate to medium height for grazing. Given that a deer needs to consume 1500-2000 kg (fresh weight) of lichen per winter, and that the optimal productivity of medium-cropped lichen is around 120-160 kg ha^{-1} year^{-1}; it follows that about 10-12 ha of pasture are required per deer (Kärenlampi 1973). In forest types where the ground cover of lichen is not continuous, a proportionally larger area would be needed.

Reindeer are gregarious animals, tending to collect into hierarchically organized groups whose members recognize one another as individuals. Antlers, which are renewed every year, play a key part in fixing the dominance hierarchy. Since different categories of deer shed their antlers at different times of year, the hierarchy is periodically restructured. Dominant animals can generally command the best pasture spots, particularly those where the snow has already been dug away by other deer. For the pregnant females, the only deer that retain their antlers throughout the winter until calving, the ability to command the best spots in late winter, a time of scarcity, is obviously important (Espmark 1970).

The natural life-span of the reindeer is some ten to fifteen years. Sexual maturity is reached by the third year. Cows remain fertile up to the age of around ten years, whereas bulls may become impotent rather earlier. On average, one bull is adequate to serve about twenty cows. Pastoralists tend to castrate males in or after their third year, relying on the supply of uncastrated males which remain at large in the forest for the impregnation of their females.

Rutting time falls in October, when the antlers of the male have reached their greatest proportions. At this time, even the most docile deer can be dangerous to handle. Bulls attract 'harems' of cows, whilst geldings group up by themselves. Over winter, herds merge into larger units under the pastoralist's direction. Calves are usually born in May.

Traditional pastoralism

During and immediately after calving, the female separates from the
group, allowing the calf to learn to recognize its mother so that the
pair remain together on rejoining the herd, until they begin to separate
in the early months of the following year. Cows and their offspring instinc-
tively tend to return to the same spots for calving every year. As summer
approaches, deer tend to move from the forest to the higher, cooler,
regions of open tundra to avoid the plague of mosquitoes, often gathering
in great concentrations. During the summer, antlers and hide are renewed,
and the deer recuperates after the long winter. After the hottest part of
the summer in July, they disperse back to the forest, remaining fairly
scattered until the advent of the rutting season. Over winter deer prefer to
graze in sheltered parts of the forest, where the snow is loosely packed
and the lichen easy to reach.

The principal categories of deer in the pastoralist's herd comprise
castrated males or geldings (Fin. *pailakat*), including specially tamed
draught geldings (Fin. *härjät*), potent males or bulls[1] (Fin. *hirvaat*),
fertile females or cows (Fin. *vaatimet*), male yearlings (Fin. *urakat*),
female yearlings (Fin. *vuonelit*), and calves of both sexes (Fin. *vasat*).

The formal organization of reindeer management in Finland

The present reindeer-management area of Finland includes the whole of
Lapland and a part of Oulu province (fig. 4). Many of the Finnish
colonists who settled in the North during the eighteenth and nineteenth
centuries took up reindeer management as a source of supplementary
income alongside agriculture. In this mixed, sedentary economy, a joint
herding organization proved advantageous, though animals remained
under individual ownership. Deer are left to roam at liberty on common
pastures during the summer months when farmwork is at its peak, and
are gathered again through a joint herding effort in autumn and early
winter. The collected herds are driven into roundup fences, where
separation according to ownership, buying, selling and slaughtering takes
place.[2] The herds are then tended through the winter until calving-time,
after which they are again let free for the summer. The system is founded
on the tendency of deer in the low-lying coniferous zone of northern
Finland to move within restricted areas of domicile rather than to embark
on long migrations between taiga forests and tundra fells, as in the
mountainous regions of northern Norway and Sweden. Borders of common
pasture areas are thus based to a large extent on natural boundaries,
usually lakes and rivers, within which the deer are accustomed to roam
(Helle 1966).

Voluntary associations of Finnish reindeer owners were gradually
formed to meet these herding requirements; and the system later spread
to encompass Lappish pastoralist groups whose traditional migration
patterns had been blocked by international border closures and policies
of sedentarization. In 1898, association membership was prescribed for

all reindeer-owners in Finland. Associations also federated on the parish level to deal with matters such as joint separations, pasture regulation and the registration of earmarks. In 1926, a central union for Finnish reindeer management was set up, which subsequently took over the functions of the parish federations. The present structure of associations (Fin. *paliskunnat*), each controlling a territorially delineated range of pasture, and capped by the Reindeer Associations' Union (Fin. *Paliskuntain Yhdistys*), was ratified by law in 1948 (Alaruikka 1964). Today, the total reindeer-management area includes 57 associations, of which only the 12 northernmost have a majority of Lappish members.

The *paliskunta* has two principal sources of income. The first is from the membership subscriptions of reindeer owners reckoned per head of deer. For the purposes of levying this subscription, deer are tallied each winter according to ownership as they appear in the separations. This levy thus ignores the variable proportion of deer which each year escape the herders and fail to pass through the separation fence. The second income source is from the auction of unidentifiable deer found at separations. The majority of these are without earmarks (Fin. *peurat*[3]), the grown offspring of cows which failed to enter the separations or come otherwise under the husbander's control during the period of attachment of the calf.

Paliskunta expenditure falls into four main categories: payments for hired herding labour, costs incurred in projects such as road- or fence-construction, wages to association officers, and compensation payments to landowners for crop damages caused by reindeer. In the far North, above the climatic limits of agriculture, the last category is insignificant. It is usual for association herders who gather the deer for separations to be paid at piece-rate according to the number of animals collected. The rate is set at the same level as the per head subscription, such that the amount paid out to herders exactly balances the amount levied from subscriptions. Income from *peura* sales is allocated to remaining forms of expenditure. The subscription level varies from one *paliskunta* to another, according to the burden of joint activities undertaken by the association. When this includes all gathering and herding work, the subscription is relatively high. In the associations of the mountainous north-west ' arm ' of Finland, where the old pattern of migratory pastoralism is still followed, the separated herds are supervised independently by their owners throughout the year, and the *paliskunta* budget is consequently extremely small. The subscription level may also be affected by fluctuations in the income from *peura* sales. If this rises above a certain point, the money may be redistributed in the form of reduced subscriptions whilst herding payments are kept at their former level.

To every association is assigned a maximum limit to its deer total which is based on estimates of pasture capacity. A certain number of deer always stray onto neighbouring *paliskunta* territories, especially when home pastures are inadequate. Compensation is paid to the

association on which strays are found by the association to which their
owners belong at the same, or a slightly higher, per head rate as the
subscription. Consequently, subscription payments for strays are directed,

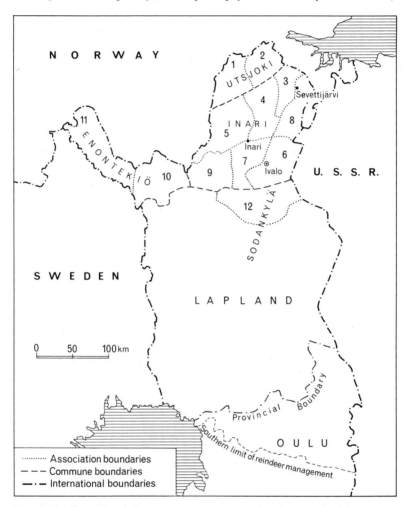

Fig. 4. The Finnish reindeer management area, showing provincial, communal
and associational boundaries. Only the twelve northernmost associations,
with a majority of Lappish members, are shown:

Utsjoki:	1. Paistunturi		7. Hammastunturi
	2. Kaldoaivi		8. Vätsäri
Inari:	3. Näätämö		9. Sallivaara
	4. Muddusjärvi	Enontekiö:	10. Näkkälä
	5. Paadar		11. Käsivarsi
	6. Ivalo	Sodankylä:	12. Lappi

23

via the associations concerned, to the herders of the 'host' association who were responsible for finding them. Under normal circumstances, stray deer are either slaughtered or driven back to the home territory after separation.

In its formal constitution, each association has an executive committee headed by the association *chairman* (Fin. *poroisäntä*, literally 'reindeer master'), and including the *vice-chairman* and from two to four other elected members. Financial business and other paper-work is managed by the *treasurer*. These officers are all elected for three-year periods; members' votes are weighted in proportion to the number of deer owned. In addition, the association may elect a number of other officers, including *foremen* who recruit herding forces and direct operations in the field, *delegates* who attend distant separations in neighbouring *paliskunnat* in order to represent the interests of association members, an *assessor* responsible for dealing with compensation matters, and *recorders* who list deer found in separations. Other posts may be created on an *ad hoc* basis as required.

General *paliskunta* meetings are held at least twice a year, once in spring and once in autumn, preceded by meetings of the executive. In these meetings, officers are elected, budgetary matters are handled, and plans for the coming season are discussed. The whole cycle of *paliskunta* activities is organized around the 'reindeer management year', beginning on 1 June and ending on 31 May.

Traditional herding practices among the Skolts and their neighbours

The traditional economy of the Skolts of Suenjel was based principally on fishing, supplemented by the hunting of wild reindeer. Small herds of tame deer were kept as transport, milk and decoy animals. In order to prevent tame deer from mixing with the wild herds, they were kept near dwellings all year round; in summer within fenced areas, where they were provided with shelters against the sun and mosquitoes. As wild deer stocks declined during the nineteenth century, expansive pastoralism began to develop in place of hunting. Enclosed summer pasture areas had to be progressively enlarged as herds grew in size, until perimeter fences were abandoned altogether on extinction of the wild deer population. It is estimated that the Suenjel herds multiplied by a factor of thirty in the period 1830–1910. However, Skolt reindeer holdings varied considerably: whereas some specialized in pastoralism, building up herds of several hundred head; many continued to concentrate on fishing and kept only a few tens of deer (Nickul 1953, 1970: 29–33, 40).

During the First World War, the Suenjel herds dropped catastrophically from their estimated peak of 8000 head to about 1500. By the outbreak of the Second World War they had risen again to 4000 (Itkonen 1948, II: 141). Suenjel was formed into a *paliskunta* when it became

Traditional pastoralism

a part of Finland in 1921; but in practice this had a negligible effect on Skolt herding procedure. Deer which had been let loose to graze over summer were collected in early autumn and brought to agreed meeting points where they were sorted and returned to their owners. Traditionally, roundup fences were not used. Over winter, herds were kept not far from the village, and inspected at intervals. Only big-owners tended their herds continuously on more distant pastures. Before calving, the herds were moved to household spring settlements. Cows were tethered during calving, after which the herds were let free for the summer. All herding labour was recruited by the household, and hired herders were sometimes employed in cases of manpower shortage. Subscriptions to the *paliskunta* were nominal (Nickul 1948: 61-2).

In their present resettlement area, the reindeer-herding neighbours of the Skolts are the descendants of the Inari Lappish population settled around the shores of Lake Inari, mountain Lapps settled in the neighbourhood of Kaamanen, and a few colonist Finns scattered along the main communication routes. Today, much of this population is inter-mixed, and ethnic or linguistic divisions are indistinct.

The traditional reindeer economy of the Inari Lapps was essentially similar to that of the Skolts, marked by its small scale and intensivity (Itkonen 1948, II: 133-8). The mountain Lapps were traditionally nomadic pastoralists, migrating between high fell summer pastures and inland winter forest pastures. The closure of the Norwegian/Finnish border in 1853 and pressure towards fixed settlement led to the eventual break-up of nomadic herding groups. *Paliskunnat* were founded in the area during the first decade of this century; and by the 1920s all summer herding had ceased.

The area to the north and east of Lake Inari was divided into two large *paliskunta* territories: *Muddusjärvi* to the north and north-west, and *Paatsjoki* to the east and north-east. Each included one major separation fence, both dating from the beginning of this century (fig. 5A). Herding procedure in the inter-war period followed the *paliskunta* model introduced by Finnish reindeer owners. Paid association herders began gathering the deer in September, taking advantage of the natural tendency of deer to congregate during rutting-time. As the work proceeded smaller herds were combined into progressively larger units until by mid-November, when snow and ice were sufficiently thick for transport, the collected herd of some 10 000 head could be driven into the separation fence. Association gathering continued in the same way until January or February, by which time the majority of the *paliskunta* deer should have been accounted for. A second major separation was generally held in January. After the separations, deer which were not sold or slaughtered were tended independently by their owners until calving-time in May, after which they were let loose for the summer (Itkonen 1948, II: 149-51).

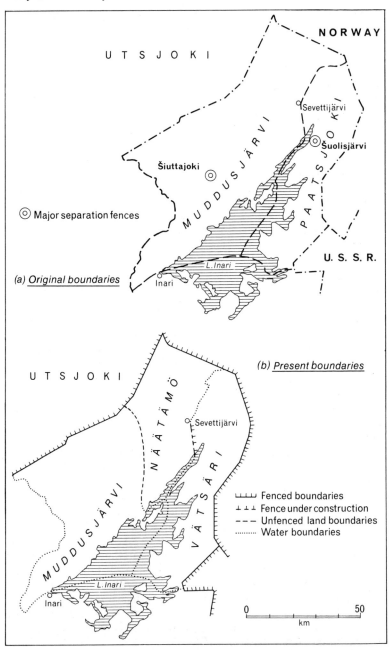

Fig. 5. Association territories in the Skolt reindeer management region.

Skolt reindeer management in the 1950s

The Skolts were twice evacuated during the hostilities of 1939–45. During the first evacuation (1939–40) their herds were transferred to the Muddusjärvi-Paatsjoki area for the winter. During the second (1944–5), there were no chances to save the herds. Most were lost, destroyed, or cut off behind the new border. On resettlement, funds were provided for the purchase of about 1500 deer, and after a decade Skolt herds had risen to their former level of 4000.

Skolts were accepted as members of either Muddusjärvi or Paatsjoki associations, according to the situation of houses: thirty-six of the resettlement houses falling within the territory of the former, fifteen within that of the latter. They formed a minority in both associations, and were forced to adapt to the herding practice of their neighbours. Compared with the strong homing sense of the Suenjel deer, the new animals, bought from many parts, were initially difficult to control. Deer and calves were lost when they mixed and merged with the herds of neighbouring Lappish owners, some of whom possessed considerable holdings. In an attempt to domicile the deer, a fence was constructed on the traditional Skolt pattern to surround an area of summer pasture in the resettlement area, but the enclosed pasture range soon proved inadequate.

A principal Skolt complaint at this time was that deer were gathered too late by the associations. Whereas the Skolts were accustomed to have their animals under control by the end of autumn; deer could not be retrieved from association separations before December, and frequently not until February or March. This led to a loss of calves, since by this time many calves no longer follow their mothers. Pelto (1962: 34–37) records that in 1958 the Skolts continued to practice their traditional system of collecting deer to agreed sites in early autumn for sorting among owners, independently of the *paliskunta* organization. However, only the *gelding* herds were collected by this method whilst remaining animals were gathered by the association. This practice has since been abandoned.

According to Pelto's description of herding in the winter 1958–59, the Skolts had in other respects accommodated fully to the *paliskunta* system, and were playing an active part in both associations. Skolt reindeer-men were independently responsible for gathering the herds in the northern parts of the two *paliskunta* territories, whilst their neighbours covered the southern and central regions. After separations deer were led back to home pastures. Cumulative pasture scarcity had led to the formation of loose coalitions of reindeer owners, usually nearby siblings or neighbours, who kept their herds on the same pastures, within reach of their houses. Owners made independent trips at intervals to inspect the herd. Animals might be slaughtered for domestic meat supplies, or for trade to the Norwegian exchange shop, at that time situated at

Bugøyfjord. The seller himself delivered the meat, bringing exchange goods in return. Calving took place under close supervision. Cows were roped and tethered, and not set loose until after birth and earmarking of the calves. By early June, all animals had been set loose. There were no herding activities during the summer months (Pelto 1962: 37–48).

The names and divisions of *paliskunta* territories in the Skolt reindeer-management region have undergone some changes in the last decade. Minor alterations in the common boundary between Muddusjärvi and Paatsjoki territories were made in 1964, and in 1967 the name of Paatsjoki association was changed to Vätsäri, referring to a fell district in the north-east of its territory. In 1969, the northern and eastern half of the original Muddusjärvi association territory, lying almost entirely within the Skolts' resettlement area, was split off to form an independent *paliskunta,* to which all former Skolt members of Muddusjärvi as well as the few non-Skolt residents in the area came to belong. The new *paliskunta* was given the name Näätämö, whilst Muddusjärvi association continues with its former territory reduced by half, covering the south and west of the region (fig. 5B). In the following chapters, associations will be referred to according to the present *paliskunta* map, unless the context specifies an earlier period.

3 Reindeer (2): The breakdown of intensive herding

The deterioration of pastures

The 1960s represented a critical decade for the Skolt reindeer economy, and indeed for the development of Finnish reindeer management as a whole. During this period the traditional, intensive, symbiotic pattern of Skolt herding was replaced by a more extensive, predatory form. The three most important factors contributing to this transformation were the deterioration of pastures, the adoption of the snowmobile in herding, and the growth of the commercial market for reindeer products.

Of these three factors, the impact of pasture deterioration is the most difficult to estimate. It is clear that the growth of the herds after resettlement put an increasing pressure on available pasture resources; but the pastures cover a huge area and have never been subjected to a detailed inventory. Judging from general reports today of serious overgrazing throughout Lapland, the official figures for maximum associational carrying capacities, which would still allow room for increase, appear grossly overestimated. Local reindeer-men agree that pastures have deteriorated, but differ in their interpretations of the extent and causes of overgrazing. The contrast between ' then ' and ' now ' is often exaggerated: lichen always grows whiter on the other side.

Skolt herders were apparently already troubled by pasture shortage towards the end of the 1950s. Pelto reports that winter herding coalitions were being forced to merge since the pastures were insufficient to keep herds of neighbouring coalitions from mixing (Pelto 1962: 44, 121). Many local men date the ' ending ' of the pastures to the early years of the 1960s, when a succession of 'thaw-frost' autumns which buried highland pastures under a sheet of ice drove huge herds of deer from the fells of Utsjoki over the border to northern Muddusjärvi and Paatsjoki. At the same time, Utsjoki Lapps are said to have rustled quantities of Skolt deer. After the construction of a fence along the border in 1963 this danger was eliminated, but the damage had been done.

The poverty of winter pasture in the Skolt area also stems from the ecological distribution of pasture zones. The bulk of the dry highland zone of open tundra and birch scrub, ideal for summer pasture, falls within the Skolt area; whilst the greatest areas of lowland winter pasture, within the limits of pine forest, are situated in the southern half of the region, outside the resettlement area (fig. 6). In the original Muddusjärvi territory, this division between north-east highlands and south-west low-lands is particularly striking. Deer tend to migrate yearly between the two zones. The huge mass of deer that concentrates on the tundra during the summer tramples and crushes the lichen cover which, when dry, is brittle and fragile. This represents the most destructive and permanent form of pasture damage. There is consequently a shortage of good lichen pasture within range of Skolt settlement, compared with relative abundance in the lowland forests south of the resettlement area.

Rather than bringing about catastrophic and irreversible losses through famine, the effect of pasture shortage has been to level off herd expansion before food reserves were totally exhausted, so that the overall growth of the deer population has followed an approximately logistic curve, flattening out to a ceiling level during the early 1960s. This tendency is not limited only to the Skolt reindeer-management region; the turn of fortunes from around 1960, after a period of exponential post-war growth, can be observed in the figures for Finnish reindeer management as a whole (fig 8).

There are three principal reasons for this. Firstly, the immediate effect of undernourishment is to lower birth and calf-survival rates without signifi-cantly increasing adult mortality. Where formerly at least 60 per cent of cows would be expected to calve annually, ratios of 20 per cent or less have been typical over the last decade, whilst in poor years an almost complete dearth of calves has been recorded.

Secondly, grazing conditions vary from one year to the next according to climatic factors. The freezing of lichen under ice in autumn, or the creation of a hard snow crust in spring may cause famine which can be countered only through provision of emergency food supplies; whilst exceptionally hot and dry summers can cause death from thirst or exhaustion. Although famine in one year may subsequently be compensated by more favourable conditions, fostering the impression that losses may be explained by temporarily adverse freaks of climate rather than by a permanent situation of overgrazing; heavy pressure on pastures in fact leads to a depletion of reserves, which becomes critical only when a proportion of the pasture area is rendered inaccessible. As a result, 'bad years' follow one another with increasing frequency, having the effect of periodically reducing total stock before expansion can proceed beyond the ultimate carrying capacity of pastures.

Thirdly and most importantly, the natural response of deer to increasing population density on inadequate pasturage is for herds to fragment into ever smaller and more widely scattered social units (Wynne-Edwards 1965). The pastoralist is consequently no longer in a position to keep his herd together. He is compelled to allow his animals to disperse in search of pastures of their own accord; lacking both the power and incentive to stop them. This has led to the progressive coalescence of the formerly distinct herds of winter coalitions. Deer have scattered far and wide throughout the region, mixing and intermingling at random, thus making

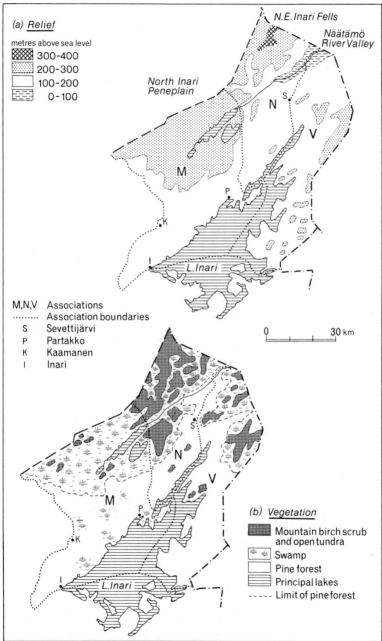

Fig. 6. The ecological distribution of pasture zones in the Skolt reindeer management region. Adapted from Piirola (1972: 12, 23).

it impossible for pastoralists to provide the security for their animals and exercise the strict selectivity that underlay the symbiotic relationship. Control over natural reproductive increase therefore breaks down before the concentration of deer on limited grazing becomes so great as to bring about a Malthusian catastrophe. The deer, for whom an attachment to man ceases to hold any advantages, revert to fending for themselves effectively as their wild counterparts did, becoming less domiciled and responsive as their contacts with herders diminish and alter in character.

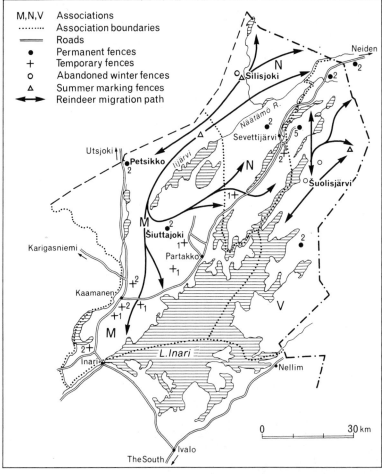

Fig. 7. Roads, separation sites and reindeer migration paths in the Skolt reindeer management region. Figures indicate the number of separations held at each site during the winter season 1971–2.

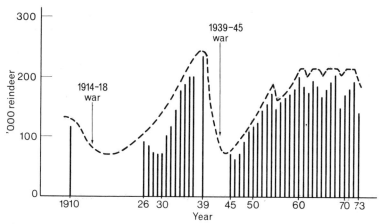

Fig. 8. The total number of reindeer in Finland, 1910–73. Vertical lines represent net totals of recorded deer, including both calves and slaughtered animals. The dashed line represents an estimate of gross totals. Note the levelling off of the gross total and the increasing fluctuation of net totals after 1960. The diagram has been adapted and extended from Helle (1966) on the basis of official reindeer association reports published in the magazine 'Poromies'. Pre-1945 figures are somewhat unreliable.

From the start the Skolts had experienced difficulties in controlling relatively undomiciled animals. However, the presence of free, mobile, deer set in a chain reaction, since they in turn disrupted those herds that were still localized and coherent. Deer tended to follow on with the mobile animals, in much the same way as in nineteenth century Suenjel, when herds could be broken up through infiltration by wild reindeer. Consequently, the system of post-separation winter herding, as well as supervised tethered calving, came to be abandoned altogether. Today, deer are simply set free after separations to go their own way, and calving takes place 'in the wild'. Winter herding coalitions have disappeared. Apart from the remnants of the tame herd of draught geldings, deer can now be domiciled only by continuous tethering or enclosure. Both techniques require a strictly limited range of abundant pasture. The few Skolts who, in winter 1971–2, tried to keep at most a handful of deer over until calving, were all eventually forced to abandon the attempt owing to the lack of available grazing.

The loss of control over herds has introduced a major new uncertainty factor into reindeer management, as to whether or not particular deer will be found and brought to the separation fence at any time during the roundup season. Under former conditions it could be assumed that the great majority of deer would be gathered and delivered to their owners every winter. Today, the task of collecting deer to separations has been made both difficult and chancy, and the proportion of animals found

The procurement of livelihood

can therefore fluctuate enormously from one year to the next. This is reflected in the marked yearly variations in net totals of deer recorded in separations over the last decade (fig. 8, 13A). Since the gross total of deer in the forest remains unknown, it is impossible to determine the exact proportion of animals found in a particular season. Taken over the whole reindeer-management area of Finland, the proportion of unfound deer has probably not exceeded 30 per cent of the gross total, but local fluctuations may be much greater, possibly leaving over half the gross stock unaccounted for.

The adoption of the snowmobile

The small, 'one-man' snowmobile,[1] originally developed in Canada, arrived on the Scandinavian market in 1961–2; and the first machines were acquired in the Skolt community during 1963. The rate of adoption was subsequently extremely rapid, reaching its peak around 1966–8 (fig.

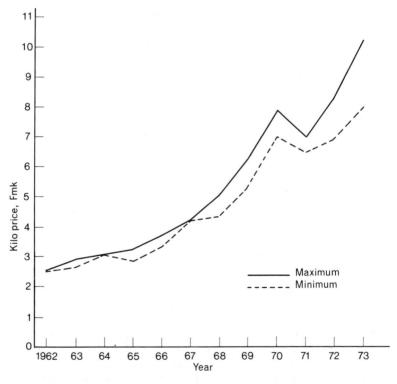

Fig. 9. The price of reindeer meat at separations in Finland, 1962–73. Year 1962 corresponds to season 1962–3, and similarly for other years. Source: 'Poromies' magazine 1964–72, fieldwork data 1971–3.

Breakdown of intensive herding

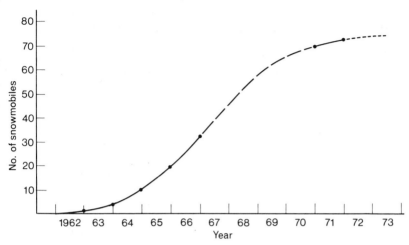

Fig. 10. The number of snowmobiles in the Skolt community 1962–73. Figures for 1962–7 are from Pelto *et al.* (1969: 13), those for 1970–2 are from my own fieldwork data. The curve has been extrapolated between these points.

10). The vehicle is powered by a small but extremely noisy petrol engine of about 15–25 horsepower, which drives a single-track caterpillar belt. Steering is managed by a pair of skis at the front. It can be used throughout the period of snow cover, and even during the summer on smooth ground. It is least effective in soft, deep snow and on rough and rocky terrain. Considerable loads may be hauled by sledge coupled to the rear of the vehicle.

The principal fields into which the snowmobile has been adopted are herding and transport. In the first case it has replaced the traditional combination of skiman and dog, in the second case the keeping of draught geldings has been rendered obsolete. Although many Skolts, especially of the older generation, are critical of the innovation; it was generally felt to be unavoidable, especially as those without became an increasingly small minority.

The adoption of the snowmobile into herding was a response to the problem of rounding up deer which were widely scattered and which, once collected, could not easily be kept under control. It was thus precipitated by poor grazing conditions. Early trials showed that with the snowmobile, herds in distant and relatively inaccessible areas, which it would otherwise not be feasible to collect, could be rounded up and driven to the separation fence in a relatively short space of time.

The effectiveness of the vehicle depends to a large extent on the nature of the terrain. It was adopted first by Utsjoki herders, who found it well suited to the smooth tundra fells of their association territories. Muddusjärvi herders learnt from Utsjoki experience. The flat expanses of the peneplain extending north from Lake Inari, which in summer form a treeless swamp, proved most suitable for snowmobile driving; whilst the uneven rocky ground within the pine-forest limit restricts manoeuvrability. The territory of Vätsäri association is least suited to the snowmobile, much of it being rough and strewn with boulders (fig. 6). Continual driving on this kind of ground causes exceptionally rapid wear and tear.

According to traditional herding methods, control was established by recognizing and taking advantage of certain innate characteristics of reindeer behaviour, such as the tendency to follow a lead, to bunch up when approached by a dog, and the attraction to the sound of a bell. Under the herder's control, deer moved at a natural pace. Snowmobile herding strategy is based on entirely opposite principles. Rather than following a lead, deer are driven from behind. Frightened by the noise and speed of the machines, they run in panic. Whereas deer bunch when approached by a dog, they scatter in all directions on approach of a snowmobile. Drivers therefore circle behind the herd, using bursts of speed as necessary in order to restrict the only line of escape for the deer to the required direction. Many animals split off and are lost on the way, whilst weaker animals drop from nervous or physical exhaustion. Those that arrive at the separation fence are in poor condition resulting from fatigue, nervousness and hunger.

As herders have gained more experience with snowmobile use, various means of combining the machine with more traditional techniques have been tried, in order to avoid its more negative consequences. The case for and against snowmobile herding has been widely discussed. Opinions, coloured by personal fortunes in reindeer management, vary widely; but amongst active reindeer-men today there is little doubt that it is an inno-vation that has come to stay. Those who consider the snowmobile to be a rash folly also hold it responsible for the loss of control over the herds. Those who defend its adoption maintain that herds were already scattered due to poor grazing conditions, and that without the snowmobile, control could not be *regained*. Causality is difficult to apportion, since the advent of the snowmobile and the deterioration of pastures were simultaneous developments, having similar consequences for the pastoral relationship. Both, whether through stress or malnutrition, depress the rate of fertility and the chances of survival of calves. Both cause scattering, and both preclude the possibility of maintaining localized, coherent herds over any length of time. Deer already growing 'wild' through lack of contact with herders became more so when attacked by snowmobiles. They have learnt to avoid 'snowmobile man' at all cost, and to hide in the most inaccessible parts of the forest. Thus, the advent of the snowmobile aggravated a situation in which herdsmen were losing control over deer, and hastened the transformation of the pastoral relationship from a symbiotic to an antagonistic or predatory form.

The enthusiasm with which snowmobiles were acquired was not merely a consequence of its perceived advantages in joint herding, but stemmed

from a highly competitive situation between herders as individual sub-
contractors hired by the association. To cover his capital costs, the snow-
mobiler is paid at twice the rate paid to the skier, on the expectation that
the former is a least twice as efficient as the latter. The size of the active
labour force is consequently reduced, and a man without a snowmobile
finds himself ineligible for herding work. Thus, although many Skolts have
vigorously opposed the use of the snowmobile in theory as a contravention
of traditional intensive herding methods, they have nevertheless found
themselves practically forced to acquire machines in order to stay in
business. Contrary to professed ideals, the actual number of snowmobiles
presently employed by the Skolts in herding, in proportion to the number
of reindeer involved (one machine per 65 deer), is by far the highest in
Lapland (KM 1973, 46: 55).

In recent years a number of studies have been made of the ' snowmobiles
revolution' in Lapland.[2] Although conclusions are clearly difficult to draw
in the present situation of change and uncertainty, three general points have
been made in all these studies. Firstly, it is claimed that introduction of the
snowmobile leads to a higher rate of slaughter of deer for sale, possibly to
a level jeopardizing the continuity of the herds. Secondly, snowmobile
herding is said to have led to a concentration of power in the hands of
big-owners, pushing the small-owner out of business. Thirdly, it is predicted
that growing wealth differences will generate new divisions of social
stratification between 'haves' and 'have-nots'.

With respect to the contemporary Skolt situation, these points call for
some qualification. Firstly, there has been no significant increase in the
proportion of deer sold by the Skolts for slaughter in the pre- and post-
snowmobile periods (fig. 13B). Indeed, few Skolts would be able to begin
paying for their snowmobiles from deer sales. It is estimated that purchase
and maintenance costs of the snowmobile are equivalent to the price of
about twenty deer per year. For the majority of Skolts, *absolute* holdings
fall below this figure (fig. 15); nevertheless 83 per cent of Skolt families
possess at least one snowmobile, and most have done so for some years.
More than half Skolt-owned snowmobiles are not used at all in herding
activities, and are evidently financed by welfare and wage-labour income.
The necessity to acquire machines has forced many men to seek additional
casual labour opportunities rather than to sell their deer.

Secondly, through the operation of the *paliskunta* system, large-scale
reindeer ownership is not a precondition for active participation in herding.
The entrepreneurial roles of the *herder* under contract to the association,
investing in the snowmobile as an item of productive capital, and the
reindeer-*owner*, whose investments in deer represent a form of reproductive
capital, are theoretically distinct; although in each case the entrepreneur
may be the same individual playing a dual role, who can therefore invest
profits from one enterprise in the other. Capital costs of herding are not
necessarily met by slaughter of the herder's deer for sale, but are covered
by *paliskunta* payments, which in turn are derived from membership

37

subscriptions. Ultimately, therefore, the costs of snowmobile herding are spread out evenly among association members according to the number of deer owned, rather than forcing an undue burden on the small-owner. Due to the contraction of the labour force, herding work has concentrated into a few hands, but not necessarily of big-owners.

The redistribution of wealth in reindeer was not so much a direct consequence of snowmobile acquisition as a result of the progressive loss of control over the herds, which in turn had been accelerated rather than initiated by the introduction of the snowmobile. Scattering and the failure to collect deer to separations leads to a high rate of generation of unmarked animals (*peurat*), opening up a channel for large-scale investment through both legal purchase and illegal appropriation. The present big-owners rose to the top from fairly small beginnings during the most chaotic herding period of the mid-sixties. They comprised the handful of younger men, without extensive domestic obligations, ready and able to try out herding innovations, and concerned at just that time with building up their herds. They used their income from continuous herding work to invest in considerable numbers of *peurat* when the supply was at its peak. On the other hand, older men who had to keep up a fairly high rate of slaughter to satisfy the needs of large families, who were not prepared to invest nor take the risks involved in innovation, found themselves losing when the calves of their deer grew into *peurat* which were no longer their property but that of the *paliskunta* for which they were no longer in a position to work. Some of these losers were among the biggest owners at the start of the decade (fig. 14).

Thirdly, although divisions of social stratification based partly on ownership of mechanical gadgetry are appearing in certain sectors of the community, stratificatory values of this kind are based on standards of status ranking through conspicuous consumption, imported from the culture of affluence. Their adherents have, for the large part, rejected the reindeer economy in favour of a regular salaried income. Active reindeer herders, for whom the snowmobile features primarily as an item of productive capital, are more concerned with accumulation than consumption. Marked differences in reindeer holdings have existed from the very beginnings of Skolt pastoralism, but have never given rise to the assertion of differential styles of life. The traditional big-owner was secretive about his wealth and renowned for his display of the outward signs of poverty, whilst the contemporary big-man is a seeker of personal prestige rather than a status-climber.

The growth of the commercial market

The traditional, highly intensive form of Skolt reindeer management, characterized by close supervision over herds and relatively small holdings, was practiced in conjunction with a subsistence and exchange economy. This required that an owner should have access to his herd throughout the winter months in order to pick out suitable animals for home consumption or to trade over the Norwegian border in exchange for goods such as flour, butter, sugar, tea, coffee and tobacco.

The Norwegian exchange shop at Bugøyfjord was at one time the most important of its kind in Finnmark, attracting traders from throughout northern Finland. Its trade declined in the 1960s after the death of the proprietor, and was finally eclipsed by a new enterprise which started up in 1962 just over the border at Neiden, then the nearest point on the Norwegian road system. This enterprise now holds a virtual monopoly in border trade with the Skolts, on which its continued existence depends.

The expansion of the road network brought with it possibilities of commercial marketing to Finnish merchants. These were opened up first by the construction of the road to Utsjoki. In 1957, a separation fence was constructed at Petsikko, where this road cuts the north-west boundary of the present Muddusjärvi *paliskunta* (fig. 7). The Petsikko fence polarized the market situation, giving access to the commercial market in the West, whilst the influence of the exchange trade remained strongest in the roadless North and East. Wealthy owners with holdings of several hundred head, above all non-Skolts of the present Muddusjärvi association, who lay outside the principal ambit of the Norwegian exchange merchant, were anxious to exploit new marketing opportunities provided by the fence. For them it was more important that the herds be gathered to strategic marketing points accessible to Finnish buyers than to have their own animals together on home pastures, available for subsistence and exchange needs. However, commercial interests accelerated the breakdown of the Skolts' pattern of intensive management as their deer, mixed in with association herds collected for separation, were forcibly driven westwards to distant marketing points, far from home pastures, where they mixed with 'stranger' animals and dispersed far and wide.

As a result of the progressive loss of control over reindeer, stemming from overgrazing and use of the snowmobile, once a herd had been gathered it became impossible to keep it localized until more could be collected prior to separation. It was therefore no longer feasible to hold a few, large separations, each of many thousands of deer, as in former years. Further, commercial interests began to favour more, smaller separations, since the quality of meat from a deer slaughtered on the spot deteriorates with the time spent in the roundup fence. Separations are nowadays held as soon as enough deer have been collected to justify the operation. The smallest separations involve only around a hundred animals, or less if the drive into the fence fails. If the herd has to be driven a long distance to the nearest permanent separation fence, it may easily be scattered and lost on the way. To avoid this risk, whilst ensuring the quality of meat for marketing, separations have begun to be held in temporary fences of sacking and wire-mesh, adequate for herds of up to around five hundred, erected at the nearest suitable point accessible to meat buyers.

The procurement of livelihood

During winter 1971-2, thirty separations were held in the region (fig. 7), compared with seven recorded by Pelto in 1958-9 (Pelto 1962: 44), although fewer deer were handled overall. Since the success of herding operations is chancy and cannot be predicted in advance, separations are announced at very short notice, whilst the smallest separations last only a few hours. The biggest separation in 1971-2 lasted only two days, compared with nearly three weeks in 1958-9 (Pelto 1962: 43).

The regional polarization of the market situation was offset by the construction of the road from Kaamanen through Sevettijärvi to Neiden, most of which was kept open from 1969 by snow-plough in winter. A number of new fences were constructed in the Skolt settlement area in order to realize marketing possibilities opened up by the new road. Vätsäri *paliskunta,* formerly entirely roadless, moved its principal separation point to within a few kilometres of Sevettijärvi village, constructing a large fence and a connecting road of a few kilometres to the site. Another smaller fence was constructed by the road near the Norwegian border. On the Muddusjärvi/Näätämö side, sacking-fence separations could be held at various points along the length of the road, or at points reachable from it by forestry tracks. The original Muddusjärvi separation site has lost its former prominence, and is used only in late winter when the main marketing season is over. Näätämö *paliskunta* also built a principal fence near Sevettijärvi village, to replace the more remote fence built by Muddusjärvi in 1961 to handle herds in the North. Up to now, Näätämö has been unable to afford the construction of a connecting road to this fence (fig. 7).

The significance of the commercial market has increased in relation to the price of reindeer meat, which has risen almost exponentially during the last decade along with the growth of demand on the north-European market (fig. 9). In recent years, a minimum initial buying price has been negotiated by the Associations' Union. As the season progresses, prices may rise above or fall below this level. In general, however, deer are meatiest and fetch their highest prices in autumn. Associations therefore try to hold their first separations as early as possible, usually in early October before the snow begins to settle. In the herding calendar, the autumn separation has replaced the traditional Skolt system of bringing deer to agreed sites for sorting among owners. Autumn separations cannot be held unless there is a road to the site, since the carcasses cannot be hauled in any other way before the snow-cover, whilst the temperature is still too high to preserve them by freezing. Näätämö *paliskunta* has been unable to hold autumn separations up to now for this reason. After the autumn separations, activities are not resumed until late November when snow and ice is adequate for movement by snowmobile, sledge and ski. The selling season is generally over by the beginning of March.

Road access became a factor of even greater significance when, in 1968, legislation was passed setting standards on the quality of reindeer meat destined for export. These demanded that certain minimal rules of hygiene be observed during flaying and butchering, which should take place immediately after slaughter, and that every carcass should be inspected and stamped by a veterinary surgeon present on the site. The consequences of these regulations for the traditional exchange trade were far-reaching. Skolts could no longer trade deer slaughtered on home pastures or hunted in the forest over the border to the Norwegian merchant. Nowadays, slaughter can only take place at the separation site, and the buyer, who is generally present on the spot, has to arrange for butchering, inspection and haulage of the carcasses. Thus, the Norwegian merchant is present as a buyer at the fence, often in competition with Finnish buyers acting as middlemen for large wholesale meat-export firms.

These Finnish buyers cover a large area, and during the season attend a different separation almost every day, hiring their own men to do the butchering work at piece rate. This degree of mobility is made possible by the *slaughter-lorry,* a unit which incorporates all the requisite equipment for butchering. The prepared carcasses are winched into the lorry, and are immediately ready for transport to the wholesaler's deep-freeze warehouse. In order to attract Finnish buyers, it is therefore essential that there should be road access to the fence adequate for the slaughter-lorry.

Even when there is good access to the site, the separation is a buyers' market. There are rarely more than two buyers, and often only one. For small or remote separations, it may be difficult to secure a buyer at all, and marketing possibilities may be lost altogether. Four principal buyers were active in the region in 1971–2: besides the Norwegian merchant, two Finnish middlemen and a local Lappish entrepreneur. Their strategic inter-relationships are covert and shifting, and are not generally known by the sellers, for whom the ultimate destiny of the meat is of no importance. Buyers acting on one occasion in collusion may act on another in competition. Quite frequently, after competing during the separation, one buyer will sell the whole of his bought stock to another at a pre-arranged price, making a small middleman's profit. Thus, a Finnish buyer will sell to the Norwegian if, owing to international price differences, the latter is prepared to offer a better price than the Finnish wholesaler. Conversely, the Norwegian will sell to the Finn if he has been unable to secure the prerequisites validating meat for export, or if his bought stock lies in excess of the quota he is licensed by the Norwegian authorities to import (amounting in 1971–2 to about 19 metric tons); whilst his presence as a buyer enables him to maintain his exclusive relationship with the Skolts, allowing them to settle debts or establish credit in his account-books.

The buying price may be established in two alternative ways: either according to a standard kilo price by weighing the carcass on delivery to the buyer's warehouse, or by haggling over the live deer on the spot. The former method gives a delayed but unequivocal result which is not open to negotiation. The buyer can arrange payment from a distance by bank-giro, and need not therefore be present in person. The latter method, although considered old-fashioned and inaccurate by the proponents of rationalization, is more general in the region; whilst the former is resorted to only when buyers have been unable to arrive owing to the remoteness of the separation site. The buyer initiates haggling by suggesting a round sum to the nearest hundred or fifty marks, and it is up to the seller to raise it by ten or twenty if he can. In effect, the quantity that is haggled is not the kilo price, which is theoretically fixed, but the weight and quality of the deer. Weighing devices, which would hardly point in the buyer's favour, are never available on the site. If more than one buyer is present, the seller may turn from one to the other; otherwise he has to face the alternatives of taking the buyer's price or not selling at all. With the kilo standard at around 6.50 Fmk, price ranges were as listed below.

Price ranges for different categories of deer

Geldings (*pailakat*)	250–350 Fmk
Bulls (*hirvaat*)	200–300 Fmk
Cows (*vaatimet*)	120–200 Fmk
Male yearlings (*urakat*)	80–150 Fmk
Calves (*vasat*)	50–100 Fmk

Since the opening of road access to separation fences, buyers have been able to arrange for bank-clerks to be present on the site. Bringing along a cash-box and a supply of bank-giro forms, the clerk can pay in cash on the spot, or arrange for the money to be held at the bank pending withdrawal. In order to remain competitive, the Norwegian merchant, too, has begun to hire the services of a Finnish bank, and is increasingly obliged to offer money payments rather than to credit the account at the shop as his customers find an ever-increasing need for ready cash. This has been made possible by the progressive relaxation of international currency and customs restrictions. Thus, the last vestiges of the traditional form of exchange trade in reindeer meat are removed: deer are bought and slaughtered at the separation fence and paid for with Finnish money.

The management of scattered herds

Under contemporary conditions, the deer of association owners roam year-round at large in the forest. Herding activity is reduced to the gathering of samples of deer to numerous, relatively small separations at many different points. Whereas the original purpose of the separation was to sort out the animals of different owners into discrete herds for winter supervision, its sole function today is to facilitate the selection and marketing of deer for slaughter. At the end of the separation, deer left alive are turned loose. It is therefore possible that deer may be subjected to two or more roundups in a single winter; otherwise no more is seen of them until they happen to turn up in a subsequent season.

Breakdown of intensive herding

Herds whose former coherence was maintained as much through established social relationships among the deer themselves as through their common link to the herder are scattered at random in the forest, broken up by frequent separations, drives to 'foreign' areas, and mixture with 'stranger' animals. Loose deer driven from their former herd and grazing area join up with other herds and in this way may wander hundreds of miles from their home territory.

The individual owner is no longer in a position to watch over the welfare or reproduction of his herd. He has little idea of the extent of his holdings, knowing only the numbers that turn up from time to time in separations. He does not know how many of his former stock have died as a consequence of fatigue from snowmobile drives, starvation, predatory spoil, disease or sheer old age; nor does he know how many are still alive but roaming 'wild' in distant corners of the forest.

Wealthy owners without pressing subsistence needs were not greatly disconcerted by the breakdown of intensive control, whilst in a position to enjoy the benefits of commercial expansion. Even if only small samples of the total deer population appear in single separations, the big-owner can be fairly sure to find enough of his own to choose suitable animals for sale according to his requirements, his unfound deer remaining as untaxed reserve stock. On the other hand, attempts on the part of Skolt small-owners to maintain their traditional economy were frustrated. Under present conditions, only the odd one or two, if any, of the small-owner's deer appear in a single separation, where decisions have to be taken on the spot, allowing little or no scope for choice. On the basis of such small samples, the factors of reindeer management cannot be estimated with any degree of confidence, whilst husbandry becomes progressively randomized. The decision as to whether or not to slaughter comes to depend not on the quality, age and sex of the deer, but on whether it happens to be found, and if so, when and where. The sizeable proportion of animals which escape the separations are automatically left alive, those that turn up at distant sites on neighbouring associational territories are generally required to be slaughtered. To satisfy immediate domestic consumption requirements, the small-owner has little alternative but to slaughter the first of his deer that turn up, whether or not they happen to be suitable with a view to the continuity of his herd. Indeed, he is more likely to adopt a policy of unconditional slaughter when found, rather than take the risk of losing his deer and their possible offspring altogether by setting them free again after separations (Ingold n.d.a.). In sum, the Skolts' traditional pattern of intensive small-holding in a domestic economy based on subsistence production and exchange trade is not viable under present conditions of dispersion and uncertainty in reindeer management.

In that the extent of interaction between herders and deer has been reduced from a maximal to a minimal level, reindeer management can be said to have undergone a transformation from an intensive to an extensive form.[3] Virtually the only vestiges of herding today are joint campaigns to drive undomiciled deer by force into fence-traps. In terms of the antagonistic quality of the relationship between man and deer as pursuer and pursued, the random or unconditional element in selection for slaughter, the team effort of the men and campaign techniques of herding, this is reminiscent of pre-pastoralist wild reindeer hunting; whereas ownership of live animals as reproductive capital defines the pastoralist complex. As the conditions for control by symbiosis have been undermined, the present pattern of reindeer management in this region may therefore be characterized as one of *predatory pastoralism* (Ingold 1974b).

4

Reindeer (3): Predatory pastoralism

The roundup fence

The plan of the roundup fence, which maps out the many activities that constitute the reindeer separation, has undergone an evolution that reflects the development of the reindeer economy from hunting to pastoralism, and the reversion of the latter to a predatory form. The basic components of the fence, the two converging wings leading to a small circular enclosure, are directly derived from early constructions used in reindeer hunting (Vorren 1965). With the development of pastoralism, the roundup fence assumed a more complex form, including a number of private corrals – twenty or more for larger fences – built around the central enclosure; and a larger, outer fence between the wings and the inner enclosure, where deer could rest prior to separation. Private corrals have subsequently fallen out of use along with the breakdown of post-separation winter herd supervision, as the animals of different owners are no longer kept apart. At the same time, new elements have been introduced into fence-construction to allow greater flexibility in location, a more speedy and efficient separation procedure, and adequate facilities for slaughter and sales on a fully commercial scale.

The principal components of the modern fence are the outer *funnel* bordered by two converging arms which may be from around 500 metres to several kilometres long; leading to the *resting-fence,* which in turn leads to the inner enclosure or *ring-fence,* possibly via an intermediate *auxiliary fence.* Around the periphery of the ring-fence are a number of *corrals,* some of which are nowadays specially equipped for slaughtering and used by the meat-buyers.

Three different types of fence are currently in use. The first, more traditional design includes a large ring-fence of about fifty metres in diameter as the central enclosure. In a fence of this size the lassoo must be used for catching deer and bringing them under control. The second type, an innovation of recent years, has a much smaller inner enclosure, known metaphorically as the ' *churn* ', of around fifteen metres in diameter. Within this enclosure, deer are handled in successive ' lots ' of about fifty at a time driven in from an auxiliary fence. The crush in the churn is so great that deer may be caught by hand. By eliminating the use of the lassoo, separation can be achieved in a much shorter time. Although during the brief periods in the churn, deer are subjected to extremely rough treatment, they are spared continual harassment from the lassoo, which induces fatigue and a consequent deterioration of the quality of the meat after slaughter (plate 1).

Some traditionally constructed fences have been converted to the new design by the addition of a churn either on the periphery or at the centre of the original ring-fence. In the first case the ring-fence serves as an auxiliary leading into the churn; in the second, corral fences have been built radially out from the churn to meet the periphery of the original ring (fig. 11). Corrals formerly belonging to private owners and later combined according to winter herding coalitions, are now allocated solely on a *paliskunta* basis, with the exception of those used by meat buyers. Many corrals have been left redundant, and are gradually falling into decay.

Fig. 11 (*opposite*). The old separation fence at Tsiuttajoki. It has been modernized by the construction of a central churn and the addition of radial corral fences connecting the churn with the periphery of the original ring-fence. Some of the old, outer corrals are falling into decay, whilst four have been adapted for use by meat-buyers. Above: detail of the core fence. A, Auxiliary fence; B_{1-4}, Buyers' corrals; M_{1-4}, Muddusjärvi association corrals; N, Näätämö corral; P, *Peura* corral. Below: general map of the fence and its associated 'village' of cabins and coffee-houses. Two cabins, shaded black, are now in ruins.

Plate 1. A crush inside the churn. The main gate has just been closed and the men are entering the fence.

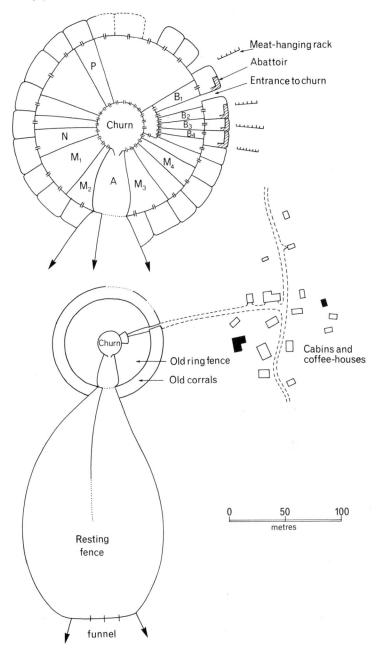

Meat-hanging rack
Abattoir
Entrance to churn

P

B₁

Churn

B₂
B₃
B₄

N

M₁

M₂

A

M₃

M₄

Churn

Old ring fence

Old corrals

Cabins and
coffee-houses

0   50   100
metres

Resting
fence

funnel

47

The third type of construction, another recent innovation, is the temporary fence of sacking and wire-mesh. In this case the entrance funnel is demarcated by *flaglines*: strings to which are attached brightly coloured plastic streamers which frighten the deer and deter them from attempting to cross. Flaglines can be quickly laid over long distances,

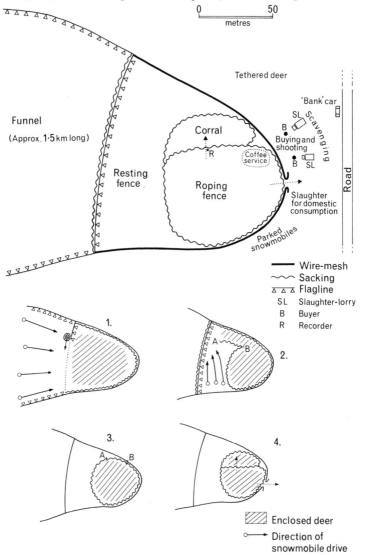

Fig. 12. Plan of a sacking-fence separation held near Partakko, January 1972. The lower diagram shows four stages in the formation of the fence.

Predatory pastoralism

strung between trees, bushes or stakes set in the ground, at a height of
about one metre. The funnel leads to a wall of sacking, partially reinforced
by wire-mesh, and laid out in a U-shape. The open end is closed off by
a flagline as soon as the deer have been driven inside. Prior to the separation
proper, the sacking fence is reduced in size to an oval of around the same
area as a normal ring-fence, and this in turn is divided to form a single
corral to take all deer left alive (fig. 12). Temporary fences have the
advantage that they can be quickly set up almost anywhere. On the other
hand, they are adequate for handling only a few hundred animals at a
time. Separation has to be carried out by lassoo, and selling is slower
owing to the absence of separate buyers' corrals in which sold deer can
await slaughter (plate 2).

The separation

Once a herd has been successfully driven into the fence, the separation
should start at the earliest possible moment, for a delay of a day or two
may be enough to render the deer unfit for immediate sale or slaughter.
Whilst formerly, pending separations were announced well in advance
in the local newspaper, today the information is distributed to association
members on the eve of the separation through the telephone exchange.
The chairmen of neighbouring associations are also informed, and they,
in turn, are responsible for sending delegates to attend the separation.

Plate 2. Roping inside the sacking fence. The wall of sacking is visible in
the background.

49

A man without a telephone or off the main communication routes is liable to arrive late or miss the separation altogether if the news does not reach him in time. The arrangement of transport to the site at short notice may be equally problematic, especially for those without snow-mobiles. The alternatives to a lift on a neighbour's sledge are to go by bus or taxi, or to hitch a ride by car or lorry, if the site is accessible by road. The active reindeer-man who hopes to attend the full round of separations must therefore not only be closely in touch with the latest herding developments, but also be prepared and equipped to embark on long journeys at a moment's notice.

An optional preliminary to the separation is the numbering of calves. Every unmarked calf in the fence has a number cut in the hide of its flank. Subsequently, owners have the chance to check the numbers on calves following their cows. Having informed the association chairman, who keeps a record of these numbers, claims may be established over calves during the principal phase of the separation, when they are often separated from their mothers and could not otherwise be identified. However, owners who fail to arrive in time to check their calf-numbers have little hope of claiming them later on.

After numbering, the deer are returned to the resting-fence. There follows a prolonged inspection period, during which more and more people begin to arrive on the site, making their way to the fence in order to take stock of their animals. Men stroll amongst the herd in the resting-fence, identifying their own and others' deer, recording the numbers on their calves, and weighing up possible husbandry alternatives. The inspection period is also a time for the exchange of greetings, often for the first time since the previous season. Men move around individually, or form small conversation groups which are always splitting and reforming in different combinations as men greet each other, exchange news and opinion on reindeer-management topics, and comment on each others' animals.

Every reindeer-man carries with him two essential items of working-equipment: a pair of binoculars and a twenty-metre lassoo. Binoculars are necessary for the identification of earmarks at a distance. The mark, viewed from behind the animal, is a particular combination of a few basic types of cuts and notches made in both ears (plate 3). Every owner possesses a unique configuration, by which his deer are recognized. Great stress is placed on the capacity to identify earmarks. A sharp eyesight is one of the most important faculties a man should command, and the ability to decipher a complex mark at a distance on a deer moving at speed represents the surpreme test of his competence. The expert must be able not only to recognize marks but also to identify each with an owner. Virtuosos in mark identification carry a repertoire of several hundred different marks in their memories. Owing to the fragmentation of holdings and the intermingling of herds, deer of as many owners may turn up in a single separation. Unidentified marked deer which are found in the fence during the separation proper provide opportunities for men to test their skill. Everyone clusters around

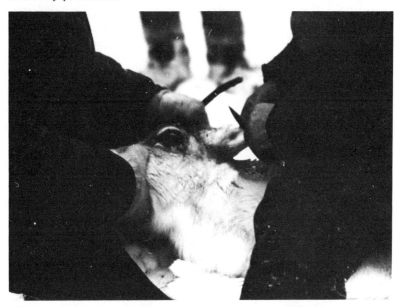

Plate 3. Cutting an earmark inside a corral during the separation.

Plate 4. Discussing a mark: the man on the left (foreground) sits astride the animal whilst the man on the right (background) fingers an ear.

the animal, all attention focused on its ears, whilst mark experts take turns to offer their interpretations (plate 4). The examination of such cases can take some time. If no conclusion can be reached, generally owing to natural decay of the mark, the deer must be sold for slaughter and its ears cut off. These are then sent to the Reindeer Associations' Union where they can be checked against a complete registry of existing earmarks.

Roping, like the recognition of earmarks, involves an element of competitive skill. When a powerful deer is caught in the fence by lassoo, a second man may be required to help bring it under control. Assistance is likewise needed when hauling animals up for presentation to the meat-buyer, and to hold them steady whilst the owner can haggle over the price. Partnerships form generally *ad hoc,* according to who happens to be nearby with a free hand at the time, but certain combinations reappear with particular frequency: most often of brothers, brothers-in-law or first cousins. As a rule, delegates from ' foreign' associations also work together.

After ample time has been allowed for the deer to rest and the men to inspect their animals, the first phase of the separation can begin. The deer are driven to the central ring-fence, or to an auxiliary fence prior to entering the churn. The drive is effected in autumn by an informally organized line of men holding a wall of sacking which closes in on the deer from behind, and in winter by a team of snowmobile drivers. Deer intended for domestic meat supplies are caught by lassoo and taken from the fence for slaughter. At the same time, any partially tame animals that are to be taken home alive, such as old draught geldings, are extracted from the fence and tethered to graze outside. Some earmarking and castrating may also take place at this stage.

After this preliminary roping and marking, the second and principal phase of separation can start as soon as the meat buyers are ready. During this hectic period, all remaining deer are either sold for slaughter or registered and thrust into the appropriate corral. In ring or sacking fences, every deer has to be roped individually (plate 2). In churn fences, deer are handled in successive lots which are driven in from the auxiliary ' roping enclosure'. During the drive the churn should be empty, and the men congregate in their respective *paliskunta* corrals. As soon as the drive has been successfully accomplished and the churn gate shut, the men surge into the churn from the corrals (plate 1). At first, the fence is densely packed with a swirling mass of some fifty deer and as many men crammed into an area of no more than 150 square metres. Deer are grabbed manually by the antlers or back legs and quickly thrust into the corral or hauled up before the meat-buyer. In this way, a fairly rapid clearance is achieved, until the only remaining deer are unmarked *peurat* which are put into a separate corral to await auction, and unidentified animals whose appearance may initiate prolonged earmark deliberations. Once the churn is eventually cleared, the next lot can be driven in. Men not involved in the drive can again retreat to their corrals, where they have a pause to talk, share drams of spirits, and examine their ' catch' more closely. A big separation may involve the handling of some thirty to forty 'churn-loads' before the auxiliary fence is finally emptied.

Beside the gate to each corral stands a *recorder* who marks down on a board the ownership and class of every deer that enters the corral, with the exception of those that have already passed through separations earlier in the season. These can be recognized by a slash which is cut in the hide of every fresh animal admitted to the corral. In temporary sacking fences, the recorder has to watch over the entire length of the wall dividing the central enclosure from the single corral, under which a deer may be thrust at any point. To maintain some semblance of objectivity, the recorder should not be allied by kinship to the owners whose corral he guards. Since those with significant holdings are fully occupied managing their own interests, the job of the recorder is most often taken by poor men, sometimes non-Skolt 'old inhabitants', who hope to earn a little money or a *peura* from the fence for their labours. Any remaining earmarking and castrating is performed on the deer inside the corral.

Meat-buyers stand before the gates leading to their respective corrals: on the perimeter of large ring-fences or, in churn fences, separated from the inner enclosure by an intermediate corral. When the separation is in a sacking fence without buyers' corrals, the buyers station themselves just *outside* the perimeter of the fence. Prospective sellers haul their deer up before the chosen buyer, waiting their turn to bargain. The buyer's final offer is treated as confidential and always made in a whisper. The conclusion of the transaction is marked by thrusting the sold deer through the gate of the buyer's corral or, in temporary fences, by killing the deer with a pistol shot through the head. Since the dead animal must be immediately flayed and butchered, the latter procedure can entail delays to enable the slaughtermen to keep in step with buying and selling. Sellers are forced to queue, sitting astride their animals, whilst losing valuable time inside the fence (plate 5); an inconvenience which the buyer can exploit to his advantage. Finally, the buyer records the seller's earmark in a special book, together with the negotiated price.

Slaughter of deer in the abattoir of the buyer's corral, and their subsequent flaying and butchering beside the slaughter-lorry or field slaughter unit parked outside the fence, is carried out by specialists hired by the buyer. Though usually local men, only one Skolt was regularly hired in this capacity. These specialists are wholly external to the system of relationships, based on the ownership of live deer, which regulates activities within the fence. In the hands of the slaughterman, the individual marked deer, formerly a vehicle for specific rights and obligations accruing to its owner, is converted into an anonymous carcass, hanging in a line of other carcasses, whose former identity is no longer verifiable nor relevant (plate 6). The boundary between these two states is physically mapped out by the fence: the reindeer-owners work inside it, the slaughtermen work outside it; and what is happening on one side of the fence is neither visible nor of any concern to those on the other. Standing

Plate 5. Waiting to sell, outside the sacking fence.

Plate 6. Flayed carcasses hanging out to dry.

on the periphery, the meat-buyer mediates the conversion from living to dead. Another specialist on the scene, distinguishable by his long white coat, is the veterinary surgeon, who has come to inspect and stamp the meat.

Around the slaughtermen, outside the fence, people may be engaged in an activity that could be described as *scavenging*: the collection of offal which is rejected in the butchering process. This includes hearts, tongues and livers, delicacies for which a small price should be paid to the slaughtermen; and brains, which may be collected without payment. It is common to see a man chopping the antlers from the skulls of slaughtered deer and collecting the severed heads in a sack. The brain is fit for consumption by both humans and domestic animals; and a man without a deer in the fence may stock up with meat for his family and for his dogs in this way. Although a poor man's habit, no negative stigma appears to be attached to scavenging. In addition to offal, housewives present on the site sometimes collect blood in buckets to make blood-pudding, and purchase rejected portions of hide cut from the forelegs which they use for making skin boots and gloves. The main part of the hide and the antlers are retained by the meat-buyers for resale, principally to enterprises in the commercial manufacture of tourist goods.

On completion of the separation process, unmarked *peurat,* which may comprise some 10–15 per cent of the herd, still remain to be handled. In churn fences, the *peurat* appearing in each lot are put into a special corral, whereas in ring or sacking fences, *peurat,* as well as any unidentified animals, are simply those remaining in the fence after everyone has extracted their own. Unidentified animals are usually sold direct to the meat buyer. Unmarked, orphan calves are given an earmark specifying common *paliskunta* ownership. Older *peurat* may be auctioned among association members, after allowing first pick to those entitled to compensation or payment in kind from the association. The auction is held within the central enclosure, with the association chairman as auctioneer. Having successfully bid for an animal, a man will drag it to his corral for marking, or outside the fence to be slaughtered for domestic meat supplies. Circumstances permitting, he may even take it to the buyer's corral for resale at a profit.

Activities within the fence come to an end on completion of the *peura* auction. Deer left live are freed from their corrals, and only the slaughtermen remain on the site to complete the accumulated backlog of butchering, working if necessary under electric spotlights powered by a mobile generator. For everyone else, the scene of activity shifts to nearby bars or coffeehouses, where men congregate in the evening for the festivities that follow every separation. Since these festivities involve a considerable expenditure of cash, in drinking and gambling, they cannot start until money has been paid out for deer sales. Representatives of the bank, readily distinguishable by their well-groomed, white-collar appearance, arrive by car at the close of the separation. A till is set up in the corner of the coffee-house, or in the nearest bar to the fence. If there are no buildings in the vicinity, payment is made inside the bank-clerks' car: each client in turn taking his place in the front passenger seat (plate 7). The seller identifies his sold deer by their earmarks, recorded in the buyer's registration book, and receives payment in cash or by credit transfer.

Beside most permanent fences are one or more coffee-houses: simple but spacious log cabins furnished with one or two long tables, a stove and oven in one corner, and a raised sleeping platform. Whole log-cabin 'villages' are found by the biggest and oldest fences, which lie dormant except during separation times, when they can suddenly come to life with a population of several hundred. Buns, coffee and meat stew are served during the separation. For the stew, a deer is purchased direct from the fence. Other supplies – stoves, logs, paraffin, pans, kettles and provisions – are hauled to the site by sledge (plate 8).

Most of the coffee-houses patronized by Skolts are run by ' old inhabitants' of the area: men without significant reindeer holdings who can afford to be absent from the fence at the height of the separation, and who are able to exact payment and maintain order in the house without offending kinship obligations. One such man operates a profitable ' chain' of identical coffee-houses at all the major separation sites, employing a neighbouring Skolt housewife as his regular assistant. Only one Skolt has attempted to establish a coffee-house, but was near to abandoning the enterprise as he was unable to control the unruly behaviour of his kinsmen and the consequent damage to custom and property.

As festivities wear on, men retire to sleep or, little by little, disperse to their homes. Desultory games of poker and bouts of drinking may still be continuing the following day: but once the slaughtermen have finished their work and the meat has been transported away, coffee-house proprietors prepare to pack up, the last of the revellers drift off, and the fence, once the scene of a ferment of activity, fades into the silence of the winter forest.

The summer marking

With the abandonment of intensive winter herding and supervized calving, owners were no longer able to mark their calves immediately after birth, but had to wait in the hope that the cow–calf pair might appear in a separation early in the following winter. If the pair appears in late winter after the calf begins to separate from its mother, or if it is not found at all during the season, the calf becomes an unmarked animal (*peura*) over which the owner of its mother has no more claim than anyone else. Consequently, the breakdown of intensive herding during the mid-1960s led to a marked increase in the *peura* supply, especially after winters with poor finds.

Summer separations began to be held in the region from the late 1960s as a response to the problem of calf-marking. The summer-marking is not a herding innovation, having been practiced traditionally by certain moun-

Plate 7. The ' bank ' operating in a car stationed outside the sacking fence. The till can be seen on the rear seat. A client is being paid whilst others cluster around, waiting their turn.

Plate 8. The proprietor of a coffee-house has arrived with supplies to last a major separation: firewood, stove, boxes of provisions, sleeping-hides, and cooking utensils.

tain Lappish groups with a more extensive form of herding; but its general adoption or revival throughout the region is recent.

Summer herding takes advantage of the tendency of deer to congregate during the hottest period from the end of June to late July on the high, bare, fells in the north of the region, where the climate is cooler and the mosquitoes less pestilent than in the forests. The greatest natural concentrations of deer are found at this time of year: herds of several thousand may congregate on a fairly restricted area of fell. However, the formation and movement of summer herds is extremely sensitive to climatic factors. The end of a heat-wave may disperse a herd as suddenly as it formed; and as herds move *en masse* into the wind, a change in wind direction can leave an area crowded with deer on one day deserted the next. Effective summer herding therefore requires that the herds are caught at just the right moment, and a sharp turn in the weather can jeopardize the whole operation. The abandonment or failure of summer herding in certain years causes ' bulges ' in the *peura* supply, which appear in subsequent, more successful, seasons.

Summer herding is strenuous work, in which only able-bodied men are fit to participate. Long distances over rough terrain have to be covered on foot, often at a run. A herding force of around ten to fifteen men is usually required. Teams of herders scan the territory from the summits of fells; and when a herd is located it is driven from behind, taking advantage of natural obstacles and water boundaries in order to direct the deer into the funnel of the marking-fence. Light aeroplanes are sometimes hired for obtaining general surveys of the deployment of deer as well as for conveying men and equipment to the site, which is far from the nearest settlement (fig. 7). Recently, portable radio telephones have been used to great effect in co-ordinating the operations of teams of herders and those waiting at ' base ' by the fence.

The marking-fence, at its simplest, includes a long funnel, extended as necessary by flaglines up to several kilometres long, leading to a moderately sized ring. An important addition for summer use is the ' drinking fence ', an enclosure leading off from the funnel including a stream of running water, without which animals might die of thirst. Separations are held in the cool of the first hours after midnight, when the sun is low on the northern horizon. Deer are handled in successive lots in the ring-fence. To prevent damage to the still small and fragile calves, they are caught with a special lassoo comprising a wooden pole some four metres long to which is attached a rope with a sliding noose. This can be gently lowered over the animal rather than thrown in the fashion of the ordinary lassoo. Once caught, each calf is marked according to the identity of the cow it was observed to have been following in the fence, and listed according to ownership. *Peurat* are either given the association mark or sold to members.

The whole summer herding operation may last some two to three weeks. Whereas in winter, snowmobile transport enables men to return home in the evenings, in summer herders live in tents or cabins near the fence, maintaining themselves by fishing in nearby lakes. Delegates sent by neighbouring associations, responsible for marking the calves of their association members, tend to reside slightly apart from the main camp.

As with winter herding, summer herders are paid by the association at piece-rate, reckoned according to the number of calves marked and *peurat* found. Owners whose calves are marked contribute to the association at the same rate, in addition to the regular *per capita* subscription which finances winter herding. With respect to marked deer the *paliskunta* thus only mediates the payment of herders by owners, whereas the sale of *peurat* gives it a clear profit. The marking rate is so small that many less active men consider participation not worth while unless a significant number of their own calves are likely to be found.

Unlike winter separations, summer marking events, owing to their physical inaccessibility, are generally attended only by those active in the herding itself. For those not present, unless represented at the fence by close kinsmen, there is little to guarantee that their calves will get marked. In the crush of the marking-fence, the number of cases of ambiguity is considerable, and it frequently happens that two or more calves may be ascribed to the same mother.

The summer separation also forms a setting for large-scale investment in *peurat*. In a successful separation, the number of *peurat* may run into hundreds. The meat of the adult deer in summer is not fit for sale or consumption, nor can it be preserved; so that *peurat* are bought up in summer entirely for their investment value. Male *peurat* may be castrated and given the *paliskunta* mark, to be sold later for meat in winter. Female *peurat* are sold at prices fixed in advance by the spring general meeting of the association. These prices tend to be slightly lower than the average for the auction of *peurat* in winter separations, and considerably lower for best quality animals that would fetch the highest prices in winter. Typical prices are: 120 Fmk for a cow/calf pair, 90 Fmk for a cow, 70 Fmk for an immature female.

From the point of view of the man seeking both to build up his herd and to ensure a maximal return on his investments, active presence at the summer marking is therefore essential not only for laying claim to his crop of calves, but also for obtaining the best and largest pick of the *peurat*. Absence from the marking is one of the most important factors behind the declining fortunes of traditional small-men.

Although important for the success of individual husbandry, summer herding is in many ways detrimental to the welfare of the herds. Young calves often die due to exhaustion and rough handling. Weaker deer cannot stand the exertions of a separation in the heat of summer, whilst harassment by herders just at a time when deer should be recuperating their strength after the hard winter leads to a deterioration in their condition which may still be evident the following autumn. In a number of recent summers, exceptional heat-waves have forced associations to abandon their summer herding plans in view of the risk of heavy losses. Summer herding is therefore increasingly discouraged by reindeer-management authorities, in favour of supervized calving and marking within movable enclosures.

Meat for domestic consumption

Under the old system of intensive winter herd supervision, a man could pick out deer as necessary from the herd gathered on home pastures in order to satisfy domestic consumption requirements. This is no longer possible, and the procurement of *lihaporo* (literally ' meat-deer ', or deer for home consumption) has become consequently problematic and uncertain. One solution is to extract suitable *lihaporo* direct from the separation fence, during the preliminary phase of the separation prior to buying and selling. However, for the small-owner it is a matter of luck whether any of his deer turn up in the fence at all when they are needed, let alone any suitable for slaughter.

Another possibility is to volunteer for odd jobs connected with holding a separation, such as hauling hay supplies to the site, cleaning up the surroundings after the event, and overnight herd supervision; for which payment in kind in the form of a *peura* from the fence is offered as an alternative to money. Men may enlist for these tasks with the specific intent of earning a *peura* for domestic consumption.

If a man finds no animals of his own that he would be prepared to slaughter, he may try to bid for a *lihaporo* in the association auction of *peurat* found in the fence, held at the end of the separation. However, those poorer men or even housewives who come to the auction in the express hope of obtaining meat for domestic consumption at an advantageous price find themselves up against the interests of active reindeermen concerned to invest in *peurat* as reproductive capital, and who are prepared to bid a much higher price for their investment-value than the poor man is prepared to offer for their meat-value. Those with limited purchase power may further be effectively excluded from the bidding by the auction of animals not one by one, but in lots of two to four, which are outside the means of the small buyer.

In theory, the general *paliskunta* meeting decides on the rules restricting bidding, which is normally limited to association members, and the categories of *peurat* available for auction; though in practice *ad hoc* rules are often made up at the separation itself to meet particular contingencies. The question of *peura* allocation tends to polarize the interests of the more successful, active herders and poorer, inactive men. The former, including the principal *peura* investors, who have by far the greatest stake in the association budget, argue that *peurat* should be allocated in such a way as to maximize association money profits, insisting that deer fit for slaughter should not be sold at prices lower than those offered by the meat-buyer, and that the rest be reserved for investment.

Thus, all *peurat* for slaughter may be sold directly to the meat-buyer, leaving only fertile cows for auction. Alternatively, any member wishing to obtain meat for domestic consumption may buy at a fixed price equal to the average paid by the meat-buyer, or the meat-buyer may be admitted to the auction in free competition with association members. The effect of such procedures is to close the loophole that otherwise exists for astute bidders to make quick money profits by buying deer in the auction and hauling them over to the other side of the fence for resale to the meat-buyer at a profit of anything up to about a third of the deer's value; a form of speculation that may provoke censure from the upholders of the association's financial interests. At the same time they force men hoping for cheap meat to match the meat-buyer's prices or to compete with the investors for deer not initially designated for slaughter.

In order to guarantee the income to the association from *peura* sales, successful reindeer-men demand that payment be made promptly, that men with debts to the association from previous *peura* purchases or without registered deer as security should be excluded from bidding, and that the association chairman should exercise without exception his legal right to sell any deer of a man with debts unpaid which may appear in the separations, whether or not he happens to be short of meat, until the debt is offset. These rules hit hardest the poorer men, no longer active in herding, but in need of *lihaporo* to feed often large families. They view the association not in terms of commercial enterprise, but as an organization whose purpose is to safeguard the welfare and security of its members; arguing that the maximization of association profits is not in the common interest when only the few, active men stand to gain as a result whilst others are left without food supplies owing to their inability to bid sufficiently high, or to make immediate payment. The poor man already saddled with debts finds himself excluded from bidding for *lihaporo,* whilst any deer of his own that turn up in the separations are confiscated in the name of the association.

In one association meeting, this polarization of interests came out vividly in a dispute over *peura* allocation. The two principal speakers were two half-siblings: one a bachelor, a big reindeer-owner and active herder; the other a housewife with nine children whose husband owned only a handful of deer, took no part in herding work and was inter-mittently engaged in casual labour. In a long, impassioned speech, the housewife complained that it was becoming impossible to obtain meat to feed the family owing to the high auction prices for cows and the stipulation of immediate payment. Her half-brother, in reply, stressed the financial interests of the association, pointing out that animals fetching good auction prices should be reserved for investment, not slaughtered for meat.

The housewife's intervention caused a slight sensation: it is not usual for a woman to speak out in association meetings, so that her special perspective as the manager of a domestic consumption unit is rarely expressed so forcibly. The debate that followed created such a sharp division that a vote had to be called, a device resorted to extremely rarely in association meetings, in which great stress is normally placed on the achievement of unanimity and consensus. The big-owner, supported by other active men in the association, defeated the small-men sympathizing with the housewife's point of view by a very narrow margin. Under normal circumstances, where votes are not counted, the big-men, with the loudest voices, invariably have the last word.

Housewives whose menfolk are now working entirely outside the reindeer-management economy, owning no more than one or two registered deer in all, sometimes travel to the separation in the hope of making a private purchase of *lihaporo* from a friend or relative at an advantageous price. Failing this they may buy direct from the meat-buyer himself. Men who are away on labour sites during the working week cannot themselves get to the fence to arrange for the procurement of meat supplies, unless the separation is held on a Saturday or Sunday.

Procurement of *lihaporo* through extraction of own deer from the fence, bidding in the *peura* auction, payment for odd-jobs or private purchase at the fence can only take place in connection with a separation. However, the individual reindeer-man cannot control the timing of separations to meet his needs. If supplies have run out at home, and there are no prospects of a separation in the immediate future, he has to look elsewhere. Sometimes, deer appear in the vicinity of a house, particularly when an old, tame gelding is kept nearby, tending to attract other mobile deer around it by the sound of its bell. If a man sees the deer of someone with whom he is on good terms by his house, he will phone the owner, who may then come to collect the deer immediately or instruct that it should be slaughtered and arrange to collect the meat.

It is not generally possible to rely on chance good fortune of this kind. As an alternative, men go out to hunt *lihaporo* at large in the forest. Hunters usually move in pairs, on foot in autumn and by snowmobile in winter. The deer is shot at long range with a rifle, flayed and butchered on the spot, and carried home packed in the hunters' rucksacks. Thus, the breakdown of intensive management, whilst reducing herding to team efforts to drive collections of deer into roundup fences for the purposes of commercial marketing, has led to the emergence of *solitary hunting* for the provision of domestic meat supplies. With solitary as with team predation, the technical forces of hunting are nowadays found in combination with the social relations of pastoralism. Likewise, both strategies of predation – team drives into fence traps and solitary stalking and shooting – were practised side by side in pre-pastoralist times (Tanner 1929).

From the point of view of the hunter, deer fall into three categories: own deer, other people's deer and *peurat*. Of these, the first category is the most advantageous to shoot. For the small-owner in need of meat, the availability of a deer of his own, whether it be found in the separation fence, seen by someone's house or spotted in the forest, is seen as a stroke of good fortune, a windfall supplying the family with meat at no apparent cost.

However, the chances of spotting his own deer at large in the forest are remote.

The second category, other people's deer, is the least advantageous to shoot. Payment is a matter for negotiation solely between hunter and owner. Some owners are known to demand exorbitant prices, others are more reasonable – for example an immediate kinsman would be expected to be relatively lenient. In any case, a privately negotiated price is likely to be considerably higher than the association fixed price for *peurat*. Small-owners tend to prefer payment in kind rather than in money: the hunter's debt to the owner persists until the hunter obtains or finds a deer of his own, which is then transferred as a repayment for the *lainaporo* ('loan-deer').

Peurat constitute the most usual category of deer to be hunted in the forest. The hunter has to pay for his kill at prices fixed at two levels, one for younger, immature animals, the other for adults, by the autumn general meeting which marks the start of the *peura* hunting season. Hunting *peurat* for domestic consumption has, however, been prohibited up to now in Vätsäri association, to which a minority of Skolts belong. Only herding teams may shoot *peurat* for a meat supply during field operations. This prohibition reflects both the predominance of more successful, active reindeer-men in this association, and the greater frequency of Vätsäri separations in the local area which provide most members with the opportunity to procure basic meat supplies. Vätsäri's *peura* policy is geared throughout to the maximization of association profits, which are fed back in the form of higher wages to herders and reductions in the subscription rate, whereas in Näätämö the inactive small-owners have a relatively stronger say in association affairs.

Formally, a hunter should be accompanied by two independent witnesses. In practice, not only is the number of unreported shootings probably considerable, but the ruling on witnesses is interpreted loosely. It is normally reckoned that the hunter can be simultaneously the second witness, and that the first witness can both take an equally active part in the hunt as his companion and receive a fair share of the kill. Hunters there-fore generally move in pairs, and divide the kill and the burden of payment equally or proportionally between themselves on the basis of their relative needs. Further, the criteria for the independence of witnesses are nowhere formally defined. The matter came up for discussion in one association meeting, in which there was general agreement that witnesses should be adult and from *separate* households. In this ruling, recognition is given to the household as an independent unit of consumption. Thus, a hunting companion may be as close a kinsman as a brother, so long as he belongs to a different household. Nevertheless, in some cases men have gone to hunt *peurat* by themselves or with their sons, claiming that partners from other households were impossible to find, and presenting the ears of the slaughtered deer to the association chairman as evidence. The difficulty of finding partners reflects both the ideal of the household as a self-sufficient consumption unit and the traditional pattern according to which visits to the home herd for picking out *lihaporo* were made individually, a man being accompanied at most by his sons.

A man intending to hunt *peurat* must obtain prior permission from the association chairman. This may be refused on the grounds that the applicant has failed to pay *peura* debts from earlier seasons, or that he has no registered deer or other means to offer as security. The problem for the association of extracting payment is the same as for purchases of *peurat* in separation auctions: a man excluded from bidding is also forbidden to hunt *peurat* in the forest. However, a debtor *may* go hunting in the formal capacity of a witness. His companion is responsible for paying the association, and the two men may then distribute the meat and settle accounts between themselves. Thus, the only practical relevance of the formal distinction between hunter and witness is in providing the debtor with an avenue for the procurement of meat when all other possibilities are closed.

Successful, active reindeer-men are also enthusiastic *peura* hunters. Although his own consumption needs are easily satisfied, the big-owner prefers the meat from a deer shot in the wild for its superior taste and quality, reserving those found in separations for commercial sale. He actively initiates hunting trips by seeking out poorer neighbours and kin in urgent need of meat, or other local buyers. For those in need, his hunting expertise makes him an invaluable companion. He may distribute the greater part of his share of the kill, keeping only a small proportion for his own consumption. By initiating reciprocities in the hunting and sharing of meat, the big-man can enhance his standing as a focal figure in the community.

Poor men, who are dependant on *peurat* for meat, frequently complain that they are becoming increasingly difficult to find. Hunters often return empty-handed, having seen no suitable deer. The decline in the supply of *peurat* is put down to high finds in summer separations, where they are acquired by private owners. Whereas the contemporary big-owners, who built up their herds through *peurat* and now wish to consolidate their holdings through control of the summer marking, are now seeking to check the production of *peurat*; the present small-owners, who lost their deer through their becoming *peurat*, now hope for an increase in the number of *peurat* (and hence often oppose summer marking), in order that they can be assured a meat supply at prices which they can just afford.

Big-men and small-men

Symbiotic pastoralism is characteristically expansive: as herds grow exponentially, so the pastoralist always pushes out into new pasture areas. Under predatory pastoralism, brought about in part by the exhaustion of pastures, herd growth levels off owing to the drop in birth and calf-

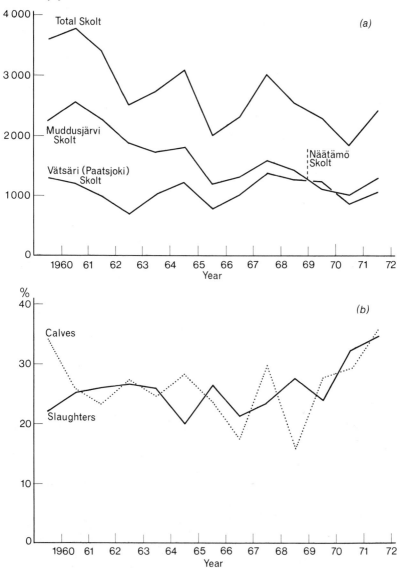

Fig. 13. *A,* Numbers of recorded Skolt deer, excluding calves, according to reindeer association (Muddusjärvi –1969, Näätämö 1969-, Vätsäri) and totalled, 1960–72. *B,* Percentage of recorded calves and slaughters to recorded total in each year, 1960–72.

survival rates, whilst a supply of unmarked animals, *peurat,* becomes available for investment. Predatory pastoralism is therefore characteristically *redistributive*: every owner automatically contributes in proportion to his herd size into the common *peura* pool, which is redistributed among investors, whilst the size of the total herds remains more or less steady.

Fig. 13A shows the total number of deer owned by individual Skolts, excluding calves, listed in winter separations between 1959-60 and 1971-2, and fig. 13B the ratios of calves found and deer slaughtered in winter to these totals for the same period.[1] An overall drop in numbers is evident in fig. 13A, but the fluctuations in total winter finds from one year to the next far exceed, or may be contrary to, those that would be expected due to a positive or negative balance of recorded calves against slaughtered deer from each previous year. As sharp increases as well as decreases are evident in the graph, it is clear that variations in winter herding success, that is, in the proportion of deer found, rather than in the absolute numerical strength of the herds, are responsible for this fluctuation. Indeed, the sizes of herds handled today in successful summer separations suggest that the actual number of deer ' in the forest' has not dropped significantly from its former level.

Variations in the holdings of individual owners over the same period show that whilst most have suffered heavy and irreversible losses, a few men have accumulated deer at a rate far greater than would be possible

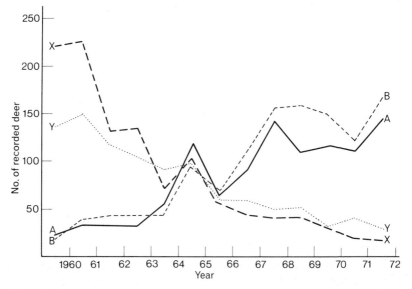

Fig. 14. The rise and fall of personal fortunes in reindeer management, 1960-72: the speculator (*A, B*) and the traditional pastoralist (*X, Y*). *A,* Aged 35, married 1967, 1 child; *B,* Aged 38, single; *X,* Aged 54, married 1952, 7 children; *Y,* Aged 44, married 1950, 11 children.

through reproductive increase alone (fig. 14). Though by themselves inconclusive, the figures are consistent with the view that poor winter finds due to the scattering of herds under predatory pastoralism have led to an increase in the rate of generation of *peurat,* particularly in the mid-sixties in the period between the abandonment of supervized calving and the adoption of summer marking, during which the snowmobile also came into general use. Owners who had based herd growth on reproductive increase found themselves losing out as their calves went to form *peurat,* whilst a path was made available for large-scale investment by those wishing to build up their herds at the time.

In addition, the total number of owners has increased as men have marked deer to their sons as a ' nest-egg' for investment.[2] In Vätsäri association, whose relative success offers favourable prospects for the small-scale investor, the number of owners has trebled in the last twelve years, whereas in Näätämö the increase has been much smaller, for few men see a future for their sons in reindeer management. The general picture is thus one of a proliferation of small ownership, a reversal of fortunes for previous large owners, and the rise to prominence of a few leading investors (fig. 15).

The losers were traditionally-oriented intensive herders of the older generation, with already established holdings, who were excluded from participation in herding owing to their failure to adapt to snowmobile mechanization and the consequent contraction of the labour force, and increasingly unable to meet extensive domestic obligations in the subsistence and exchange sector owing to the scattering of their herds. Today, they form a category of ' small-men ', forced to enlist on the unemployment register or to engage in casual labour on the roads and construction sites in order to acquire a nucleus of money income. To the extent that the small-man has lost control over the reproductive increase of his herd, he becomes a hunter who must pay for his kill, relying on a supply of *peurat* as a source of relatively cheap meat when his own herd is no longer adequate nor available to satisfy domestic consumption requirements. Like the hunter (Paine 1971a), he is above all concerned with the consumption rather than the accumulation of stock.

Those who gained were men of the younger generation, without major domestic commitments, who could afford to take the risks of investment. Initially without large holdings, their contribution to the common pool of *peurat* was correspondingly small. Keen to try out new techniques and exploit new commercial outlets, these men have dominated association herding for the last decade, and the most prominent have amassed considerable wealth (fig. 14). Having reached this position, their proportional contribution to the *peura* pool is increased, and it is therefore in their interests to consolidate their holdings, above all through control of the summer marking.

Today, a decade after the initial breakdown of intensive herding, the majority of active herders are men in their late thirties. As consumption

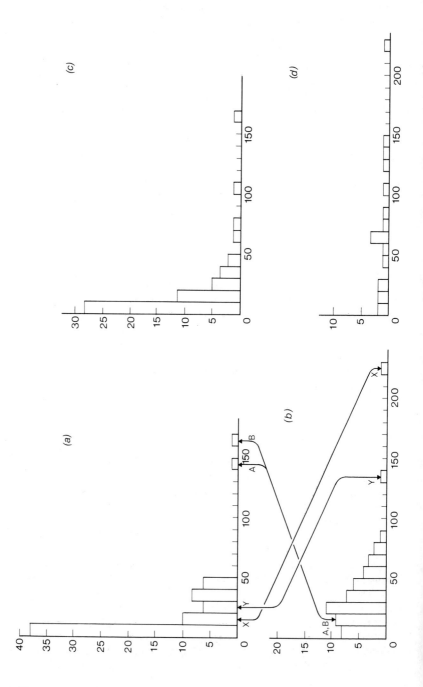

dependants are a hindrance to expansion, they have married late, if at all, and their children have not yet reached adolescence. The present junior generation, now entering their twenties, were still too young to be along in reindeer work before their fathers abandoned active herding, and therefore lack experience and training in reindeer management altogether. Many have joined their fathers on the unemployment register and in casual labour. Active herders therefore constitute a rather clearly demarcated generation set (fig. 16).

The expertise, caution and foresight whereby the pastoralist of the older generation controlled the growth and welfare of his herds was rendered redundant as herding took on an exclusively predatory form. It was this loss of control which led traditional men to cease further investment in reindeer management, at the same time opening up a career for the kind of man who thrives not on caution but on risk. Changes in the overall herding situation have thus thrown into prominence a personality contrasting vividly with that of the declining small-man reduced to hunting *peurat* for his subsistence needs. This is the reckless adventurer, identified with that rugged, individualistic and highly competitive form of leadership constituting the style of the 'big-man'.

The contemporary 'big-men' of reindeer management are the few most conspicuous of the present generation of active herders, who have accumulated both considerable private holdings and personal prestige, surrounded by a following of active but less outstanding men. Their *peura* investments represent a gamble in which the biggest men play for the highest stakes, publicly demonstrated in the bidding at auctions. Where the traditional pastoralist accumulated wealth through his control over the reproduction of his herd, the big-man enriches himself through a risky policy of wholesale speculation, mediated not by natural increase but by financial profit. The former was typically reserved and evasive in his relations with others. As extension of social relationships could only lead to dissipation of the herd, he preferred to gloat alone over his amassed fortune. However, under predatory pastoralism, a man's wealth is dispersed in the forest and apparent only in small samples at separations, never in its entirety; whilst in herding activities, the emphasis shifts from the control of discrete herds by individual owners to joint campaigns to drive collections of deer of assorted owners into fence-enclosures. Whereas the traditional pastoralist took pride in the size of his collected herd, the contemporary big-man

Fig. 15. The proliferation of small-ownership among the Skolts, between 1959–60 and 1971–2. Horizontal scale: number of deer owned; in classes 1–10, 11–20, ... Vertical scale: number of owners in each class. *A*, Näätämö Skolt 1971–2. 70 owners. *B*, Muddusjärvi Skolt 1959–60. 53 owners. A, B, X and Y are the owners shown in Fig. 14. *C*, Vätsäri Skolt 1971–2. 53 owners. *D*, Paatsjoki Skolt 1959–60. 18 owners.

exults in the success of the hunt: in the number of deer he and his
followers have found and brought to the fence, representing a challenge
to his rivals. Where the former was an isolationist, the latter invests all
his personal energies in expansive sociability, seeking prestige and followers
as a leader of herding campaigns. For the big-man, extension of relationships opens up channels for the amassment rather than the dissipation of
desired resources.

In associational campaigns, the big-man is the focus of a team of hunter-
herders, rarely more than a dozen men. He may occupy the position of
association foreman, carrying the responsibility of directing operations
in the field. Even if he occupies no formal position, he is nevertheless
the effective boss in practical herding matters. In order to meet quickly

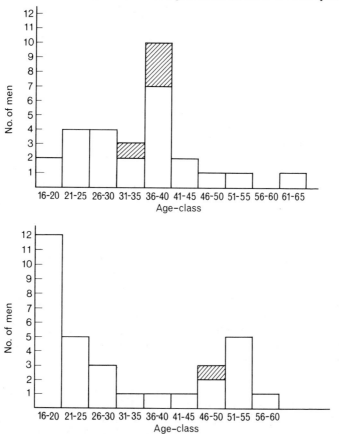

Fig. 16. Age/frequency distributions of men actively involved in herding
(above) and those on the unemployment and casual labour circuit (below).
Shaded areas refer to non-Skolts.

changing and unpredictable situations in the deployment of deer, herding demands flexibility and individual initiative rather than a formal and rigid structure of command. Thus, whether or not the big-man is the recognized foreman, during the campaign he is a leader among peers, whose authority lies not in the formal status but in personal prestige and experience. Other herders look to him for initiative and direction, and by seeking his approval to gain admission to the team, they become his followers. Likewise, the big-man not only becomes a focus of *peura*-hunting partnerships but dominates in the summer marking, the most important arena for the accumulation and consolidation of wealth in reindeer holdings.

Few men can hope to reach positions of influence in practical herding except under the shadow of the big-man. Anyone attempting to ' go it alone ' is unlikely to find support and risks personal humiliation. Thus, one man who attempted to collect deer to a separation independently of the big-man and his team was barred from bringing them himself to the fence, and from claiming credit for finding them. In the separation, he was openly prevented from bidding in the *peura* auction, and during the subsequent festivities, he was beaten up and robbed by the big-man and two of his followers. On another occasion when the same man attempted to stage a separation on his own, he was able to recruit only a motley assortment of redundant older generation small-men who were normally excluded from herding campaigns. The attempt, involving the traditional herding combination of skis and dogs, attracted widespread derision and ended in fiasco: the only deer found in the fence had wandered there by accident.

Unlike the somewhat reserved and introvert traditional pastoralist, the big-man is a loud-mouthed extrovert: boastful, extravagant, generous and sociable, a man who makes himself the centre of attraction. Renowned for their heavy drinking in post-separation activities, where spirits flow freely and the norm of reticence is lifted, rival big-men publicly vaunt their respective prowess, exploits and achievements in herding campaigns, engaging in boasting matches in which they have been known on occasion to come to blows. The coffee-house by the separation fence becomes a setting for the display and affirmation of prestige. In association meetings, too, the big-man asserts his dominance, having the last word when others have had their say. He makes the loudest, longest and most rhetorical speeches, leaving his audience to murmur assent or dissent but not to question his pronouncements.

Big-men claim that their aim is to get as many people as possible along into reindeer management, not to push them out. They complain about the phlegmatic indifference of the small-men, sitting at home reflecting on the past, whilst they themselves are constantly looking to the future, for ever planning new operations and experimenting with new techniques. In the ideology of the big-man, it is his own unflagging energy that keeps reindeer management alive; and in his own personal success and prosperity lies that of the community as a whole. Through his investments he contributes the most to the wealth of the association, and through the initiative and success of his herding operations he brings a share in the rewards and a boost to the morale of his active followers. If in the long run the small-man loses, it is due to his own lack of ambition and enthusiasm, whilst the active may partake in the big-man's prosperity, as long as they accept his dominance.

This view is in sharp contrast to the co-operative ideal of the formal association structure, in which individual welfare is seen to stem from a common commitment to a clearly defined set of rights and obligations, backed not by the might of the big-man, but by formal legal sanctions. Two contrary systems of power and control thus appear to be operating side by side: the one informal and unstructured, based on personal prestige and influence, dominated by the big-men who pull their followers along in their wake to take a share in their fortunes; the other a formal structure, based on impersonal legal rules, and with an organizational arrangement of elective offices. These two systems tend to counterbalance each other. The association, having resort to the law, keeps in check the growth of the wealth and power of big-men; whilst the operation of the latter maintains a markedly uneven distribution of wealth despite the levelling-off effect in the generation of *peurat*. Whereas active herders look to the big-man for direction, the small-man seeks security in the reindeer management law and the *paliskunta* rule-book, claiming his rightful benefits irrespective of personal allegiances. Where the ideology of the small-man stresses the contrasts of honesty and dishonesty, legality and illegality, in the terms of the big-man, men are stupid or cunning, unambitious or enterprising.

The pivot between the two systems is the office of association chairman. The chairman must enjoy the trust of the small-men, be a man of their generation without outstanding personal ambitions and interests. At the same time, he must be prepared to bend to the demands of the big-man in practical herding matters, where effective power rests with the latter. Although at the apex of the formal association structure, in practice the chairman has little sway over the course of events, and little authority to influence decision-making. His efforts are concentrated in maintaining his own credibility and the facade of association consensus and unity symbolized by his leadership. His task requires a large measure of diplomatic skill. Whilst remaining acceptable to the big-man, the chairman must not appear to sacrifice his moral integrity as an upholder of association law in the eyes of the small-man.

It is now possible to sum up the transformation of the reindeer economy to its modern associational form, and to piece together a complete picture of the management strategies that have been generated in the process.[3] The traditional pastoralist increased his herd by maximizing the reproduction of existing stock. Deer were slaughtered only to satisfy domestic necessities of meat, money and exchange credit. *Peurat* had no place in this economy: growth was achieved through natural increase, whereas money and credit were involved only in the procurement of livelihood. To this traditional pattern, associational organization separated the roles of herder and deer-owner. The financing of herding labour through membership subscriptions allowed a man to herd for wages without owning deer, or to own deer without taking part in herding.

As low finds created a high *peura* supply, the 'interest rate' on deer correspondingly decreased. For the association, herding costs increased owing to mechanization, but the income through subscriptions decreased. The balance was made up from the auction of *peurat*. The availability of *peurat* in large numbers enables active herders to pursue a policy of investment, whilst the expansion of the commercial market removed the traditional illiquidity of reindeer holdings, opening up a new growth spiral based on financial profit rather than natural reproduction. The investor can buy *peurat* at cheap association rates, reselling at higher prices to the meat merchants when they are found in subsequent seasons. Quick profits may even be made by resale in the same separation. Through the enlistment of followers and control of key herding operations, above all the summer-marking, the big-man is able to build up and consolidate sizeable holdings, ensuring an intake of calves and *peurat* well above the natural or even legal level. Meanwhile the small-man, whose herd dissolved as his deer scattered and calves grew to *peurat,* finds himself dependent on *peurat* for domestic meat supplies. *Lihaporo* may be obtained either by hunting *peurat* in the forest and paying a fixed price for the kill, or by bidding in the auction.

5 Reindeer (4): Associational diplomacy

The three local associations

Although the transformation from symbiotic to predatory pastoralism is apparent throughout the Skolt reindeer-management region, its effects have not been equally felt within the region's three constituent associations: Muddusjärvi, Näätämö and Vätsäri. The mood of optimism that currently prevails among active reindeer-men of Vätsäri association is not shared by their fellow-Skolts of Näätämö, for many of whom the whole future of reindeer management still appears to hang in the balance. The difference is apparent from a comparison of the number of men in each association who remain active in herding: of able-bodied Skolt men in Näätämö today, only 21 per cent are active reindeer-men, compared with 32 per cent in Vätsäri. To account for this difference, it is necessary to probe some of the intricacies of associational politics; above all the history of conflict within the original Muddusjärvi association between the Skolts and their Lappish neighbours, which led to its eventual fission and the creation in 1969 of Näätämö as a separate 'Skolt *paliskunta*' in the northern and eastern part of the territory. Against this, the lack of internal dissension within Vätsäri has been impressive, and largely accounts for its present relative prosperity.

The territorial extent and principal ecological zones of the three associations are shown in fig. 6. The extent of Skolt membership and holdings in each are presented in relation to the overall figures in Table 1. Although a majority of Skolts became members of Muddusjärvi on resettlement, they owned only around a quarter of the total Muddusjärvi herd immediately prior to fission; whereas Skolt members of Vätsäri to-day own nearly half the total herd of their association. After fission, no Skolts remained in Muddusjärvi, but a few 'old inhabitants' of the Skolt resettlement area resident on Näätämö territory were incorporated in the new association.

Muddusjärvi before fission: the polarization of interests

The original Muddusjärvi association was among the biggest in Lapland, with an official carrying capacity of ten thousand animals. A large part of its non-Skolt membership was made up of former mountain Lapps with a tradition of large holdings and extensive management, but also included

74

Associational diplomacy

relatively wealthy owners of Inari Lapp or Finnish background with
holdings running into several hundred. Besides the Skolts, a few other
elements of the displaced population of Petsamo were accepted as members of the association, having obtained plots of land in the south-western
part of the territory.

On resettlement, Muddusjärvi admitted the Skolts as members of the
association on the understanding that 'no damages or losses are sustained
as a result of their reindeer-management activities'. Winter pastures in the
sparsely populated north-eastern part of the territory, to be included in

Table 1. *The proportions of Skolt ownership and holdings in the three
local associations*

Association	Vätsäri	Muddus-järvi	Muddus-järvi	Näätämö	Näätämö + Muddusjärvi
Year	1971–2	1968–9	1971–2	1971–2	1971–2
Total number of owners	124	203	138	82	220
Number of Skolt owners	53	66	—	70	70
(as percentage of total)	(43)	(33)	—	(86)	(32)
Total number of recorded deer	2215	5388	5417	1630	7047
Number of Skolt-owned recorded deer	1044	1403	—	1317	1317
(as percentage of total)	(47)	(26)	—	(81)	(19)
Highest permitted number of deer on association territory	4500	10000	6000	4000	10000

the resettlement area, were little grazed; and were expected to suffice to
support the additional numbers of Skolt-owned deer. Nevertheless,
relations between the Skolts and their neighbours in Muddusjärvi have
never been good. From the time of resettlement, the Skolts and their deer,
justifiably or unjustifiably, were felt as a burden on the resources of the
association. The Skolts, for their part, complained that calves were being
lost as their animals mingled with the large herds of neighbouring owners,
and that the late retrieval of deer from association separations was
jeopardizing the success of traditional intensive-management practices.

75

The procurement of livelihood

The situation was aggravated by the construction, in 1957, of the separation fence at Petsikko, on the north-west perimeter of the territory. Unlike their neighbours, Skolt small-owners were more concerned with the continuity of their subsistence and exchange economy than with new commercial outlets; and resented the forced abduction of their herds westwards from their areas of domicile to distant marketing points from which many never returned. The consequent clash of interests already threatened to split the association; but the Skolts were temporarily appeased by the construction in 1961 of a new fence at Silisjoki, in the heart of the northern fells, where deer gathered by Skolt herders could be separated on home ground (fig. 7).

During the years that followed, tensions continued to build up within the association against the backcloth of overgrazing, the loss of control over herds, and the adoption of the snowmobile. South-west Muddusjärvi herders were quick to acquire snowmobiles, and were ruthless in their application. Skolts who would not, or could not, manage a snowmobile were summarily excluded from herding operations. On a number of occasions, snowmobile teams of south-west Muddusjärvi men used their technological superiority to seize control over herds collected by the Skolts ready for separation at Silisjoki, driving them at breakneck speed across the tundra to market at Petsikko, a journey of over fifty kilometres during which many animals were lost.

Older Skolts, frustrated at their failure to put into practice strongly held ideals of intensive management, regarded such operations as flagrant raiding. They saw their animals taken out of their hands, driven to distant parts, only to be let loose in the forest, perhaps never to be seen again. As the number of animals appearing in separations declined from year to year, the obvious conclusion was that they had either been driven to death by the snowmobile or become completely wild. Whatever the real reasons for the collapse of intensive herding, the cause was seen to lie in continual harassment and interference from dominant south-west Muddusjärvi herders.

Matters came to a head in March 1967, when a meeting of the Skolt assembly – the council of householders in the resettlement area – approved a proposal that Muddusjärvi be divided to create a new association in which Skolts could manage their animals in their own way without hostile interference. Lacking an independent voice within the formal association framework, Muddusjärvi Skolts presented their case through the assembly in terms of ethnic solidarity; although a third of the Skolts in the assembly, members of Vätsäri, had no more interest in the resolution of the dispute than a sympathy somewhat tempered by perennial quarrels with their neighbours over common territorial borders. Negotiations within Muddusjärvi association, held early in 1968, failed to produce any area of agreement between the Skolts and the association executive; and the proposal was forwarded to the Provincial Government in Rovaniemi, which is empowered to pronounce final judgements on matters of this kind.

In their proposal, the Skolts claimed that the existing Muddusjärvi territory was too large. Deer were allowed to wander so far afield that they could be neither collected nor kept under adequate surveillance. In reply, the Muddusjärvi executive pointed out that the northern fells constitute an essential area of good summer pasture; and that the effect of dividing the territory, such that the best summer pastures would lie on one side of the new boundary and the best winter pastures on the other, would be to reduce very considerably the number of deer that could be maintained on both sides.

The Skolts went on in their proposal to claim that extensive herding operations mounted by the association were incompatible with their traditional intensive management methods, which they wished to perpetuate within the security of an independent, territorially enclosed, association. Most of all, they objected to the new techniques of herding with snowmobiles. The Muddusjärvi executive argued back that active Skolt herders were using snowmobiles in herding as much as, if not more than, everyone else; and that since the construction of the Silisjoki fence, they had been free to participate on an equal footing with other members of the association. However, it maintained that since so many Skolts had given up reindeer management in recent years, the active herding force would hardly suffice to gather the deer on their territory without external intervention. Though facts could be adduced to substantiate both points of view, the Skolt case ignored active herders of the younger generation firmly committed to new methods and with increasing reindeer holdings; whilst the Muddusjärvi executive failed to point out that snowmobile operation had become a precondition for active herding, or to take into account the reasons behind the abandonment of reindeer management on the part of more senior Skolts. Likewise, the Skolts were able to claim that their holdings had fallen during the sixties, whilst the Muddusjärvi executive claimed they had risen.

Both sides courted support from Vätsäri. The Skolts claimed that Muddusjärvi herding activities were a harassment to their neighbours in Vätsäri, but at the same time demanded the return of an area of pasture at the north-east extremity of the territory which had been ceded to Vätsäri in 1964. The executive, on the other hand, claimed that the association had no quarrel with its neighbours; and further that since the transfer of pasture to Vätsäri, which was no longer disputed, the association could not withstand any further territorial reduction. In a characteristically double-edged statement, Vätsäri raised no objection to the division of Muddusjärvi, but refused to return any of the territory previously ceded to it.

After consultations with other interested bodies, the Provincial Government accepted the reluctant verdict of the Reindeer Associations' Union that since the two parties appeared unable to co-operate, division represented the only viable solution. The formation of Näätämö *paliskunta* was announced in August 1968. The line of division, cutting the territory

approximately from North to South, was less generous to Näätämö than
that suggested in the Skolt proposal, cutting off some 40 per cent of
original Muddusjärvi territory. The common boundary with Vätsäri
remained unchanged.

Näätämö: old hand, big-man and politician

Näätämö *paliskunta* began operation in June 1969 under very different
conditions from those prevailing in the early days of the Petsikko conflict
when the idea of division was first broached. By this time, all intensive
management had ceased, and the snowmobile was firmly established as an
instrument of herding. The opening up of the road through Sevettijärvi,
and the construction of nearby fences, equalized opportunities for
commercial marketing with those of Muddusjärvi in the West, eliminating
one of the major initial sources of conflict. On the other hand, with the
revival of summer-marking separations and the growing economic significance of *peurat,* control over summer pastures and separation sites in the
North became an issue of crucial importance.

Whereas the Skolt case had been framed in terms of traditions of
intensive management, the dominant interests in Näätämö came to be
those of the Skolt big-men and their active followers. The initial incom-
patibility between extensive management geared to the market and
intensive management geared to subsistence production and exchange
trade reappeared *within* the new association in the form of disputes over
peura allocation between big speculators and small-men in need of meat.
At the same time, rivalry between Skolt and Muddusjärvi Lapp big-men,
operating within a commonly accepted pattern of extensive mechanized
herding, was raised to an *inter*-associational level.

Under their leadership, the herding teams of each association compete
to maximize finds of deer, and above all of *peurat,* in their respective
separations. Just as the original *peurat* that were hunted in pre-pastoralist
times, so modern *peurat,* the unmarked offspring of the pastoral herds, are
initially the property of the group on whose territory they are found: once
of the *siita,* now of the *paliskunta.* This form of competition, in which
prosperity is measured by the number of animals that can be captured on a
given territory, can thus be regarded as a product of the transformation to
predatory pastoralism.

Näätämö continues to be referred to today as the ' Skolt *paliskunta*',
although only 57 per cent of Skolt owners are included in it, and although
membership is open to non-Skolt ' old inhabitants '. Prior to fission, the
ethnic label had been used to define a cultural contrast in economic goals
and management strategies, a contrast that applied only to Skolts trained
under ' traditional' conditions in pre-war Suenjel. After fission, it ceased
to represent an informal minority interest, denoting instead a *paliskunta*
unit formally identical to adjacent units of the same order, and represented
in the field by younger men whose goals and strategies matched with,

rather than differed from, those of their neighbours. 'Skolt' and 'Muddus-Lapp' refer to two teams competing within a framework of rules of neither Skolt nor Lapp, but Finnish, and hence ethnically neutral, derivation.

The foundation of Näätämö really came about through the convergence of three quite distinct interests. Firstly, traditionally-oriented Skolts still hoped for a revival of intensive management, if only 'foreign' deer could be kept off the pastures, and their own deer kept on, by constructing a fence along the overland boundary with Muddusjärvi. The vision of the association's older members, tainted with nostalgia, is of a closed-in exclusively Skolt area, free from snowmobiles, the deer tame, and lichen thick on the ground. In view of the state of the pastures, and the activities of big-men within the association, the possibility of realizing this vision appears remote, even if a boundary fence were to be built. For some, the projected fence has assumed exaggerated significance as a symbol of defence against hostile neighbours: a barrier against people rather than reindeer. On the other hand, many Skolts whose main concern today is to obtain meat for domestic consumption privately admit the injustices of the policy enforced by big-men of their own association towards those with *peura* debts, claiming that in Muddusjärvi a poor man is never denied meat when in need.

The second interest was that of dominant or aspiring big-men. Whilst paying lip service in public statements to the vision of their elders, their support for the Skolt cause had little to do with a wish to revive intensive herding methods. Rather, they used the pretexts of ethnic solidarity and respect for tradition to win a decisive competitive advantage over their neighbours, by gaining exclusive control over the summer pastures and separation sites within Näätämö territory, and thereby increasing their fortunes at the expense of both their Muddusjärvi rivals and their fellow Skolts. It is a matter of common knowledge in the association that big-men and their followers, whilst extolling the virtues of traditional ways and paying tribute to the expertise of their elders, are putting their ear-marks on as many calves and *peurat* as can be found. In order to defend their advantage, big-men depend on the maintenance of ideological consensus on the local level, and on the continued representation of the Skolt cause at higher levels of administration.

A third and formative interest behind the creation of Näätämö was a personal one: the political career-objectives of the Skolt headman and chairman of the community assembly, whom we shall call M. This man, who lives outside the area and who has not been actively involved in reindeer work since his youth in Suenjel, has throughout the resettlement period sought advancement within the political and administrative framework of the wider society through a claim to be the sole representative of his people.[1] He was the architect of the original proposal for a separate Skolt association; and the acceptance of this proposal, followed by his election as secretary to the new *paliskunta,* represented a personal triumph to which he drew much public attention. M has vociferously defended the cause of Näätämö in the press, in general meetings of the Reindeer Associations' Union, and in memoranda to the Provincial Government. His writings and speeches, couched in pompous rhetoric, are calculated to rouse the collective guilt of an outside audience sympathetic to the plight of small minorities. The Skolts are portrayed as the victims of malicious prejudice: despised, distrusted and downtrodden by all and sundry.

That such prejudices exist against the Skolts cannot be denied, yet they are equally reciprocated. To denigrate one's neighbour and to be a little bit dishonest oneself is, indeed, an accepted element of the business of reindeer management; and there have been successful reindeer-men among both the Skolts and their neighbours. Thus, whilst M fabricates a picture of ethnic stigmatization in order to impress the administration and the general public with the moral legitimacy of the Skolt cause, active reindeer-men in Näätämö are planning strategies of cunning and deceit with which to outwit their Muddusjärvi opponents. They depend on M to win concessions from the administration, just as he must be able to call on the unanimous support of his association members in order to maintain his credibility and increase the stock of political capital that he can apply outside the local arena. Both rely on the perpetuation of an ideal, the restoration of traditional practices amongst a generation of 'old hands' who have been left largely as spectators whilst politician and big-men have pursued their separate but complementary objectives. It is amongst these small-men, disillusioned by the failure of the new regime to bring any material improvement in their situation, that the first cracks in the facade of association unity are appearing. Only the threat from Muddusjärvi, which persists as long as the border fence remains unbuilt, prevents the emergence of an open split.

The three interlocking yet partially incompatible interests behind the formation of Näätämö *paliskunta* are borne out in the choice of association officers. The election and subsequent re-election of the politician, M, as association secretary and treasurer went unopposed. Association positions demanding an involvement in field operations, such as foremen for the direction of herding campaigns and delegates to attend separations on neighbouring territories, were mainly filled by big-men and their followers. For their first chairman, the Skolts chose an old hand, an acknowledged expert in traditional reindeer-management practices and firmly committed to their restoration. For reasons of health, he did not stand for re-election at the end of his first term of office in 1972. Four candidates were nominated for the post. One, a Lapp married to a Skolt but with many relatives in Muddusjärvi, was excluded on the grounds of his ethnic identity. It was felt that if the idea of Näätämö as a 'Skolt *paliskunta*' were to mean anything, the chairman must at least be a Skolt himself, whilst kinship ties across the border would naturally compromise loyalty to the association. On the other hand, the executive

Associational diplomacy

has always included one non-Skolt member to act as an intermediary in negotiations with Muddusjärvi; and also to convey information that he may receive through private channels. The other three candidates were a big-man, a younger brother of M with rather similar political ambitions, and the elder brother of the retiring chairman – a man already in his fifties. The third received overwhelming support. Like his predecessor he is a moderate and easy-going but not ambitious man, with a great deal of experience behind him: an ideal puppet for the dominant interests that voted him in.

Näätämö: fences, flaglines and the threat of reunification

The creation of Näätämö *paliskunta* did not, as the authorities had hoped, remove or diminish the conflict between the Skolts and their neighbours, but merely carried it onto a different plane. The present dispute largely focuses on the projected construction of a reindeer fence along the overland boundary between Muddusjärvi and Näätämö: a project which the former has consistently opposed. In the absence of a fence, the combined herds of both associations continue to make their customary annual migrations from the forests in the south and west of the region to summer pastures in the north and east. Since Muddusjärvi deer presently outnumber Näätämö deer by more than four to one, it usually happens that only a minority of the deer found on Näätämö territory actually belong to Näätämö owners, whilst the majority of Näätämö deer are found on winter pasture in Muddusjärvi territory.

Thus, in 1971–2, 30 per cent of deer found on Näätämö territory belonged to Näätämö owners, compared with 49 per cent belonging to Muddusjärvi owners; and conversely, 29 per cent of Näätämö deer were found on Näätämö territory, compared with 47 per cent found on Muddusjärvi territory. This may be contrasted with the situation in Vätsäri, whose borders do not cut natural migration routes. In the same winter, 79 per cent of deer found on Vätsäri territory belonged to Vätsäri owners; and conversely, 88 per cent of Vätsäri deer were found on Vätsäri territory.

Mixed in with the herds are considerable numbers of unmarked *peurat*. In recent summer separations, the number of *peurat* appearing in the fence has averaged at about 10 per cent of the herd. This represents a major source of wealth for the association on whose territory they are found. For the three local associations today, *peura* profits have constituted between 70 and 80 per cent of total annual income, the remainder coming in from membership subscriptions and compensation payments from neighbouring associations for finds of stray deer. The compensation income may be quite high for an association like Näätämö, in which the majority of deer found on the territory are strays; but may be more than offset by similar outgoing payments for deer of the association found outside its territory. For example, in 1971–2 Näätämö suffered a negative balance of 76 deer, representing a net financial loss of about 600 Fmk.

However, compared with annual incomes from *peurat* of the order of 50000 to 100 000 Fmk, gains or losses on this scale are of little consequence.

It is in the competition for *peurat* that Näätämö's control over summer pastures for both its own and Muddusjärvi deer is of critical importance, since the haul of *peurat* from a successful summer separation may run into hundreds. Muddusjärvi has repeatedly proposed that the summer-marking should be carried out jointly at Silisjoki fence by herders of both associations, and that *peurat* be divided in proportion to the total number of cows of each association recorded the previous winter. It was argued that for the Skolts to claim the lion's share of the *peurat* would be unreasonable in view of the fact that the vast majority are the offspring of Muddusjärvi animals. Näätämö has rejected this mode of division, suggesting instead that the find of *peurat* should be split equally between the two associations.

In practice, having failed to reach agreement, the two sides have held separate summer separations: Näätämö at Silisjoki and Muddusjärvi at the nearest point to its present north-east extremity, just over the border from Näätämö, where herds could be intercepted on their return migration south-west from the high fells at the end of the hot spell in July. However, a large proportion of animals reaching the Muddusjärvi fence were found to have already been through the Näätämö marking. The strain imposed on these animals was, as a result, doubly severe, and was felt by the deer of both associations to a like extent.

In summer 1971, Näätämö handled about 3500 animals at Silisjoki, obtaining a haul of about 350 *peurat*. The figures for the Muddusjärvi fence were approximately the same, giving a similar numerical result to that which would have been obtained had a joint marking been carried out on the lines proposed by Näätämö. On the other hand, had Näätämö accepted the Muddusjärvi proposal, its share of *peurat* would have been only about 170 animals. Through its control over the Silisjoki site Näätämö was thus able to ensure a net gain of some 180 *peurat* at Muddusjärvi's expense, representing in financial terms a profit of around 16 000 Fmk. Clearly, the argument over *peura* allocation involved more than the mere recognition in principle of Näätämö's territorial autonomy; for the benefits of a joint operation in minimizing damage to the deer were obvious to both sides. Yet, when herds were reported returning north-east after the Muddusjärvi marking in 1971, Näätämö was still prepared to stage a second separation at Silisjoki. The reports proved false; but had the operation succeeded, many deer would have had to suffer three separations in succession, an ordeal which weaker animals could hardly have been expected to survive.

Both sides have deployed temporary flaglines as a strategic device for summer herding. In the summers of 1970 and 1971, Muddusjärvi put a flagline across the reindeer migration ' corridor ', just within its territorial border. At this point the corridor is at its narrowest, forming a bottleneck some eight kilometres wide flanked on one side by the Utsjoki boundary fence and on the other by the great lake Iijärvi at the head of Näätämö river (fig 7). The line was set up after the deer had moved south, away from summer pastures; the object being to prevent the deer, including Näätämö animals, from returning to Näätämö territory, and therefore to ensure a good find of deer, calves and *peurat* the following winter. The results of the strategy were not altogether in Muddusjärvi's favour. The deer found on Muddusjärvi territory in winter 1971–2 were in much poorer condition than those found on Näätämö: firstly because many of these were animals that had been through the summer-marking twice, the others having remained behind; secondly because the flagline had made it impossible for them to return to good summer pasture, essential for recovery and growth, whilst many of the deer deterred by the flagline had drifted westwards onto neighbouring territories. The condition of the deer was in fact reckoned so poor that both associations were compelled to abandon their separation plans for the following summer, in the face of substantial losses had they been carried through.

The agreement to forgo summer-marking separations in 1972 did not, however, extend to summer herding with flaglines. In an attempt to foil Muddusjärvi tactics, Näätämö planned a similar flagline across the migration bottleneck on its own side of the border. The operation had to be carefully timed, to catch the deer after they had arrived on the fells and before they returned south. In the event, the plan was wrecked by unusual weather conditions which brought an exceptionally early southward movement. A survey carried out by light aircraft after the line had been laid revealed Näätämö territory to be practically empty of deer, and the line had to be lifted in order not to prevent them from returning later in the season. In the use of tactical devices of this kind to compete for a mobile resource, it is clearly the reindeer themselves who, wittingly or unwittingly, hold the balance of power (Ingold 1974b: 532).

Following the successful Skolt initiative in establishing a separate association, it fell on Muddusjärvi to make representations to the administration in order to win back its advantage. A long memorandum, recommending that the two associations be reunited, was drawn up by a ' committee of four' and sent to the Provincial Government in July 1971. Drawing attention to the conditions under which the Skolts were originally admitted as members of Muddusjärvi, the committee pointed out that their activities had resulted in a loss to the ' host' association of not only a large part of its territory, including the best summer pasture, but a quantity of calves and *peurat* to which it was entitled. By juggling the figures, the committee purported to show that Skolt summer herders at Silisjoki had marked four times as many calves to their own as to Muddusjärvi animals, although the latter outnumbered the former two to one. In addition, the duplication of summer-marking, due to the Skolts' refusal to accept proposals for co-operation, was inflicting severe damage on the herds. Proposals for joint winter herding had been rudely rejected, despite the inadequacy and inefficiency of the present Skolt herding force and the high management costs consequently incurred in Näätämö. Finally, the committee declared that the construction of a border fence would be catastrophic for the association. Deer reaching the fence on their annual migrations would trample and ruin the pasture in the vicinity, and migration routes would be deflected westwards, taking deer onto neighbouring territories. The number of deer that could be kept on association pastures would be drastically reduced.

The Muddusjärvi complaint drew a characteristically rhetorical response from M. How could the north-eastern pastures be so essential to Muddusjärvi, he argued, when they were virtually ungrazed at the time the Skolts first arrived? He accused the 'committee of four' of gross distortion of the figures for the size of Näätämö territory, the rate of calf-marking and the scale of management costs; reminding them that compensation due to Näätämö for strays found on its territory since the division, amounting to some 12 000 Fmk, had not even been paid. Joint herding he considered equivalent to collecting deer free of charge for Muddusjärvi. The only way to stop the conflict and live in peace with troublesome neighbours was to build a border fence that would keep the deer of each side permanently apart. The Muddusjärvi memorandum was just an example of the lengths to which people will go to pour abuse and insult on the Skolts. Branded as dishonest, incapable, and less than human, they were being pushed beyond reasonable limits of endurance.

In May 1972 the Muddusjärvi case was brought before the 'Reindeer Parliament', the Annual General Meeting of Finnish reindeer associations, where it received overwhelming support. Only one opposing statement was put on record. M, the Näätämö delegate at the meeting, accused the chairman of bias, and declared that the Skolts had once again become the victims of racial discrimination. Reporting back to a meeting of Näätämö association in June, he received unanimous backing for his resolution, submitted to the Provincial Government, that 'Näätämö *paliskunta* wishes to remain independent'.

Unofficially, the Reindeer Associations' Union supports the Muddusjärvi case in the name of efficient herding and the rational use of resources, considering the earlier decision in favour of the formation of Näätämö to have been a mistake. A Union working party recommended that the two associations be legally bound to co-operate in both summer and winter herding, dividing costs and *peurat* in proportion to their respective totals of recorded deer. The future of an independent Näätämö is still therefore very much open to question. Whether the administration is finally persuaded by the arguments of ecological rationality or of inter-ethnic harmony, the fortunes of the mass of small-men are unlikely to change; nor, given the extreme improbability of a border fence ever being built, will big-men of both sides cease to seek every opportunity to further their respective positions, both through tactical operations in the field, and, through their representatives, in the arena of public debate.

Associational diplomacy

Vätsäri: composition, terrain and markets

Compared with its western neighbours, Vätsäri has had a remarkably trouble-free history, and its Skolt members have, on average, fared a great deal better than their fellows in Näätämö: many owners having managed to retain their total herds at much the same level over the past decade. The factors responsible for this difference are not immediately apparent. Skolts in Vätsäri, as in Muddusjärvi, were in the minority within their own association, though this imbalance has been all but offset by a threefold increase in their membership numbers following the acquisition of earmarks and deer for their many children. Pastures are overgrazed in Vätsäri as throughout the region, though perhaps not so seriously as in Näätämö. Intensive management ceased at roughly the same time in both areas, snowmobiles have been brought into use for herding, and summer separations have been held in recent years on the fells of the north-eastern margins of Vätsäri territory. Despite these apparent similarities, Vätsäri differs from its western neighbours in respect of three factors: the ethnic composition and distribution of its membership, the extent and nature of its territory, and the location of separation points with access to road transport.

The ethnic composition of Vätsäri membership is tripartite. The Skolts are represented by the fifteen northernmost households in the resettled community. At the other extremity of the territory, in the remote area extending north from Nellim between the eastern shores of Lake Inari and the Soviet border, live around twenty Inari Lapp families. Like the Skolts, whose homes were no further away in pre-war Suenjel than today in Sevettijärvi, their economy was based largely on fishing, supplemented by relatively small-scale, intensive reindeer management. Between these two settlement areas at the northern and southern poles of the territory respectively, the only habitation consists of four related households whose members trace a common connection through descent or marriage to a Finnish 'colonist' couple who arrived in the area towards the end of the nineteenth century. Vätsäri reindeer holdings, as well as key positions in the association organization, have for long been concentrated in this latter group, although some Skolts have succeeded in building up herds of comparable size.

The sons of these 'Finnish' families are, for the most part, middle-aged bachelors, and their fathers are now old men. Living in utmost domestic simplicity, they have earned a reputation for having carried the pastoralist ideal of accumulation to the point of miserliness: hoarding their animals on the pastures without the justification of securing an inheritance for future generations. In recent years, they have attempted to impose severe constraints on the auction of *peurat* to individual association members in order to ward off the challenge from aspirant big-men. Today they hold 36 per cent of Vätsäri deer, compared with 47 per cent owned by Skolt members, and a mere 14 per cent owned by the Inari Lapps.[2] The presence of this group as a dominant, centrally-placed, 'third party' has tended to prevent the emergence of an ethnically defined north-south polarization of interests as in Muddusjärvi. If anything, the Inari Lapps in the south have been the most vulnerable to changes of the past decade, and the extent of their holdings and participation in the association has indeed dropped considerably.

The land area of Vätsäri territory is a good deal smaller than that of the original Muddusjärvi, with an official carrying capacity of only 4500 animals. Much of the terrain is extremely rugged. The southern part is densely forested, whilst with the exception of the fells on the north-eastern periphery, beyond the pine limit, the whole is cleft by countless ridges and furrows, and littered with boulders. To collect deer on such terrain requires a far greater herding effort than on the smoother ground of Muddusjärvi and Näätämö. There has therefore never been a shortage of work in the association, and Skolts have always been able to participate to the full. The snowmobile was brought into use with much less haste in Vätsäri than in Muddusjärvi, being difficult to manoeuvre on rough country. It was initially employed to transport herders to the field of operations; and only in the last few years, largely owing to pressure from leading reindeer-men amongst the Skolts themselves, has the mechanization of herding become almost complete.

The predominantly forested and low-lying nature of Vätsäri territory also affects the migration patterns of the deer. Although a large proportion of the herd collects every summer on the north-eastern fells, there is no long-distance migration 'corridor' as between Muddusjärvi and Näätämö (fig. 7). The majority of deer are accustomed to roam in the northern part of the territory, making only short-distance movements between the fells and nearby pine-forest, whilst many of those remaining in the south do not migrate to the fells at all. Consequently, Skolt herders working to collect deer in the north have a considerable advantage over the south Vätsäri herding team.

Perhaps the most significant difference between Vätsäri and its western neighbours lies in the location of winter separation fences. The southern part of Vätsäri territory remains entirely roadless, whereas the new road through Sevettijärvi affords access to a newly constructed principal separation site close to Sevettijärvi village. There has been no regional polarization of marketing facilities comparable to that created by the Petsikko fence. At the new fence the Norwegian exchange merchant is invariably present himself in competition with Finnish meat-buyers.

In all, Vätsäri Skolts could not lay the blame for the breakdown of intensive herding on the activities of their southern neighbours, and the heavy labour requirements of collecting deer on rough terrain meant that they were not automatically excluded from herding work as a result. The concentration of deer in the northern half of the territory, coupled with the opening up of commercial outlets within easy reach of Skolt settlement, have played very much in their favour, whereas Inari Lapps in the south have been left at a severe disadvantage.

Vätsäri has been involved in a number of minor boundary disputes with Muddusjärvi, and now with Näätämö. Most often these have revolved around the alleged failure of Muddusjärvi herders to collect deer in peripheral regions of their territory into which Vätsäri animals tended to stray, resulting in a loss of calves. An application lodged in 1962 for a large block of winter pasture adjoining Skolt settlement towards the south of the community was refused, but in 1964 Vätsäri made a successful claim to two smaller areas: one near Sevettijärvi, the other adjoining the Norwegian border. The legitimacy of these claims has been disputed by Näätämö, which does not recognize the results of negotiations carried out under the former Muddusjärvi regime. However, Vätsäri has already built a fence along one of its new overland borders, which has proved of some assistance to Näätämö's herding work. Small disputes of this kind maintain a situation in which association loyalty counter-balances ethnic loyalty. Vätsäri Skolts look on their Näätämö neighbours with a sympathy laced with mild contempt for the absurdities of Näätämö herding practice, whilst the big-men of each association vie with one another for personal prestige. Although Vätsäri gave its support for the formation of Näätämö *paliskunta,* its attitude towards Näätämö's current problems has remained diplomatically neutral.

The scope for rationalization

It is clear that pastoralist expansion in the region has reached its limits. Controlled herd growth has been replaced by a form of competitive redistribution inimical to the functioning of the association as a unit of co-operation, and to the regulation of management activities between associations. As the objects of competition, deer are subjected to treatment that is damaging both to their welfare and productivity, whilst the element of herd protection that characterized traditional pastoralism has entirely disappeared.

A way out of this impasse in the development of the reindeer economy would seem to lie in a more rational use of resources, geared to the maximization not of herd size but of meat production for the market. This could be achieved through closer regulation of pastures and much stricter policies of selection. In order to maintain an optimal input from pastures, reindeer stocks should not be permitted to exceed their ideal carrying capacity, and the extent of grazing should be carefully regulated according to a rotation schedule which would allow adequate time for regeneration. At present much of the growth potential of lichen is lost through overgrazing in some parts, possibly undergrazing in others, and destruction by trampling due to the failure to keep herds off lichen grounds in summer.

The rate of growth of the reindeer is highest in its first summer of life, falling off to a negligible level after two years for females and after three years for males (Varo 1969). Since the carrying capacity of lichen pasture cropped to medium height sets a maximum limit to the size of the herd that can be maintained over an extended period, it is only worth keeping over winter, with regard to meat production, those deer that are expected to grow significantly during the subsequent summer, or which have been selected for breeding in order to maintain the supply of calves at a steady, optimal level. All female calves not selected for breeding should be slaughtered at the end of their first summer, castrating all non-breeding males at the same time. The latter still have considerable growth potential and may be slaughtered after the first year. Only breeding animals should be allowed to survive to maturity. As well as making full use of the summer growth season without overstocking winter pastures, the rigorous application of a slaughter policy of this kind would make it possible to rear a breed of deer specially selected for its qualities as a meat-producer. In addition, the ever-present risk of natural loss, which increases with the age for slaughter, would be minimized. The age-sex composition of a herd that might be obtained under such conditions would differ radically from the typical pastoralist pattern, according to which the vast majority of animals are allowed to survive well into maturity (Ingold 1974b: 536). It should be possible by these means to increase productivity to at least twice its present level.

The success of any rationalized production and selection strategy would ultimately depend on the virtual elimination of the random element in husbandry. At present, only a fraction of calves are ever found after their first summer of growth. It remains in the interests of every owner to retain female calves in order to increase his herd, whether or not this is beneficial in terms of selection. It also pays him to slaughter or castrate all his male deer when they are found, since the greater part of their breeding potential would otherwise only be spent on the impregnation of cows of other owners, from which he would derive no benefit. Thus, selection for breeding, as well as for slaughter, largely depends on the chance outcomes of herding operations – on whether or not particular animals are found. It is difficult to see how the random factor can be eliminated under conditions of acute pasture scarcity without the introduction of costly artificial feeding on a large scale. A precondition for rationalization would thus seem to be a major curtailment of existing stock coupled with strict pasture regulation which would allow the lichen to regenerate.

Stock-rearing, defined as a rationalized strategy for the maximization of reindeer-meat production through calf-slaughter and selective breeding, represents an entirely new development in Finland. Despite encouragement and incentives from reindeer-management authorities, the idea of stock-rearing has yet to be accepted in the northernmost associations dominated by pastoralists and ex-pastoralists. The causes of their resistance lie not so much in the technical problems of overcoming randomization as in the separation of responsibilities incorporated in the associational system of reindeer management, and in basic contradictions between the goals and values of pastoralism and those of stock-rearing.

Firstly, associational management separates the complementary activities of herding and husbandry along two organizational axes.[3] Sole responsibility for herding, including pasture management, is borne by the association, whereas husbandry is left up to the individual owners concerned. Consequently, the owner carries no responsibility for the pasture his deer consume, and by excluding this from his reckoning, he is logically more concerned with the size of his standing crop than with the rate of production. Conversely, the association has no powers to control the husbandry decisions of its members, precluding the formulation of any coherent selection strategy on the associational level. Effective stock-rearing can be achieved only by a reorganization that would make the units of herding and husbandry congruent, such that husbandry decisions would be taken in accordance with an integrated pasture regulation and selection policy, rather than as at present, by a multitude of independent owners whose holdings are often too small to allow scope for rational choice.

Secondly, whereas pastoralism recommends a man to slaughter only the minimum of deer needed to maintain his family, stock-rearing requires him to leave alive only the minimum needed to maintain his herd. Both involve principles of selection, but whereas the former aims to maximize the resources available for deer consumption whilst maintaining the human population at a stationary level, the latter aims to maximize the resources available for human consumption whilst maintaining the deer population at a stationary level. The definition of stock-rearing obviously implies that meat is to be produced primarily not for subsistence but for sale and export, and therefore assumes the existence of a fully developed market structure as well as the acceptance of commercial values.

The evolution of Skolt reindeer management has been traced from the initial transition from hunting to pastoralism during the last century, a transition defined by the grafting of an ideology of scarcity and accumulation to a domestic mode of production. A period of growth interrupted by successive European hostilities culminated in a situation of overgrazing which undermined pastoralist attempts to control the reproduction of their herds. The simultaneous penetration of the commercial market opened up channels for risky speculation; initiating a phase of redistribution without growth, which brought an ever greater proportion of meat onto the market whilst generating a class of men dispossessed of their holdings. The step from this to a fully capitalist ranching economy would appear short and inevitable. Paradoxically, however, although the associational system has provided a framework for the transformation of the reindeer economy to its present state, it has delayed the working out of this transformation to its logical conclusion, through the perpetuation of an uneasy and shifting balance between the principles of individual profit and collective responsibility.

6 Fishing

Fish as a source of food and the dynamics of the fish population

For most subartic peoples dependent for meat on a fugitive game resource fishing provides a basic element in the diet, replacing the reliance on a diversity of wild or cultivated plants typical of more temperate latitudes (Lee 1968). In this, the Skolts were traditionally no exception. Only with the expansion of reindeer pastoralism did fishing begin to lose its dominant position in the subsistence economy of those households most actively involved in herd management (Nickul 1948). At the time of resettlement it was recognized that the fishing potential of the Sevettijärvi area did not match the richness of Suenjel waters, but it was intended that this would be adequately compensated by a developing reindeer economy (Nickul 1956). However, as the collapse of symbiotic pastoralism rendered the meat supply again chancy and erratic, many poorer households unable to afford expensive processed foods from the shops have had to fall back on fishing as a source of essential protein.

In contrast to the tenets of pastoralism, whereby the value of animals as food is subordinated to goals of accumulation, fishing is essentially a food-getting activity. Whereas pastoralism incorporates an intrinsic growth dynamic in the reproduction of herds, the scale of fishing is geared to, and limited by, the consumption requirements of the domestic group, developing beyond this level only to the meagre extent of penetration of the market for fish products. Consequently, fishing lacks the complex organizational structure of reindeer management; rather, it is carried on by individuals and households acting independently and without co-ordination. In sum, whilst the main significance of reindeer lies in the structuring of society, that of fish lies in the provisioning of its members.

The quality of fish that renders them at once eminently suitable as a source of food yet unsuitable as embodiments of wealth is their enormous reproductive potential. One female may spawn from several thousand up to half a million eggs, but only a tiny fraction of the hatched larvae will actually survive to maturity. The population is thus immediately constrained by environmental limitations such as water temperature, availability of nutriments, and pressure from predation. Two conclusions follow. Firstly, the supply of mature fish does not depend so much on the annual 'input' of hatched fry as on the abundance of nutriments and the species composition in a particular habitat. Secondly, unless a locale is subjected to extremely extensive fishing, the fish population may be relied upon to reproduce itself; indeed regular and systematic exploitation may have the effect of *increasing* productive capacity to match demand. This second point requires some explanation.

Most freshwater fish will eat eggs, larvae or fry of their own just as well as of any other species. Consequently, under natural conditions, the population tends to be punctuated by numerically dominant year-classes, separated in time approximately by the life-span of the fish. As long as members of one dominant class remain alive, they will suppress future year-classes by feeding on their young. The death of the majority of the old dominant class removes this pressure, thereby favouring the emergence of a subsequent dominant class from the young of the following year. The effect of regular fishing, by removing older fish too big to pass through the mesh of the net, is to augment surviving numbers in younger year-classes to a steady, high level. Nutriments such as larvae and plankton, which would otherwise be monopolized to the point of exhaustion by an ageing and deteriorating dominant year-class are liberated for the growth of younger generations going through the most productive phase of the life-cycle. Thus, up to a point, the more intensively a locale is fished, the more may be harvested in the future.

Experiments in fish-stocking carried out in the Skolt area over the last decade have had limited impact, owing to two widely held misconceptions about the need for stocking and the results to be expected. Firstly, it is often claimed that poor yields are due to overexploitation. Fishermen report catches of only a handful of old individuals, often so thin as to be scarcely edible. This, of course, is exactly the result that might be expected from *under*-fishing; and it is significant that poor catches are reported in just those neighbourhoods where fishing, and in particular seine-sweeping, has all but ceased as a regular activity. Whilst the exhaustion of the fish supply through past exploitation is used as a rationalization for the cessation of fishing activity, energetic fishermen continue to report good catches, and are quick to attribute the increasing lack of interest in fishing not to diminishing returns but to contagious laziness or snobbery, an aversion bred of wealth and status aspirations. Fish are to be had to the extent that one is prepared to fish for them. Secondly, just as poor stocks may result from under- rather than over-exploitation, so conversely the addition of large numbers of fry will not, as is often assumed, increase the future yield, since the population is limited in the first place by competition for food resources rather than by reproductive potential. Fish-stocking at best confers a measure of control over the quality and composition of the yield without bringing about any dramatic increase. At worst, it may jeopardize future catches by disrupting the delicate balance of the aquatic ecosystem. One consequence of the lack of co-ordination of fishing activity is that no record exists of fish catches, their extent and quality, that could be used as a guide for fish-stocking policy. Experiments have inevitably proceeded through trial and error.

The water system, species of fish and techniques of fishing

An abundance of lakes lie within the Skolts' resettlement area, ranging
in size from hundreds of small tarns to massive lakes such as Iijärvi,
Pavdijärvi and Tsuolisjärvi, and the lengthly inlets of the great Lake Inari.
One major river runs through the area, draining the greater part of it.
This river, Näätämö, crosses the Norwegian border, flowing into Varanger-
fjord north of Neiden (fig. 17).

The waters of the region tend to follow three narrow bands running
roughly parallel from south-west to north-east, following grooves cut out
in the landscape by glacial action. Permanent Skolt settlements are strung
along the shores of the 'home lakes' constituting the middle band, whilst
fishing cabins are scattered around the waters of the flanking bands:
Näätämöjoki and its feeder lakes to the north-west and the inlets and lakes
draining into Inari to the south-east.

The most common species of fish to be caught in the lakes of the region
are whitefish, grayling, pike, perch and brown trout. In addition, Näätämö
is one of the major salmon rivers of Finnish Lapland. Stocks of non-
migratory trout exist in some waters, but are not well established. Burbot
is caught occasionally, but whereas in the south it is regarded as a delicacy,
the Skolts consider it fit only for animals.

The species composition, and habits of the fish as regards diet, seasonal
movements and spawning, vary enormously from one lake to another,
giving every lake its own unique character. In general, the best catches are
obtained as the fish rise to shallow waters for spawning, though after the
exertion of spawning their condition is often poor. Apart from whitefish
and some trout populations, which spawn in autumn or early winter, most
species spawn in late spring The most productive periods for fishing are
therefore a brief spell in June, as soon as the ice breaks up but before the
heat of the summer sets in, when the main catch is of perch, pike and
grayling; and in autumn, first before the ice forms and then after the ice
is strong enough for laying under-ice nets, when the main catch is whitefish and brown trout.

Two types of net are in use: the simple gill-net and the seine. The task
of setting and checking gill-nets never requires more than two people, and
it is quite possible for one man to manage on his own. They can be used
throughout the year, except when waters are inaccessible during the
breakup and formation of ice in spring and autumn respectively. However,
in high summer, catches tend to be poor, apparently because the fish are
lethargic and are able to see the nets in the sunlight. Since dead fish putrefy
after more than a day in warm water, nets have to be checked regularly
during this season, and fresh catch must be salted or cooked and eaten
immediately.

In winter, gill-nets may be laid under the ice by cutting holes with an
ice-pick and threading the nets between them using a long flexible wooden
strip, often improvised on the spot, as a 'needle' (plate 9). The ends of the

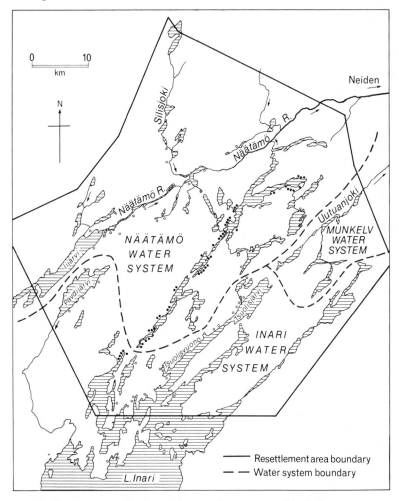

Fig. 17. Water systems in the Skolt resettlement area. Black dots represent Skolt permanent dwellings, open dots represent fishing cabins.

net are fixed with sticks which freeze into place. Once laid, it is easy to draw them in for checking, and to reset them again afterwards. However, if adequate stocks of fish have been built up to last the winter, nets are withdrawn by around January or February, when the most productive season is over, and when the thickening ice increases both the labour of setting the nets and the risk of their becoming frozen in.

Most Skolt families possess from ten to twenty gill-nets, representing an outlay of between 500 and 1000 Fmk. Old cotton nets are gradually being replaced by nylon, which is both stronger and less visible in the water. Boats, which are hauled by sledge in early spring to strategic points for fishing or transport, are nearly all made locally, if not at home. Some men who are acknowledged experts in boat-building may take on commissions for others. The outboard motor in summer and snowmobile in winter have reduced the time and effort involved in reaching netting sites, as well as opening up possibilities for commercial exploitation of more distant waters when profits from sales adequately compensate for increased petrol costs.

Whilst gill-nets are inexpensive, lightweight and versatile, seine-nets are costly, heavy and cumbersome, and are only suitable for use during the warmest months of summer, from late June to early August. Every family received one seine-net on resettlement, but as these gradually wear out, no families have felt it worthwhile to invest in new ones, whilst some have even sold or given away their seines. Use of the seine has thus declined considerably in recent years. For those who can afford to dispense with it, seine-sweeping belongs to a primitive and rejected past, and is considered a mark of traditionalism. It persists only in poorer neighbourhoods where it remains indispensable for providing the daily meal during the leanest months of summer, when meat no longer keeps and when gill-nets yield poor or rotten catches. At present, twelve seines are in use in the community, some of them shared between two households.

Due to its size and weight, the seine is used only in home lakes not far from the household. The best time for sweeping is towards midnight, when the sun is low in the sky, and the net least visible to the fish. The water should be warm and calm, dulling the senses of the fish. A team of four is required, in two boats. The net is divided between the boats, from which it is paid out from its mid-point as they diverge in opposite directions and slowly make for nearby points on the shore. The ends of the net are brought together on the shore, so that it forms a large loop in the water. As it is hauled in, the enclosed fish are forced towards the sack at the mid-point of the net, at the extremity of the loop, and are finally thrust into the sack with a wooden pole before it is lifted from the water (plate 10). The catch tends to be of smaller fish, mostly whitefish of around 10–15 cm which swim in shallower waters near the shore; and may vary in quantity depending on whether or not the net has encircled a shoal.

In contrast to gill-netting, seine-sweeping not only involves a greater co-ordination of labour, but brings immediate returns, destined for immediate consumption. When sweeping is completed around midnight, the main meal of the day is ready between three and four o'clock in the morning, and families are ready for bed at around seven o'clock. It thus happens that during the summer months different households in the community are entirely out of phase in their daily routines, with regular seine-sweepers at one extreme and wage-labourers at the other, the one rising when the other is preparing for bed.

Other fishing techniques are of little importance. Wire-netting cage-

Plate 9. Threading a gill-net through a hole in the ice. The pick is for making the hole, the shovel for removing snow and ice-chips.

Plate 10. Seine fishing. The fish are thrust with a pole into the sack at the apex of the net as it is about to be hauled in.

The procurement of livelihood

traps are scarcely used, although common elsewhere. Rod and line fishing is carried on entirely for sport, mainly by youths, and the catch is too small to be of economic significance. Fishing with a line through holes bored in the ice is a popular sport in spring, often organized in competitions. Salmon-fishing is regulated by a number of special procedures laid down by international treaty between Norway and Finland. Though important as a tourist attraction, salmon is not caught in great quantity by the Skolts, and is reserved for luxury consumption.

Fishing cabins

The traditional seasonal migrations of the Suenjel Skolts were laid down by their primary dependence on the fishing economy. Every household had built one or more fishing cabins within its customary territory, moving from one to the other in accordance with the spawning times of the fish in different waters, returning to the winter village only for the slack period from the New Year to the end of April (Nickul 1970: 21). Although on resettlement this migratory pattern was abandoned in favour of the compromise of relatively dispersed permanent dwellings whose construction was modelled on those of the old winter-village, provision was made in the legislation for the establishment of fishing cabins on traditional lines. Cabins could be freely set up on State land within the resettlement area at the rate of one per adult male.

Most households have established cabins, and in some cases men of the same households have built separate cabins, enabling them to operate more or less independently. The majority are situated at distances of ten to fifteen kilometres from the permanent dwelling; that is, the distance separating the outer 'bands' of fishing waters from the string of home lakes (fig. 17). In a few cases the connecting distance is longer – up to about 30 km – particularly when men who have been separated by the resettlement plan into different neighbourhoods from their close kinsmen wish to establish cabins nearby those of their relatives. Thus, the flexibility of siting for fishing cabins provides one means of partially circumventing the residence constraints imposed upon resettlement.

Most cabins are of traditional design, measuring about 2.5 metres wide by 3.5 metres long, with a sleeping platform along one wall and a worktop and shelves for cooking utensils along the other. An open stone fireplace is fitted into the corner next to the door at one end, and a small table is lit from the only window at the other. Supplies of salt, sugar, crispbread and dried fish, and often a battery radio, hang from the roof-beams. Around the cabin, rather widely scattered, may be a number of tiny outbuildings. Store-sheds for fish and equipment are raised off the ground to prevent incursions by animals, and often incorporate the remaining stumps of old trees as uprights. Other constructions include the *sauna,* cellar, baking oven, cooking frame, wood store, hay-loft, net-drying racks and latrine.

Footpaths connecting fishing cabins to permanent houses acquire something of the personalities of the particular men and women who walk them, marked out by the imprint of countless journeys: the odd bough broken beside the path, old fireplaces, a tin can or a bottle stuck on a twig, a fish-head or reindeer antler wedged between branches, or a stroke with an axe in the bark. These diverse and often subtle signs provide guidance over long distances on terrain that is often featureless and monotonous.

The use to which cabins are put varies a good deal from one household to another. Some cabins have been abandoned as older household members have grown infirm and unable to manage the journey, when younger members no longer have an interest in fishing. Few families nowadays spend long periods at their fishing cabins, and individuals may often leave independently or in pairs for short trips of a few days to a week or more. The most intensive use falls during the cloudberry season in late July and early August, as many cabins are situated by excellent gathering grounds. At this time, whole families may leave for a week or two at the cabin. At other times of the year the cabins are used sporadically as the need arises: perhaps merely as a base for a weekend fishing trip to stock up subsistence supplies between weeks on labour sites.

In the summers of 1971 and 1972, six households made particularly extensive use of fishing cabins. In three of these cases, only certain members of the household would leave for frequent trips lasting from a week to ten days, returning home for intervals between trips in order to take some of the catch to those left at home and to replenish supplies. In only the three remaining cases were long-term migrations undertaken, the longest being from May to October. In general, for a lengthy stay away at the cabin, the husband-wife team represents the minimal self-sufficient production/consumption unit. For larger nuclear families with young children who have special educational and health-care requirements, a long stay away, remote from the lines of supply and communication, is nowadays increasingly difficult.

A number of Skolts have built cabins on or near the Näätämö river, which are used fairly intensively during the salmon-fishing season. Recently, a number of young men have applied for cabins by the river. This does not represent a revival of the traditional fishing economy: on the contrary, most of these young men are regular wage-earners. Rather, the cabins have been redefined as 'summer cottages', a place to spend holidays away from work. As well as aspiring to the style of life of the affluent Finnish bourgeoisie, for whom fishing is recreational and the summer cottage a major status symbol, these men have an eye on the lucrative business of catering for salmon-hungry tourists who flock to the river-banks in ever-increasing numbers.

Fishing for sale

Nearly all fishing activity is carried out primarily for subsistence. Since people throughout the region obtain much of the fish they consume in this way, the demand for fish on the market remains low, and prices are rarely adequate to cover high transport costs. Unlike reindeer meat, fish holds no exotic value in the south of Finland or abroad, and no significant export market has developed.

However, a few more active, specialist fishermen, especially those operating from fishing cabins by rich waters, aim to obtain a reasonable surplus for sale, over and above subsistence requirements. In the past, fishermen with cabins on the Inari water system have sent fish to market by the post-boat that plies Lake Inari between Nellim in the south-east and the headwaters of Tsuolisvuono and Tsuolisjärvi. However, fishing in these waters has much declined over the years. Today, the most productive fishing grounds are in lakes forming the headwaters of the Näätämö river. Fish for sale has to be transported in summer by taxi-plane to the nearest point on the road, and thence by post-bus to the Finnish merchant at Inari. In addition, the fisherman has to fly in barrels of petrol for his outboard motor. The cost of air transport is so high as to impose a severe constraint on the viability of commercial fishing in the more inaccessible areas.

The allocation of rights over fishing waters

The Skolts' fishing waters in Suenjel were divided such that every household was entitled to exploit waters within its customary territory, subject to ratification by the *siita* assembly. As the old pattern of settlement and migration was lost on the move to Sevettijärvi, household territorial divisions were not re-established in the new environment. In practice, however, vaguely defined customary rights have developed, based on the habit of particular households or groups of households to exploit particular waters. Large ' home lakes ' are exploited in common by the neighbourhood of households located around their shores, smaller and more distant lakes by clusters of closely related households, by individual households or even independently by particular household members. No advantage is to be gained by placing one's nets close to those of another, and with ample waters available, there is little encroachment or competition over fishing grounds. Exclusive customary rights over waters immediately adjacent to houses or fishing cabins are generally respected (Pelto 1962: 48-9).

The development of fish-stocking in the region has added an extra dimension to the definition of informal fishing rights. Although sacks of fry can be obtained free of charge from the fish-farming department at Inari, in exchange for eggs and milt ' milked ' from mature fish, the time and effort invested in stocking are felt to justify an exclusive right to the product for the stocker. The fish-stock thus comes to acquire the character of a capital asset. Not only can this lead to a sharper conception of ownership over stocked water resources, but even to the possibility of separation of ownership and management of stocks.

Fishing

The few long-established residents who held land in the area prior to the arrival of the Skolts are in a special position as regards the management of fishing waters. In all except the three northernmost communes of Finland – Enontekiö, Utsjoki and Inari – fishing waters have been parcelled out amongst land-owners, as an extension of territorial boundaries established in the general reallotment of agricultural land (Fin. *isojako*) which replaced the old pattern of strip-farming. It was recognized that in the extreme North, where fishing and reindeer management outweigh agriculture, and where some 97 per cent of the total land area is registered as State Forest, a water allotment based on land boundaries would apportion parcels too small to meet local fishing requirements. At the same time, the legal position is complicated by the recognition of certain unwritten customary rights of usufruct on behalf of the indigenous Lappish population to their traditional fishing grounds.

Towards the end of the nineteenth century, five 'colonist estates' (Fin. *uutistaloja*) were established in the Sevettijärvi area, not only by immigrant Finnish families but also by indigenous Lapps who wished to take advantage of the favourable terms offered to colonists at that time. According to an ordinance of 1848, provisional title was granted to lands on what was then Russian Crown territory, pending the general land reallotment which had not yet reached the region, and on the understanding that these grants should not prejudice final boundaries to be established in the future. 'Colonists' were exempted from tax for a period of twenty years on condition that they cleared hay meadows, tilled the soil, and erected permanent buildings. In addition, they were granted extensive and similarly provisional rights of usufruct to fishing waters in the surrounding region, but on condition that these were to be shared with any future colonist who might settle in the area, and with any indigenous Lapps who had traditionally fished in these waters. In effect, the waters of the Sevettijärvi area were apportioned between the five colonist estates, but with a great deal of overlap, and with only vaguely defined borders (fig. 18). Essentially, this pattern persists today, as throughout the three northernmost communes where water-boundaries remain to be surveyed.

The general land reallotment was carried out in the region between 1936 and 1944. 'Colonist estates' were given full title to mapped lands ranging from 150 to 200 hectares in extent. At the same time, land was allotted to other long-established households in the area that had not previously set up colonist estates, having remained as tenants on State Forest. Each was promised rights to fishing waters to be specified in the future water-allotment. The Skolts, on resettlement in 1948–9, were entitled to fish anywhere within their resettlement area, accommodating themselves around the fishing habits of established landowners. Under these rather confused legal circumstances, a fairly equitable, informal and flexible distribution of fishing grounds has emerged. No major conflicts have appeared between the Skolts and the 'colonists' in whose waters they habitually fish, although the latter sometimes complain about the heavy pressure on fish stocks resulting from Skolt settlement.

In each commune, the 'colonist' landowners or their heirs form an association (Fin. *manttaalikunta*), a rather anachronistic institution whose sole function today is the partial management of fishing waters attached to the old 'colonist estates'. Income from fishing licences sold in the region is split equally between the landowners' association and the State Forestry Authority. The two bodies theoretically share responsibilities for the management and surveillance of fishing, to which this income is allocated.

A series of committees appointed by the State have attempted to draw up a legal basis for the allotment of waters in the northernmost communes. The report of the latest of these was published in 1971 (KM 1971, B69) and aroused a storm of protest, above all from the landowners' associations, and is unlikely to be implemented as such. The burden of the report was to reject the case for a permanent retention of rights to those fishing waters named as belonging to the 'colonist estates' at the time of their establishment. It stressed the many anomalies to be found in the old charter documents. The same water was often allotted to several different estates, whilst some of the earliest estates to be founded laid claims to vast expanses of water before other colonists arrived. Given permanent recognition, these claims would generate endless legal confusion. In addition, the report pointed out that the original division of waters had been explicitly provisional, pending a final allotment. No legal grounds could therefore be found to justify claims for the retention of this division.

Instead, the report suggested a geometrical apportionment of waters on the 'central line principle', such that the boundaries would run along lines equidistant from the banks of adjacent estates. This would be included to cover the Skolt estates established on resettlement. The bulk of waters, including those adjoining State Forest and the open expanses of large lakes, would remain in State hands. These would come under the exclusive management of the Forest Authority, but could be freely exploited by local pastoralists or agriculturalists for subsistence supplies. Unwritten customary claims to particular fishing grounds would be respected in the water allotment, but only when clearly definable. The report surmised, to the astonishment of much of the Lappish population, that such cases would be rare.

The objections from the point of view of the landowners' associations are obvious. The allotment would transfer the greater part of the waters to which the 'colonists' felt entitled to the Forestry Authority, and strip the landowners' associations of their only remaining powers. It would also put a stop to the profitable business of selling plots of land, with full net-fishing rights attached, for summer cottages; a business in which practically all landowners are involved despite their overt denunciation of tourist fishing. In the Sevettijärvi area alone, thirteen plots have been sold in this way within the last three years. However, the fact that the predominantly Lappish landowners' association membership is using the

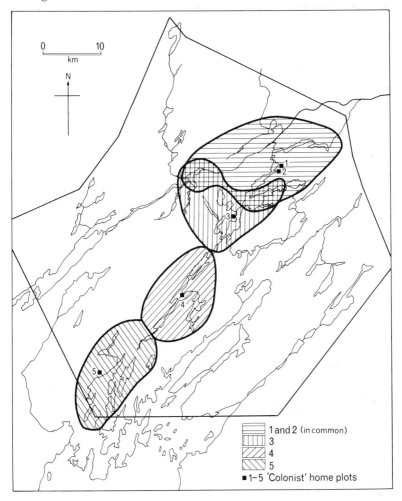

Fig. 18. The approximate apportionment of waters in the Skolt resettlement area between the five 'colonist estates'. Shaded areas enclose waters
belonging to each estate. Based on the original charter documents preserved
in Oulu provincial archives.

issue of Lappish minority rights as political capital to advance their cause
illustrates the paradoxical nature of the situation. It was above all the
indigenous Lapps who legally registered as 'colonists' in the last century.
In so doing, formerly unwritten traditional rights of usufruct to customary
fishing grounds were codified not only as having been established at a
particular date, but as being strictly provisional. It is the descendants of
these people who are objecting to the removal of their 'traditional' rights,

using the claims of the Minority Movement for the recognition of such rights in an attempt to freeze a situation originally designed to encourage colonization.

The water allotment debate has had little impact on the Skolts, few of whom are in a position to comprehend the confused legal arguments. Some felt that the present arrangement, if ambiguous, is sufficiently flexible to allow for the practicalities of fishing, and that rigid boundaries laid down in a future water allotment could cause embarrassment and perhaps conflict. The increased value accruing to the three-hectare Skolt estates through the attachment of areas of private water would be essentially theoretical when too small to satisfy more than a fraction of the households' fishing requirements. On the other hand, the development of fish-stocking has made the perceived need for a water allotment more acute. Along with the formulation of ownership of living fish stocks in the expectation of a delayed return, appears the possibility of theft. Complaints, that stocks put in by one man have been fished out by another with small-mesh nets before reaching maturity, have become common-place. Accusations are directed as much against local people as against tourists fishing illegally. Men are not prepared to go to the effort of stocking and surveillance when they can neither be guaranteed a right to the product nor apprehend an offender guilty of encroachment. It is thus increasingly felt that effective fish management can only follow the demarcation of water boundaries.

The interminable arguments over the water allotment exemplify the legal and bureaucratic penchant for the establishment of boundaries that can be drawn unambiguously on the map. It is symptomatic that whereas the discussion draws on a certain depth of legal history, no more than lip-service is paid to the technicalities of fishery management, whereas for the fish, these elaborately derived lines are obviously of no concern whatsoever.

7 The exploitation of subsidiary natural resources

The allocation of resources

A formal, legally-defined distinction exists between land and water areas under full or partial State control, and the household plot. Within their resettlement area, the Skolts are guaranteed common rights of usufruct over State resources: for pasturing reindeer and livestock, fishing, hunting and trapping, berry-picking, cutting wild meadow-grass and obtaining wood for domestic fuel and building requirements. The three-hectare plot of land is the only basic resource specifically under household control: its productive value is limited to the provision of fertility for cultivation and hay for stock-rearing. It is in this respect that the present organization differs most markedly from that of Suenjel, where all land and water resources were apportioned between members of the *siita* on a household basis. On resettlement the most important primary resources in the Skolt economy, above all, fishing waters and reindeer pasture, became dissociated from the household. It is therefore no longer possible, as it was in Suenjel, to regard the household in general as a corporate unit of production.

Although certain customary claims to exclusive usufruct have become vaguely established in the resettlement area, their significance in adding to the stock of household productive assets is limited. Thus, the division of winter reindeer pastures disappeared along with the abandonment of winter herding and the scattering of herds. Customary divisions of rights over water, except in 'home lakes', are more often on the basis of fishing cabin than household affiliation. Gathering grounds are as vaguely defined as fishing waters, and may similarly be apportioned more between nuclear families than between households, where the latter are of complex structure. There is effectively no apportionment of hunting territories, since in any case the hunting team frequently comprises two men from *separate* households, as is the rule with *peura*-hunting. Traps are usually laid along a *line* connecting two points such as the permanent dwelling and a cabin, so that an areal apportionment would be inappropriate. The provision of domestic firewood supplies is the only form of primary exploitation of common land which is organized exclusively on a household basis. In this case, the allocation of logging areas is more formal: every household has to negotiate a site with the local forest warden.

The procurement of livelihood

Hunting and trapping

The emergence of solitary reindeer hunting for the procurement of domestic meat supplies, as a response to the breakdown of symbiotic pastoralism, has already been described. Other forms of hunting have almost disappeared, and game in the area is scarce. Elk were already rare a decade ago (Pelto 1962: 58), and now appear to have been eliminated altogether in the area, although still common over the Norwegian border. Animals that are predatory on reindeer are hunted to protect the herds and for the bounty paid as a reward. A few men took foxes, receiving a price for the skin and a small bounty. The bounty on the wolverine is very high due to the wanton damage it can inflict, but it is very rarely shot. Bears and wolves, also a menace to deer, are often encountered in regions adjoining the Soviet border, but have hardly been known to penetrate the resettlement area. Although figuring prominently in traditional mythology, only a few of the oldest Skolts can claim to have met with them.

Of wildfowl, the ptarmigan is of greatest economic significance. During the autumn, from September to November, it is hunted with rifles in the pine-forest. It is most vulnerable when the plumage begins to change colour from brown to white, as winter camouflage, before the snow-cover sets in. At this time, the bird is most conspicuous, and hunters may bag some three to four birds a day. Fowling is popular amongst young men in this season, and may provide an important addition to the household diet.

When the snow-crust forms, the ptarmigan move from feeding on berries in the pine-forest to the higher tundra where they eat the buds and shoots of birch scrub. Here they may be trapped during February and March. The snare consists of a wire noose set in a gap between barriers of twigs, rich in shoots, laid between adjacent bushes. Each snare takes less than a minute to set up, and about a hundred can be laid in a day, placed along the line of a familiar route in order to aid retrieval. One stretch around ten kilometres long may contain several hundred snares (plates 11, 12).

The ptarmigan population undergoes major oscillations, and catches vary accordingly from year to year. One man who bagged nearly four hundred in 1971 took only twenty in 1972 from the same number of snares. Ptarmigan trapped in this season may be traded over the Norwegian border or sold to local merchants, through whom they eventually reach the tables of high-class restaurants. Current prices are about 6 Fmk a piece. In good years, trapping may therefore show a handsome profit, in bad years it may barely suffice to cover the extra expenses nowadays incurred in covering the stretch by snowmobile (Müller-Wille 1971: 277-9). In 1972, only six men in the area, two of them non-Skolt, felt it worth their while to trap ptarmigan, and all experienced poor results.

Plate 11. A turf cabin used as a base for ptarmigan trapping.

Plate 12. Setting a ptarmigan snare in a barrier of birch twigs.

Gathering

The Skolts gather three species of berry: the cloudberry (*Rubus chamae-morus*), bilberry (*Vaccinium myrtillus*) and whortleberry (*Vaccinium vitis-idaea*). The picking seasons follow in that order: cloudberry for a very short period of about a fortnight in late July and early August; bilberry from mid-August until it is killed by frost in September; whortleberry – which is frost resistant – from mid-September until the onset of snow-cover in mid-October.

Cloudberry is almost entirely sold for export, destined for manufacture into highly valued jams and liqueurs, for which there is an expanding international market. Bilberry has no such exotic value. It is relatively laborious to pick, difficult to preserve, and lowly priced on the market. It is therefore gathered only on a limited scale for home consumption in season. Whortleberries, which are much quicker and easier to pick, are gathered on a larger scale for domestic supplies, since they keep throughout the year and add an important nutritive element to the diet in the absence of fruit and vegetables. Any surplus over domestic requirements may be sold at a moderate price, though whortleberries lack the exotic value of cloudberries. In 1972, average prices paid per kilogram were 7 Fmk for cloudberries, 3 Fmk for whortleberries and 1 Fmk for bilberries.

Cloudberry-picking holds a very important place in the economies of those households which aim to procure the bulk of basic raw materials for domestic consumption through the traditional channels of subsistence production and exchange trade. The reindeer herd of the ' small-man ' is inadequate not only for the provision of meat to his household but for the maintenance of his former level of trade with the Norwegian merchant. As the hunting of reindeer in the wild has replaced the extraction of animals from the herd as a source of meat, so the trading of cloudberries has replaced the sale of deer, nowadays no longer possible outside separations, as a source of flour, butter and sugar. The small-man is no longer a pastoralist but a hunter and gatherer, intermittently involved in casual labour. Cloudberry sales to the Norwegian merchant have increased in inverse proportion to sales of reindeer. Only a fraction of the pick is marketed to Finnish merchants, and then only when they can offer prices so high that it pays to sell for cash in Finland and buy goods in Norway with the money rather than with credit.

The whole family, down to the smallest children, combines for picking, often residing in the fishing cabin for the two-week gathering period. The berries are packed in 25 kg barrels which, if necessary, are transported to the roadside by air. The size of the pick varies from year to year according to climatic conditions, but these variations are partially compensated by contrary price fluctuations. In 1972, most families collected between 100 and 250 kg of berries; gaining between 700 and 1750 Fmk worth of credit with the Norwegian merchant. This is equivalent to the price of some four to ten reindeer, more than the total number that many reindeer-men were able to sell the previous winter.

For the merchant, the cloudberry season is a hectic time. Within a fortnight he may handle some 10 000 kg of berries, about half of which come from the Skolts. The sellers, who may have to arrange an expensive trip by taxi to transport their produce, usually wish to take back an equivalent volume of supplies on the return trip. He therefore has to carry stocks of goods to full capacity, and may have to borrow money to tide him over until the berries can be resold.

Commercial berry-picking, though relatively lucrative, is often regarded as a poor man's activity. Wealthy reindeer-men on the one hand, and regular wage-earners on the other, seldom bother with gathering, except for luxury consumption. For the one, the herd is adequate to satisfy domestic requirements, for the other they are covered by the money income.

Logging

Although the biggest source of employment in Lapland province as a whole, commercial logging on State Forest is limited in the far North by factors of economic viability and environmental conservation, and is conducted in the region on a very minor scale. Three Skolts who had received training in forestry were more or less permanently engaged on a logging site not far outside the resettlement area. Many more are intermittently employed by the Forestry Authority in local jobs. These include planting seedlings, and supplying the substantial fuel demands of the local primary school. In the rare years when pine-cones grow in super-abundance, all the available manpower in the community may be mobilized to gather the cones, which the Forestry Authority buys in huge quantities as a source of seed. Such a year fell in 1973, when the supply of cash in the community apparently rose far above its normal level.[1]

Nearly all mechanized logging work is carried out on a sub-contract basis. The more complex jobs involve a heavy investment in skills and machinery, beyond the financial means of any Skolt. On the most basic level, both the motor-saw and snowmobile represent widely available assets that can be applied in felling and haulage respectively. The sub-contractor, at once the owner, manager and operator of small-scale motorized equipment, is paid at piece-rate, covering estimated purchase and running costs of the equipment as well as the cost of his own labour.

The Skolts are freely entitled to exploit the forest resource within their resettlement area, but only for domestic purposes. There is no shortage of otherwise worthless dead or dying timber that can be gathered for firewood. On the other hand, provision of wood for building involves the felling of large numbers of sound, standing trunks: up to 150 for one cabin or house enlargement. The trees have to be selected and stamped by the Forest Warden. The Forestry Authority is allowed to market timber from the area, but the policy has been to sell only to local institutional buyers with occasional needs, such as the reindeer associations, in order to conserve the scanty stands of high-grade pine.

Skolt logging privileges are not extended to long-established indigenous landowners, who are expected to satisfy their own wood requirements from their extensive landholdings. They are, however, entitled to *sell* timber growing on their land, as many have done in order to clear themselves of mounting debt.

Resources of the plot: stock-rearing and cultivation

The Skolts, as Finnish citizens, are subject to a legal system rooted in the traditions of peasant agriculture, attaching supreme importance to the definition of rights to land. Elaborate rules govern the delineation, transfer, partition and inheritance of estates. On resettlement, Skolt plots were carefully mapped out and measured up in conformity with the standards of the land registry, but today this exercise appears to have been of little purpose. Much of the land included within plots but not immediately surrounding the complex of buildings has been left untouched: only forgotten border stones placed here and there in the forest serve as a reminder of the omnipresence of the legal mind. Besides providing foundations for buildings, plots are valued only in so far as the Skolts themselves participate in activities of an agricultural nature: namely keeping livestock and cultivating the soil. Both are marginal to the Skolt economy.

Three households kept milking cows in Suenjel (Nickul 1948). On resettlement, only the three Skolt households of Pattsvei origin continued to keep cows, but gave it up over the last decade as hay supplies proved inadequate to cover the long winter. Most indigenous landowners with ample hay-meadows used, until recently, to own a few cows; but they, too, sold their animals as the death or infirmity of ageing housewives, whose daughters had long ago left the community and whose sons remained bachelors, left no-one to do the women's task of milking. The local diet is still deficient in fresh milk; but the new road has now made possible weekly deliveries from the shops to most households.

Sheep-rearing played a more important part in the traditional economy. In Suenjel, every household kept a few sheep, principally for their wool, which was woven into blankets and knitted to make clothes. On resettlement, each house was provided with a sheepcote, but most of these have since been converted into extra bedrooms. Sheep-rearing declined as woollen clothing became readily available from the shops. Today, only eight Skolt households and one 'indigenous' household continue to keep sheep. The size of the flock varies between five and twenty animals, and is strictly limited by the supply of winter fodder. The animals are kept over winter in separate sheepcotes, and over summer on nearby islands or peninsulas.

Subsidiary natural resources

Shortage of hay is again given as the principal reason for the decline of sheep-rearing. When supplies from the home plot are inadequate, hay has to be bought, either locally from an indigenous landowner or imported at a high price. Since their cows were slaughtered, landowners have more hay to dispose of, but most is sold to the reindeer associations which use it as fodder for deer during long separations. Although the Skolts are theoretically entitled to cut wild meadow-grasses growing on State land within the resettlement area, few do so, possibly because the best and most accessible natural meadows producing hay suitable for animal fodder were long ago appropriated as scattered 'forest plots' by the indigenous inhabitants, in the general land reallotment. Many of these have now been sold to summer-cottage builders.

Under the exclusive management of the housewife, sheep-rearing has traditionally formed a sector of the domestic economy. Today, however, when sheep are kept more for their meat than their wool, sheep-rearing provides an avenue for independent economic initiative on the part of the housewife. Some of the mutton is consumed at home, but most is sold, either to the local boarding school or to the wholesale delivery lorry, which sells it on to shops trading on the international border. A few Skolt housewives are keenly interested in the prospects for a revival of sheep-rearing on a commercial basis.

Neither the soils nor the climate favour cultivation. After resettlement, the Skolts were strongly encouraged to grow their own potatoes on their plots. Most households cultivate only enough to last a few months of the year; only one grew a year-round supply, and several had not cleared potato-patches at all. Many lack adequate frost-free cellars for storage, and the harvest is often allowed to rot. No attempts are made to grow any other crop.

8 The sources of money income (1): Local fields of employment

Constraints on the growth of private enterprise

Possibilities for Skolts to set up independent enterprises outside the sphere of primary production for an external market are limited by both social and economic constraints. On the economic side, Skolts lack investment capital, and have nothing to offer as security for bank-loans. An enterprise may well prove uneconomical on account of remoteness from supply centres and the lack of such essential service inputs as electricity. Any venture geared to the local market is inevitably risky amongst a sparse population accustomed to self-sufficiency. Business may be hard to build up in the first place, and may be lost in quite unpredictable ways.

Socially, the scope for entrepreneurship is limited by the involuted network of kinship and neighbourhood ties within which every Skolt finds himself enmeshed. These ties are grounded in a morality of generalized reciprocity in direct contradiction with the rules of commerce governing the market for goods, services and labour. Consequently, an entrepreneur exploiting the local Skolt market must be prepared to accept the costs of a socially marginal position if the enterprise is to pay off financially, let alone if it is to expand to incorporate additional labour beyond that of the entre-preneur himself. Given the general and persistent shortage of cash in the community, he faces the alternatives of either handing out unlimited credit, with the consequent threat of bankruptcy, or of making precipitate demands for payment and risking loss of custom as a result. These difficulties may be illustrated through two examples.

One innovative Skolt attempted in 1968 to set up as the local taxi-driver: he was the first Skolt to obtain a driving licence and to purchase a car. He expected the extension of the road to open up a potential demand for rides, especially to the Norwegian exchange shop. However, within a year the enterprise fell through. Upkeep of the car on bad roads proved expensive, and he was having to give too many free rides to neighbours and relatives. Today, the whole length of the road is covered by a single Lappish operator from Partakko, who hires a Skolt to drive one of his two cars.

The second example concerns a Finnish mechanic who, having married a Skolt and settled in the neighbourhood of his affines, was much concerned to establish good relations with them. Outside his dwelling he built a snow-mobile repair-shop. Though there was no shortage of potential repair-jobs, it proved difficult to attract custom. Skolts, who are not experienced

110

mechanics, are used to fixing their own machines in makeshift fashion, taking them to the workshop only when beyond repair. Most of the Finn's clients were his own affines and neighbours who regarded his work as a form of generalized assistance rather than as a specialized commercial service, even to the extent of coming along to help in the work themselves. Rather than sacrificing good relations in the neighbourhood, he chose to abandon the enterprise in favour of entering into partnership with his brother-in-law, a powerful reindeer-man, for whom his mechanical expertise represents a major asset.

The history of commercial development

The most significant field of expansion in the private sector has been of shops and bars. After resettlement, two shops were established in the ' central village' of Sevetti. The first was a branch of a leading co-operative chain, run by a Skolt family. The shop ran into all the difficulties that beset Skolt entrepreneurship: it was handing out too much credit to neighbours and kin, its accounts could never be made to add up, and transport costs incurred in supplying the shop were prohibitive. Eventually, it had to close. The second shop, the ' general stores ', was a subsidiary of a larger Finnish business based at Inari. The merchant, on his regular journeys to Inari to collect supplies, has been able to do business with Skolts living along the route. An additional asset for the ' stores ' has been its combination with the local post-office.

In 1965, the wife of the Forest Warden opened a small shop in one of a group of cabins which had been set up by a Skolt entrepreneur to provide tourist accommodation. As the shop prospered, she took over the tourist venture, which had run into disrepute under its Skolt management. When the road was extended to Norway in 1969, she embarked on a major project of expansion, building a large complex including a modern supermarket-style shop and bar, as well as private quarters. The 'Sevettijärvi Trading and Tourist Centre' was completed in 1970, becoming the biggest enterprise in the entire area. Besides holding a monopoly over the mushrooming tourist business, in which her husband's position in the Forestry Authority conferred a decisive advantage, the shop was aimed to attract the new wave of Norwegian customers driving over the border to buy meat, clothes and fancy goods at cheap Finnish prices. To satisfy the enormous demand for meat, a deep-freeze running off the shop's own electricity generator was installed, allowing stocks of fresh meat to be held throughout the year. Faced with such overwhelming competition, and unable to invest in its own electricity supply, the shelves of the ' general stores ' became ever more empty, and custom barely sufficed to keep it going.

The hegemony of the Trading and Tourist Centre was short-lived. The income from tourism began to fall off as more and more tourists took to driving straight through the village, stopping only for petrol and coffee.

The procurement of livelihood

In 1971, a mobile shop from Inari began to serve the length of the Sevetti-järvi road once a week, absorbing most of the Skolt clientele, save those living in the immediate proximity of the established shops. The greatest blow to the enterprise, however, came from the extraordinary commercial development that took place on the Finnish side of the international border during the same year.

On a bleak and desolate stretch of open tundra, near the frontier station where the new road crosses the border, two large supermarkets were built almost adjacent to one another, each incorporating a bar and café section. The first, hampered by lack of funds, was slow to be completed, but opened with a flourish during Easter 1971. The second opened later the same year. Both were aimed exclusively to capture the Norwegian market, although nearby Skolts also started to shop there. The previous flood of Norwegian customers to the Sevettijärvi Trading Centre dwindled to a trickle. There followed a scramble to obtain permits to set up businesses on the border. One merchant set up a clothes shop in a marquee tent, in anticipation of obtaining a building plot, and other enterprises were projected. The new commercial centre has the unrestrained and aggressive atmosphere of a frontier town, notorious for cut-throat competition, extravagant drinking, and violent brawls, not infrequently between the merchants themselves. As a social centre, it attracts visitors from a wide catchment area on both sides of the border; whilst its commercial impact has been to undermine the trade of Norwegian merchants in Kirkenes and throughout the South Varanger region. Only the exchange merchant on the other side of the border has remained virtually unaffected.

The growth and decline of these various commercial enterprises indicates their extreme precariousness and susceptibility to competition when dependent on such highly specialized forms of clientele as Norwegians, tourists or Skolts, each with their own particular demands. A single, unpredictable development can subvert an entire body of custom. Factors of distance and mobility are all-important: the mere placing of a shop in relation to its competitors can be decisive for its fortunes.[1]

Both border supermarkets and the Sevettijärvi Trading and Tourist Centre employ a certain amount of Skolt labour, particularly girls who serve as shop assistants and barmaids. The work offers social attractions, but wages are low, hours long, and working conditions rough. The turn-over is consequently very high. One merchant lost his entire female labour force after a violent row over working hours. Nine Skolt girls were employed at various times during 1971–2 on the border, and four older women have taken part-time work in the shops. Four Skolt youths have held jobs as van-drivers for the merchants, but for many youths the expense of obtaining a driving licence is prohibitive.

Employment in the public sector

A very small number of salaried positions are held in the community in

112

connection with local administration and public services, most of which
are concentrated within the ' central village '. An inventory of these
positions (table 2) indicates that the majority, especially those requiring
paper qualifications, are held by immigrant Finns. This confirms the

Table 2. *Positions in local administration and public services*

| | Male | | | Female | | | |
| | | Skolt | | | Skolt | | |
	Non-Skolt	Full-time	Part-time	Non-Skolt	Full-time	Part-time	Total
Frontier patrol	6	2	.	1	.	.	9
Primary school	2	.	1	4	3	1	11
Health centre	.	.	.	1	.	1	2
Post and telephone	.	1	.	1	.	1	3
Forestry	1	.	.	.	.	..	1
Road maintenance	1	1	.	.	.	.	2
Totals	10	4	1	7	3	3	28

general picture that, up to now, Skolts have either not had or not taken
advantage of opportunities to acquire professional training in fields offering possibilities of local employment.

The frontier patrol stations constitute an important source of employment throughout the remote border regions of Finnish Lapland. One such
station is located within the resettlement area, where the route to Neiden
crosses the frontier with Norway. In the absence of any restrictions of
movement across this border, the main function of the patrol is to police
the surrounding wilderness. The frontier station has exerted a strong
influence on the lives of many Skolts, especially in the more northerly
neighbourhoods where contacts with the station are most frequent.
Patrolmen have been prominent in the organization of youth and sports
activities, whilst nine Finnish patrolmen formerly or currently stationed
in the area have found themselves Skolt wives, including three from a
single family. Patrolling projects the attractive vision of a career offering
a good salary and a measure of authority combined with the freedom of
outdoor life in a familiar environment. Of the eight men currently employed
at the station, two are Skolt, and several more Skolt youths are presently
training or intending to train as patrolmen.[2]

The staff of the primary school includes three teachers, matron, caretaker, and cook, as well as three Skolt women employed as dormitory

assistants. In addition, the school employs a part-time wood-chopper, and one housewife as a part-time cleaner. The sister in charge of the local health centre is Finnish, but has a resident Skolt assistant. The post-office is managed by the Finnish wife of a local merchant. One Skolt trained as a telephone engineer when the construction of a new line through the area offered prospects of local employment. His wife managed the village telephone board as a part-time job in the home. The only permanent position in forestry is that of the Forest Warden. The road maintenance department employs an engineer to supervise construction work on the Sevettijärvi road, and one Skolt is permanently employed to carry out routine maintenance.

Casual labour

There are broadly three fields of casual labour in the local region, defining the latter by a circle of around 100 km radius, centred on Sevettijärvi. The first includes unskilled jobs on road-building and construction sites, obtainable through the State Employment Agency: these will be discussed in the following chapter. The second includes a variety of jobs obtainable locally through personal contacts. The third, work over the Norwegian border, includes haymaking, mining and fish-packing. Local casual labourers are distinguished from short-distance migrants and emigrants on the basis of their having no established place of residence apart from their Sevettijärvi homes, to which they generally return for weekends and holidays.

Most local jobs in the second category are available through the patronage of local officials and merchants. By far the most munificent patron in the community is the Forest Warden, who is periodically able to hand out logging jobs, mostly of rather short duration, to his personal clients. From the same source come opportunities to benefit from tourism by ferrying tourists by boat or snowmobile to their chosen destinations, and by looking after wilderness cabins set up for them; whilst a limited amount of work is always available in the shop, bar and in odd construction jobs connected with the enterprise. It is significant that the majority of labourers taking jobs in this category come from the neighbourhood of the Trading and Tourist Centre. For girls, the greatest concentration of local casual employment is in the supermarkets and bars on the border, which draw labour from throughout the more northerly neighbourhoods of the community.

Casual employment for male labour in Norway is mainly seasonal. For many years, from seven to ten Skolt youths, drawn mainly from neighbourhoods nearest the border, have gone to work on the farms around Neiden during the brief haymaking period in late July. They earn some 50 Nkr a day in addition to free board and lodging. For the farmers, faced with pressing labour requirements, Skolt hands are the cheapest to employ. In some instances, farmers have established enduring links with particular Skolt families. The huge iron mine in Kirkenes also attracts a few Skolt men each summer, where they are needed to compensate for the reduction in the regular workforce over the holiday months. The work is hard, but extremely highly paid. In summer 1972, five men were working in the mine, returning home every weekend by taxi. All were bachelors whose aim was to earn quick money for themselves. Two were active reindeer-men over the winter months, and a part of the money earned was to be invested in the herds. For girls, employment is available in the fish-processing factories of coastal towns throughout Finnmark. The nearest of these, in Bugøynes and Vadsø, fall within the local region, but work in more distant towns around the northern coasts involves longer-term migration. A shortage of female labour in fish-packing exists throughout northern Norway, and an active advertizing campaign has been conducted to attract the reserves of labour in Finnish Lapland.

The great majority of casual labourers discussed in this section are younger generation, unmarried men and women. Unlike many of the men who register with the State Employment Agency, they do not have to sustain a regular contribution to the expenses of domestic consumption and household maintenance; so that the temporary nature of the work is no disadvantage. Short spells of remunerative work enable the youth to invest in personal equipment, clothing, and the like, which can be enjoyed during the long spells when there is little or nothing else to do.

9 The sources of money income (2): Unemployment and welfare

Unemployment compensation

Unemployment is endemic in Lapland, as throughout the 'underdeveloped' provinces of northern and eastern Finland. In the far North it ranges between 5 and 15 per cent of the total labour force, though with marked local and seasonal variations. However, in communities that can fall back on a part-subsistence economy, unemployment is not the clear-cut phenomenon that simple figures would suggest. Only after the first local branch of the State Employment Agency was established in 1964, did Skolts begin to become 'unemployed'. They were told that, by registering at the Agency, either work would be found for them in the local region, or they would become eligible for unemployment compensation.

Over the years, more and more Skolts, many of whom had previously gained the bulk of their livelihood from reindeer management and fishing, have appeared on the unemployment list. They include former herders of the generation made redundant through mechanization and the cessation of winter herd supervision, family men responding to the growing inadequacy of traditional primary sources to meet household income requirements swollen by demands for modern equipment, and youths without experience in the traditional sector, for whom the alternative of applying for vocational training would imply long-term migration. During 1972, thirty-one men were periodically switching between enlistment on the unemployment register and employment arranged through the Agency. This figure represents 30 per cent of the formally able-bodied, non-migrant male labour force. This may be compared with the 24 per cent still actively involved in associational reindeer herding, and 5 per cent regularly employed in the public sector.[1] The picture for female labour is radically contrasting, reflecting a difference in both aspirations and opportunities for training and employment. Only one woman, with a rather exceptional career, was on the Agency list in 1972.

After registration, the applicant is expected to report to the Agency once a fortnight to confirm that he is still looking for work. Every alternate fortnight he must appear in person, otherwise he may report by telephone. So long as no work is available, he receives unemployment compensation which in 1972 stood at the rate of 15 Fmk per day for bachelors and 20 Fmk per day for married men. If he fails to report without good reason, compensation automatically ceases. Until recently,

116

a maximum of 120 days' compensation could be granted in a single year, but today it may be paid if necessary throughout the year. Officials at the Agency complain that it is notoriously difficult to keep track of Skolt applicants, who frequently fail to report for months at a stretch, only to reappear some time later when again hard up for money. Whilst bound by law in their administration of compensation, they reluctantly admit that whereas the urban unemployed labourer needs every penny of his dole to meet the basic costs of food and housing, the Skolts not only have no rent to pay, but continue to obtain almost as much of what they need from the natural environment as they did before becoming 'unemployed' in the first place.

The regular trips to the Agency at Ivalo have become an integral part of life in the Skolt community. The trip involves a return journey of 320 km: a full day's ride by bus. It may even start from a distant fishing cabin. One man, who combined visits to the agency with intensive fishing for both subsistence and sales, walked 20 km overnight to catch the morning bus, whilst on the return trip he carried back potatoes and other supplies to last his family until the next journey. Whilst at Ivalo, the commercial and administrative centre for the whole region, the visitor may conduct any other business he has at shops and offices. This usually includes a call at the bank to cash a part of his money, much of which he spends at the store of the State Alcohol Monopoly (ALKO), conveniently housed in the same building as the Employment Agency. Here, he stocks up with a supply of spirits, to be consumed before, during, and in the aftermath of the return journey. Monthly trips to the Agency are thus integrated with personal festive cycles.

Most work projects arranged through the Employment Agency are financed by a special State fund set aside for the absorption of excess labour in local regions of high unemployment. There is no shortage of potential projects: work stops either when a job is completed, or when the fund runs dry. In practice, jobs can last from a few weeks up to several months. When only a limited amount of work is available, preference is given to men with families, but all applicants were 'unemployed' for a few months of the year in 1971-2. Work is most difficult to find for youths aged 16-18, who by law can be employed for only six hours a day, and towards whom the employers bear a special insurance liability.

During 1971-2, Skolts were employed as unskilled labourers with picks and shovels on a number of road building projects in the region, both for the Roads Department and the Forestry Authority. Other projects included the construction of bridges and snowfences, a reindeer fence at Utsjoki, a hospital extension at Ivalo and a new runway at Ivalo airport. Workers live in transportable barrack accommodation on the site during weeks, returning home every weekend. Pay packets are distributed every fortnight. The pay, by general standards, is very low. Unskilled labour on the roads earns a minimum rate of 4 Fmk an hour, making a wage of about 700 Fmk a month, of which a variable proportion is removed at source as tax. On

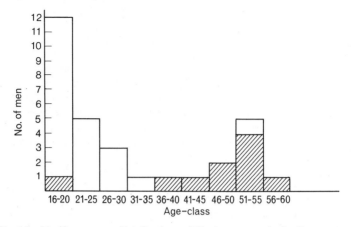

Fig. 19. Age/frequency distribution of Skolt men periodically on the unemployment register during 1972. White areas, bachelors; shaded areas, married men.

average, take-home pay for work in which Skolts were involved ranged between five and six hundred marks a month. This may be compared with the income from unemployment compensation of from three to four hundred marks a month. Over time, income thus oscillates between these two extremes: a maximum defined by the wage during periods of work, and a minimum defined by compensation during periods of unemployment.

The age-frequency distribution of the thirty-one men registered with the Employment Agency shows two separate clusters; one of youth in the age-bracket 16–25, and the other of older married men concentrated in the age-bracket 46–60 (fig. 19). Most of the latter have large families to support, whilst their reindeer herds, once considerable, have dwindled and scattered. Unable to secure an adequate supply of basic raw materials for domestic consumption through the traditional channels of subsistence production and exchange trade, they must be guaranteed a minimum of regular money income to make up for this deficiency, even to pay for reindeer shot in the forest or purchased for meat at the auction. They cannot afford to fail to report for work, as this would automatically result in the forfeiture of unemployment compensation as well. Nevertheless, road work is tough for men in their fifties, especially during the harsh mid-winter frosts and storms, and they are often very reluctant to take it on. Unlike full-time salaried earners, who have deliberately chosen to reject the traditional economy in favour of a regular income almost entirely within the monetary sector, these men are led into wage work as a result of having been forced to compromise in their attempt to *sustain* the traditional economy, under conditions that militate ever more strongly against it. Money income is intended to complement, not to replace, traditional sources; and is sought only to the extent that the latter alone no longer suffice to satisfy the constant component of household budgetary expectations.

Others without such heavy domestic commitments, including bachelors of mature years, are more likely to be able to withstand temporary forfeiture of unemployment compensation. Their original motive for registration may have been to find money to cover the hire-purchase of a new piece of equipment, such as a snowmobile or motor-cycle, rather than to satisfy the recurrent costs of subsistence. They may even fail to report to the Agency once the urgent need for money is passed. Faced with the choice between loss of compensation and going to work, they would take the former course. They may perhaps ' taste ' the job, but are in no way committed to it. Finding it not to their liking, they may give it up after a few days, preferring to be able to continue subsistence production back at home.

It is these transient applicants who cause the greatest headache for the officials at the Agency. Their irritation is understandable as long as they regard payments as ' unemployment compensation ' rather than recognizing their practical function as a means of subsidizing subsistence production. Whereas officialdom, whose categories are derived from the urban-industrial context, takes a negative view of unemployment, for the Skolts a situation of lasting unemployment represents the ideal compromise. It allows a man to keep up his productive activities in the traditional sector of the economy, whilst receiving sufficient income as unemployment compensation to honour regular monetary obligations: for the purchase of additional food, raw materials or equipment. This compromise breaks down when work is provided. If he is to prevent income from falling below minimal requirements, he may have to go to work rather than forfeit compensation. Consequently, whilst earning cash in excess of household requirements, he is forced to neglect or curtail activities in the field of primary production. It could be argued that the replacement of unemployment compensation by a subsistence subsidy would eliminate this dilemma, thereby promoting a fuller and more rational use of local natural resources, as well as giving full recognition to the sophisticated native skills that Skolts already possess (Ingold 1973).

Youths aged between around 16 and 25, who make up over half the Skolts registered at the Agency, are in a rather different position from that of their seniors. They belong to the generation that have received little or no training in traditional skills from their fathers, most of whom have also enlisted on the register. Their motive for registration is the chance it gives them to get work and become independent earners, rather than the possibility to combine subsistence production with a money income. Significantly, all the youth in this category are from neighbourhoods far from the Norwegian border and outside the normal range of local patronage: for them the Agency is the only source of opportunities for casual labour.

For many youths, registration is the first step after leaving school. They are often encouraged in this by their parents, who hope that some of the income they bring in can be applied towards household maintenance. At the same time, since these youths are in fact *least* employed, parents hope that the opportunities to earn locally might induce their sons to stay at home to help out in everyday household tasks whilst fathers are away at work. In practice, the aspirations of youth are contrary to their parents' expectations. The youth's primary concern is to break loose from the constraints of his natal household. Much of the money he earns may be saved up for a snowmobile or motor-cycle, or consumed outside the household. Very little of his earnings or his labour is contributed towards household welfare.

Youths are nevertheless strongly attached to the freedom of their native environment. Although made increasingly aware of the necessity to obtain additional qualifications in order to secure stable employment in the future, they are reluctant to apply for technical college or a vocational training course when this normally means going at least as far as Rovaniemi, 450 km away, to learn a trade for which vacancies exist only in the industrial South. They are thus inclined to take the easy course of registration, indefinitely postponing any decisions about their future careers. Until training schemes are instituted on a regional basis to provide qualified instruction in locally applicable skills, to replace the handing down of obsolescent tradition from father to son, there seems little prospect for the youth to break out from the impasse of the unemployment and casual labour circuit.

Vocational training

In response to the growing labour demands of industry and the high level of unemployment in marginal regions, a State fund has recently been set up to finance courses of vocational training for those finding themselves either continually or periodically unemployed, or whose current occupation is proving inadequate to secure a livelihood. Participants receive board and lodging, a small daily wage, an allowance for family dependants, and free travel. Recruitment to the courses is arranged through the State Employment Agency.

Applicants to the Agency are presented with a choice: either they can remain at home, switching between unemployment and local casual labour; or they can go away to attend a course designed to equip them for more stable employment. Unemployment compensation effectively pays a man to stay at home, whilst the benefits of vocational training pay him to migrate to the industrial centres. The liberality with which local employment agencies have been prepared to hand out compensation payments has come in for some criticism from labour officials in the south. In their view, too many potential workers are being allowed to idle away the best years of their lives at home, whilst an abundance of training and employment opportunities await them in the cities, where they could both earn a handsome salary and contribute to the national productive effort. Vocational training courses, most of which are heavily undersubscribed, have evidently not been as effective in promoting the redeployment of labour as was intended by the industrialists.

Since autumn 1970, nine Skolts - eight men and one girl - have been directed to vocational training courses by the State Employment Agency at Ivalo. One was continuing his course in autumn 1972, but of the remainder, only two had gone straight on to a steady job: both working as garage mechanics at Tampere in the industrial heart of southern Finland. The remaining six have all returned: one after a brief spell of work, the others directly after ending the course, in one case having even failed to complete it. After the initial 'bright lights', they had felt lonely and home-sick in the cities. Only one trainee found that he could use his newly acquired skills locally, building log cabins for the market. Others have remained unemployed or become casual labourers on the same pattern as before, re-enlisting at the Employment Agency. Clearly, as far as these Skolts are concerned, efforts to promote urban migration by offering training inducements have been of little avail.

More recently, efforts have been made to set up vocational courses within the region to serve local - and in particular Lappish - interests, rather than those of the industrial South. Courses in bone, wood and leather work as well as in small-motor repairs were instituted at Inari in autumn 1972, and two Skolts are to attend the first course in reindeer management to be held at Rovaniemi in 1973. Further developments along these lines, providing modern skills to complement traditional expertise, could do much to secure the future viability of Lappish communities.

Welfare benefits

In most Skolt households, the domestic economy rests on the assumption of an income in both subsistence/exchange and monetary sectors, and an expectation of the proportion from each sector in the total budget. In a household including a number of productive members, the maintenance of generalized budgetary expectations is made possible by the placing of members in different occupational sectors. Some may concentrate on earning wages, whilst others specialize in hunting or trapping, fishing and reindeer management. However, co-ordinated specialization of this kind rarely reaches more than a rudimentary level. Whilst the nuclear family is expected to be potentially self-sufficient, fathers can exert little control over their sons' earnings. Only in one household comprising a group of unmarried adult brothers was a measure of productive co-ordination achieved. Most often, and particularly for larger nuclear families with high consumption requirements, the maintenance of a diversified income is problematic, and the attempt may lead to irregular switching from one sector of economic activity to another when combination is not possible.

The importance of welfare benefit in the domestic economy lies above all in the ability of the receiver to continue activities in the field of primary production, as long as he is physically fit, whilst simultaneously receiving a money income. Receivers of unemployment compensation are in a relatively insecure position, since the provision of work may at any time jeopardize this combination. Pensions and child allowances, on the other hand, furnish a regular, unconditional money income. In the last decade, the significance of the child allowance as an income source has dropped, whilst pension payments have increased. In 1959, 30 per cent of Skolt households received their main money income from child allowances, and 18 per cent from pensions. In 1969 these figures were 7 per cent and 33 per cent respectively (Koutonen 1972). This shift is due in part to a relative rise in the level of pensions, and in part to changes in the population structure towards a lower birth-rate and a higher proportion of old or disabled people left at home.

The pensioner who is still active and able to produce much of what he or she consumes is an enormous economic asset to the household. A large part of pension income may be allocated towards the purchase of equipment enjoyed by junior members of the household, possibly relieving them of pressure to seek wage employment. In 1972, sixteen Skolt men and twenty-eight women were receiving retirement, disablement or widows' pensions, ranging from 150 to 440 Fmk a month, depending on particular circumstances. In addition, nine men below retiring age were receiving a wartime service pension of a similar scale of value. Only fourteen, or 28 per cent of Skolt households did not include at least one pensioner.

Whilst pensions supply a sizeable money income irrespective of the number of consumption dependants in the household, child allowances are directly related to this number. Some ten children are necessary to bring in as much welfare income as a single pensioner. Since in addition, allowances are nowadays paid directly to the mother, they are allocated more often towards the recurrent costs of provisioning the household than towards the purchase of consumer hardware.

In the years of greatest poverty immediately after resettlement, a fair number of households received maintenance allowances from Commune funds. Even today, the extent of these allowances is twice the Communal *per capita* average and four times that of the nation as a whole (Koutonen 1972). However, some 90 per cent of this amount is nowadays spent in providing institutional care: in hospital, and in children's and old people's homes. Thus, very little of this amount enters household income and then only when needed to care for a sick or disabled member. It does not therefore constitute a significant factor in the normal household budget.

Despite the importance of welfare income in the domestic economy, not all those eligible for benefits are in fact receiving them. Some older Skolts are unaware of the full extent of their rights to benefit, or have been unable to sort out the complex bureaucratic procedures of application. In this, they have received little assistance from social workers in Ivalo, who are only superficially in touch with the Skolt community.

Charitable assistance

The existence of the Skolt community has long provided a means for the more wealthy and fortunate cosmopolites of the South to make demostrations of merit, which are often extensively publicized in the national press. Various organizations have indeed competed in recent years to capture shares in the Skolt charity market, a competition which has not reflected to their credit. The community has become accustomed to the arrival every summer of several different voluntary workcamps in search of building projects and a first-hand view of ' Skolt Culture '. Before Christmas, the post-office is overwhelmed by gift parcels, usually containing old clothes and toys, from a host of different sources. The Salvation Army, probably the organization most actively involved in ' helping ' the Skolts, has supplied vast quantities of used clothing as well as old, often defunct, sewing machines. In some households, this has sufficed to satisfy all basic clothing requirements for the older generation and for the children, whilst the excess has been left to rot, or has even been burnt. Naturally, young people conscious about their appearance refuse to wear charity clothing, and buy their own.

Most charitable organizations are very poorly informed about local conditions, and their assistance often both inconveniences local people and comes uninvited. It is assumed that a need exists for the goods and services they supply: unskilled student labour, old clothing and even spiritual or moral guidance. With isolated and highly publicized exceptions, the effects of charity on Skolt material welfare have been marginal. The commodity in greatest demand within the community, namely money, is not one that the charitable are inclined to give away.

The Skolts themselves tend to regard charitable assistance with the same objective pragmatism as towards other external and impersonal features of their environment. No relationship is felt to exist between giver and receiver: consequently there is no recognition of debt, no obligation to receive nor gratitude towards the giver. The Skolt is not concerned or insulted by the condescending tone in which assistance is given. As long as the goods continue to arrive for no apparent reason, he takes what is useful and rejects the greater part that is not.

10 The sources of money income (3): Migration and emigration

The pattern of migration

Of the total number of Skolts either resettled in, or native to the Sevetti-järvi area, up to a fifth are temporarily or permanently absent from the community. The locations of migrants and emigrants[1] in 1972 are shown on the map (fig. 20), and fig. 21 sets out their age/sex distribution against that of the Skolt population as a whole. A striking difference in the pattern of migration between men and women is immediately apparent from these data. Whereas over the last decade the majority of young women have eventually left the home community, married, and settled outside the region, the majority of men have stayed at home as bachelors, whilst of those who have left, a smaller proportion have married.

Single female migrants are concentrated at short-distance range where jobs are available in local regional centres and in fishing towns around the Finnmark coast, but a number have sought work as far away as in the capital city, Helsinki. Single male migrants are concentrated at long-distance range in the industrial heart of southern Finland where the labour shortage is most acute: in Helsinki, Tampere, and Rauma. Married women are widely scattered throughout Finland, as well as in Norway and Sweden, depending on their husbands' home towns and places of work. Many of those who married local frontier patrolmen have moved to other national border points as their husbands have taken up new posts: at Utsjoki, Virtaniemi, Kolari and Pello.

Several Skolts have joined the massive flow of Finnish migrants from regions of high unemployment to industrial centres of southern Sweden, which are heavily dependant on the supply of Finnish labour. Whereas firms in southern Finland are rarely prepared to provide for the needs of a married migrant's dependants, Swedish industry is generous in providing family accommodation, as well as in offering a much higher salary and material standard of living than in Finland. Emigration to Sweden represents an alternative for couples, perhaps with young children, who married and attempted to settle locally *prior* to departure, only to find it impossible to gain an adequate livelihood to support a family. Most of the Skolt emigrants to Sweden, as spouses in local mixed marriages, were in this situation; and a number of other couples facing similar circumstances have

Fig. 20. The locations of migrants and emigrants.

contemplated the move. As well as abnegating ties with kin at home, the emigrant family has to come to terms with an entirely alien cultural and linguistic environment, an experience which, for Skolts, must be doubly severe.

In general, the scatter of migrants and emigrants follows the availability of employment opportunities; depending on age, sex, marital status, and domestic circumstances. The pattern of migration is typical for rural communities throughout ' under-developed ' northern Finland (Naukkarinen 1969), and does not appear to be significantly modified by the factor of Lapp or Skolt ethnicity. Authors concerned with the special problems of Lapps as an ethnic minority have stressed the element of stigmatization in accounting for similar features in the pattern of migration from other Lappish communities, arguing that migrants avoid the medium-distance range where they are subject to strong negative stigma, and have no

Fig. 21. Age/sex distribution of migrants and emigrants, set against that of the total Skolt population. Age-classes, 0–4, 5–9, 10–14,....

Migration and emigration

recourse to an exclusively Lappish social milieu (Eidheim 1958). Although Skolt migrants undoubtedly suffer personal problems of adjustment, these are probably similar to those of anyone leaving a remote, rural home environment to live in an industrial city. If they are subject to feelings of stigma, these are more likely to follow on from the experience of migration than to enter into the decision to migrate. The pattern of migration results from the attraction to zones of opportunity, not the avoidance of zones of stigma.

The female emigrant

The divergence between male and female career orientations begins already during the final years at school. Girls are eager to reject those traditional constraints that tie the woman to the domestic sphere as a housewife and mother of a large family. Like modern schoolgirls everywhere, they both expect, and are expected, to take advantage of the widening scope to follow independent careers of their own. Their aspirations are largely consistent with the kinds of training and employment perceived to be most readily available in the region. There is an overwhelming preference for jobs in the fields of domestic help and child-care, followed by work in shops, offices and catering (Vaarama 1973). Much of the teaching they received at school supports these objectives. At the same time, despite their apparent rejection of the traditional, the preference for domestic work fully accords with female role expectations learnt at home. For girls, therefore, school acts as a fairly effective bridge between the home community and placement in jobs on the quasi-urban fringes of the local region, or in towns and cities further afield.

To fill the initial void after leaving school, many Skolt girls have been encouraged to apply for the one-year course offered by the Lappish Christian College at Inari, an institution with a strongly puritan religious bias, whose aim is to promote a generation of nationalistically conscious young Lapps. Skolt pupils at the College find the religion irksome, and have little use for ethnic nationalism. In retrospect, however, they have found the teaching in practical subjects valuable, and generally leave with a clearer idea of what they intend to pursue in the future. Those aiming at a career in domestic or catering fields can go on to acquire additional qualifications by attending courses offered by the Schools of Domestic Science in Ivalo and Kemijärvi, and by Rovaniemi Technical College. These courses have been rather popular among Skolt girls.

In the intervals of summer holidays or perhaps whole years between attendance at formal courses, girls may take casual jobs within the local region to earn extra money: as domestic helps in Ivalo or Inari or on the Norwegian farms of South Varanger, as packers in the fish-factories of the Finnmark coast, or as attendants in the shops and bars on the international frontier. Others, attracted by the lure of the capital city, have left for Helsinki, where they have had no difficulty in finding employment as domestic servants of the well-to-do, through whose patronage they have become familiar with cosmopolitan life-styles. Two Skolt girls have travelled as far as London, working in an *au pair* capacity in opulent surroundings.

During their late teens and early twenties, girls thus spend most of their time away from home: in local regional centres, in north Norway, in the provincial centres of Rovaniemi or Kemijärvi, in the national capital of Helsinki, or even abroad. At this stage they still depend on their links with home to provide support, including money, when needed, and a place to which they can return between forays in the outside world. Whilst they have yet to commit themselves to a life outside the community, their whole outlook points only in that direction. Thus, value orientations of the future are dislocated from personal and emotional bonds from the past. Visits home, becoming progressively shorter and less frequent, are no more than temporary episodes filling the intervals between phases of a career of incipient emigration.

At any point in this early stage of her career, a girl may find her future husband. Marriage, sometimes precipitated by the arrival of a child, confirms her future as a permanent emigrant from the Skolt community. The high rate of female emigration thus results from an opportunity situation which places girls outside the local community at that stage in their careers when they are most likely to be seeking marriage partners. The decision to marry involves a more or less permanent commitment: there has been only one case of divorce followed by a return to the community. After marriage, the residence of the Skolt wife is largely laid down by the career prospects of her husband. She may settle permanently in his native town where they first met, follow him to a posting in another part of the country, or emigrate with him to the south of Sweden. In this fashion, Skolt emigrants have scattered as far and wide as Helsinki, Gothenburg and Hammerfest.

At this distance, ties with the home community, once a lifeline, become no more than a memory as they are replaced by a new set of affinal kinship links and a network of local friends and connections. The emigrant wife has a permanent home, she or her husband has a steady job, and probably children at school. An emigrant to Norway or Sweden may have even acquired a foreign nationality. Parents back in the Skolt community seldom hear from their daughters, and are left to form a mental picture of their grandchildren and of their daughters' domestic surroundings from infrequent letters and family photographs. Very occasionally, a daughter may travel with her family to spend a few weeks' summer holiday visiting 'old folks' at home. Parents are then allowed the rare or perhaps unique opportunity to see their grandchildren, but for too short a period to establish any real relationship, whilst if the family comes from Norway or Sweden, grandparents and grandchildren may have no common language. The visitors arrive in large, expensive cars, and show every sign of newly found material prosperity. In their well-groomed appearance and urban sophistication, they present a stark contrast to parents and siblings left at home. They may be classified, along with other occasional arrivals from the same origin, as ' tourists' rather than kin.

Probably, few Skolts have made a conscious, irrevocable decision to emigrate. Rather, emigration is the cumulative result of a number of smaller steps starting with placement in training or employment outside or on the periphery of the local region, followed by marriage and a growing commitment to home and family in the new place of residence. Likewise, it is improbable that incipient emigrants are motivated by a desire to reject their Skolt cultural background, since it is not until personal connections with the home community have been completely severed that they begin to perceive their background in the external, cultural idiom of a minority/majority opposition. However, the loss of reproductive potential to the community undoubtedly does threaten the continuity of the Skolts as a culturally distinct group. The demographic consequences of emigration are already apparent in the drastic fall in the birthrate during the last ten years, compared with the ' bulge' of the previous decade (fig. 21). This result is no more than would be expected in a community of four hundred under modern conditions of personal mobility and free marriage choice. It is only reasonable that a young woman should put her individual material and emotional interests before any consideration of the reproduction of her ethnic group. What is remarkable is not so much the extent to which women leave the community as the preponderance of men who stay at home.

The male migrant

Boys, who value the freedom of life offered them in the home environment, seldom find the experience of school a rewarding one. School presents, but does not resolve, the dichotomy between ' traditional' and ' modern'. Career expectations, in line with the national profile, are based on mechanical and industrial skills, but bear little relation either to traditional economic pursuits or to local regional employment opportunities. For many boys, the first and obvious step after leaving school is registration at the State Employment Agency. A few have attended the Lappish Christian College, but have left without any clearly defined career intentions. Further education at technical college is not available nearer than Rovaniemi; only one youth had applied to study there in 1972. Some of those who registered at the Employment Agency have been directed to vocational training courses, but most have returned rather than taken jobs in the South.

Thus, during the first ten years after leaving school, whilst most young women are away from home in employment or training, the majority of youths are living at home, either unemployed or engaged in local casual labour. The exodus of marriageable women prevents the establishment of new conjugal units in the Skolt community, leaving a large excess of bachelors, many of them now in their thirties and forties, with no future prospects of marriage. Only five men have successfully followed the typical career of emigration: leaving to take jobs outside the community, marrying, and settling in the place of work. Two live as near as Ivalo, and keep in close touch with the Skolt community; but the other three are scattered in distant towns. The remaining two married male emigrants are both in Sweden: one left with his family after marrying locally and attempting to establish a home in his natal Skolt dwelling, the other left after becoming a widower.

A few younger men have gone to try their fortunes in the southern towns, where the availability of women has been a major attraction. In three cases, youths have gone to live with their older married sisters, who have provided provisional accommodation and domestic attention to tide over the period of initial insecurity. Their plans for the future are un- certain, depending on the extent to which they are prepared to commit themselves to personal relationships in the new urban setting. Skolt youths both lack confidence in urban styles of sexual competition and are reluctant to cut off connections with home. A break with a girlfriend or the failure of a marriage bid may signal an abrupt return home after many years away.

A number of older bachelors in their thirties and forties, with neither a family nor old parents to care for, have embarked on careers of periodic long-distance migration to southern industrial centres. Unlike younger prospective emigrants, they do not leave in order to seek a new set of personal relationships or to realize a new, externally derived set of values. Their departure may be sparked off by tensions inherent in the process of domestic group fission; in particular by inter-sibling tensions generated through the preferential treatment bestowed upon the younger son by old parents in accordance with the institution of ultimogeniture. A house- hold including a number of adult bachelor brothers, whose sisters have already married or emigrated, can split up only as the older brothers either marry into other local households, or migrate, leaving the youngest at home. Opportunities for the former alternative are strictly limited by the supply of both women and housing.

A man may thus become a periodic migrant as the pressures of home life become intolerable, when no alternative home is available locally. He does not, however, break off connections with the community. His ulti- mate intention is to return home to live on the money he has earned, some of which he may have sent back in anticipation. In practice, the expense of city life, in the absence of domestic help, is so high that little, if any- thing, can be saved; and the goal of retirement may recede to an ever more distant future.

Periodic migration represents an alternative to the combination of local casual labour, subsistence production and welfare, for those who are socially but not residentially tied to the community. Migrants are directed to jobs through the State Employment Agency, which pays the costs of travel, including holiday visits home. However, once in the South, migrants often switch from one job or town to another, remaining uncommitted to any particular workplace. As a labourer in the factories, building sites or docks, he is one of a mass of men similarly recruited from the surpluses of technically unskilled labour in the rural margins of Finland. In the city, he shares barrack-type accommodation with his fellow migrants, accumulating no possessions, and investing neither in personal relationships nor in property.

From the perspective of the home community, the world in which the periodic migrant moves whilst he is away lies outside society. It is a world where there are no personal relationships, only multitudes of people. Men disappear into it, and reappear from it as though nothing had happened. Little is known of the migrant's circumstances whilst he is away, and nothing is said about them when he returns. Only one periodic migrant was exceptional in writing long letters home. Otherwise, contacts between the migrant and the home community are limited to remittances of money from the migrant, sometimes with instructions as to how it should be spent; and parcels of food and tobacco from home, possibly including shares of reindeer meat to which he may be entitled. Unless they are working in the same place, contacts between migrants are also restricted, owing to their small number and wide distribution.

Part II The social relations of resettlement

11 The structure of resettlement

The resettlement map

The details of the Sevettijärvi resettlement plan were prepared by a committee of experts set up by the Ministry of Agriculture in 1946. In accordance with this plan, the 51 cottages built for the Skolts are scattered along the shores of a string of lakes such that from one extremity of the community to the other is a distance of about fifty kilometres (fig. 22). Although Skolts were entitled to build fishing cabins, the cottages were intended as year-round dwellings, and the traditional organization of centralized winter village and dispersed family areas was rejected. The resettlement map represents a compromise between the principles of centralization and dispersion (Nickul 1956: 94). The ' radial' pattern of Suenjel settlement had to be transposed into a linear form dictated by both spatial geography and established communication routes, whilst retaining some congruence between spatial and kinship groupings. The element of centralization was retained by building most houses in small clusters of from two to five, linked by a winter road; the element of dispersion by the linear scattering of these clusters. Larger groupings of several clusters, which we shall call neighbourhoods, are also apparent on the map, representing structural units on the level of the clan, although there is no one-to-one correspondence between clan and neighbourhood. The central neighbourhood along the line (Sevettijärvi) took on the remaining functions of the old winter village: here were built the school, health-clinic, church and shops.

It must be emphasized that the resettlement map is the result of a single major piece of decision-making; not of the numerous minor and separable decisions, spread out over time, that normally govern the developmental process of a settlement. The Skolts were consulted in the planning process, and were represented by an elder with unrivalled knowledge of kinship matters, who devised the final house allocation scheme. As an attempt to map out the total kinship network along a line, the solution is ingenious but not without anomalies. When the families arrived, the allocation of cottages had been made, leaving no possibilities for choice.

Definition of units

The *house* is defined as the physical structure, including the *dwelling* and *outbuildings*. If an additional dwelling is built to house a newly established family, this has formally to be regarded as subsidiary to the parent dwelling, since two ' main buildings' are not technically permitted to stand on the same plot. We define it then as a *sub-dwelling*. The *estate* refers to the house and its associated plot of land viewed as property. We define the *household* as the unit of social organization associated with the house.

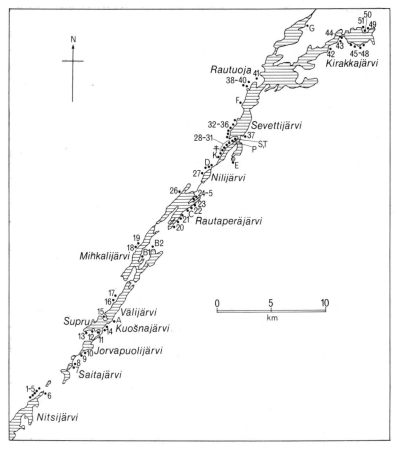

Fig. 22. The resettlement map. Skolt houses are numbered 1–51, houses of original inhabitants are lettered *A–G*. *K* refers to the house of the Forest Warden and the trading centre managed by his wife, *P* to the general stores and post office, *S* to the school buildings complex and *T* to the health clinic. House references are indicated in greater detail in fig. 23. ‡ represents the location of the orthodox church.

Structure of resettlement

It may normally be equated with the units of consumption and residence. However, with regard to both the allocation of rights of usufruct over productive resources, the ownership of capital assets, and the recruitment of labour, the household does not, in general, function as a corporate unit of production. The personnel of the household constitute the *domestic group*.

Above the level of the house/household, we define the *house-cluster* as a group of houses built immediately or almost immediately adjacent to one another, and the *household-cluster* as neighbouring or near-neighbouring households in close everyday interaction. Above the household-cluster we define the *neighbourhood* as the wider field of regular social interaction. The boundaries of the neighbourhood tend to be imprecise when they are not clearly delineated by the physical layout of houses. It could be viewed as a variably dense network of relationships involved in everyday life, incorporating clusters characterized by high density and a high frequency of activation of relationships. Inter-neighbourhood relationships, in contrast, tend to be activated only in the context of special visits or occasions.

A broad picture of the pattern of households, household-clusters and neighbourhoods that make up the overall structure of the community is shown in fig. 23. House-clusters and household-clusters are usually congruent, except where houses are vacant. Some of the cases where this is not so will be examined in ch. 16. In a few cases, relatively isolated households outside the house-clusters are incorporated in household-clusters. A few clusters are not included in neighbourhoods, largely owing to physical isolation, but still have fairly frequent contacts with one or more of the clusters of adjacent neighbourhoods: these are indicated on the diagram.

Kinship and spatial proximity

The household cluster and neighbourhood, as social units introduced through resettlement, have modified traditional patterns of social interaction. In Suenjel, all households were equally dispersed in summer and, with the exception of a few families, equally together in the winter-village. The resettlement plan imposed its own structure on the pattern of social interaction through the constraints of spatial distance and proximity which have tended to override kinship as a principle of organization. Although neighbours are nearly always kin, physical proximity selects out from the much larger category of an individual's kin those with whom he is in everyday interaction.

The household cluster is generally based on a sibling group, or sometimes on two or even three interlocking sibling groups. Reflecting the norm of virilocality that applied in Suenjel, these sibling groups are most often of brothers, but may also be of brothers and sisters or just sisters. In only three anomalous cases are immediately neighbouring households unrelated, and in two cases households belonging to a cluster are linked to the dominant sibling group by more distant kinship connections. A fair proportion of immediate kin is thus found among members of the household-cluster. The remaining repertoire of close kinship links is activated in inter-cluster or inter-neighbourhood relationships. To the extent that cluster sibling groups are of brothers, relationships involved in extra-cluster interaction are traced through sisters. Rarely does a visitor to another neighbourhood have to activate kinship beyond the first cousin range in order to establish a connection.

In the period between the two world wars, when the Suenjel Skolts were largely cut off from intermarriage with neighbouring Skolt groups and before the post-war rise of inter-ethnic marriages, the *siita* became a virtually endogamous community. The result today is a very complex and highly involuted network of kinship. When kinship is traced bilaterally, the number of ego's kin at the second or third degree can be very great. It is also possible for the same individuals to be related in several different ways. As distant kinship becomes less diacritical, so its importance as a principle of social organization decreases. Today, kin-terms are regularly used only for the immediate range of kin who would be expected to reside in ego's own or his children's households; or in those of his or his spouse's siblings, parents, parents' siblings, siblings' children and first cousins. Kinship links outside this range are rarely activated as such unless backed by neighbourhood, except when the connection is 'short-circuited' through the establishment of ritual kinship in the form of godparentage.

The neighbourhood is usually designated by the name of the principal lake around which the houses are situated.[1] It is first and foremost defined by physical constraints on interaction, but is associated with the clan in the resettlement scheme. As distant genealogical connections are forgotten, the patrilineally inherited clan-names offer proof that those with the same clan-name are related. Clan-names thus define categories of mutually related people, introducing a patrilineal bias towards the recognition of

Fig. 23. Households, clusters and neighbourhoods. Households have been marked on the diagram roughly in the order that they appear ' on the ground', but the scale has been grossly distorted for clarity of presentation. Black dots, Skolt houses built for resettlement; open dots, vacant Skolt houses; crosses, post-resettlement sub-dwellings (14 x, 20 x, 21 x, 34 x, 39 x); black squares, non-Skolt houses (K2 is the trading centre, *P* is the general stores cum post office); open squares, houses or flats built by the State or Commune for local officials: *K*1, Forest Warden's house (now occupied by the family from 39 x); *S*1–6, School flats; *T*, Health clinic. Large rectangles represent neighbourhoods. Dashed rings represent household clusters (where congruent with house clusters). Dotted rings represent house clusters (where not congruent with household clusters). Straight heavy lines indicate membership of household clusters for households outside house clusters. Curved heavy lines indicate links between isolated clusters and neighbourhoods. Neighbourhood names are in capitals.

Structure of resettlement

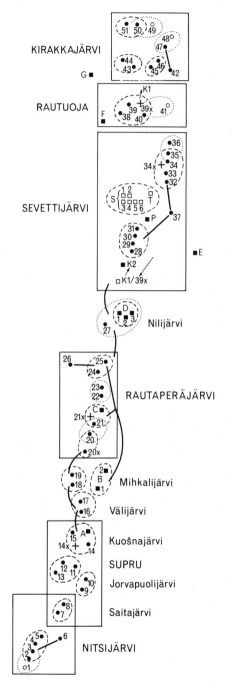

distant kinship. The association of clan and neighbourhood leads to a vague and implicit feeling of clan solidarity – of having something in common. As one member of a family not sharing the dominant clan-name of the neighbourhood put it: ' This is really an A lake, we B's are living amongst strangers here.'

In sum, the involution of the kinship-net has led to a shrinkage in the range of significant bilateral kin, and the fixed resettlement pattern has imposed a structure emphasising physical distance and proximity. Immediate bilateral kinship is divided into three sets: the first operative within the cluster, the second within the neighbourhood, the third outside the neighbourhood. Relationships activated in everyday social contact on the neighbourhood level are dichotomized into those based on immediate bilateral kinship and those based on more distant connections, whereas within the cluster and outside the neighbourhood relationships are based exclusively on immediate kinship, activated in the latter case only in the context of specific occasions. Evidence of more distant kinship is provided by patrilineally inherited clan-names, which also define clan categories associated on the same structural level with the neighbourhood. Despite the attempt to map genealogy onto settlement pattern, the significance of the former as a rationale for the latter is undermined when it is evident that people are living where they are, not as a result of the gradual unfolding of normative processes of kinship, but because they have been put there.

12 The household (1): The physical structure

The Skolt house

Most of the resettlement houses are built on a standard plan, modelled on the houses of the Suenjel winter village. This comprises a two-room dwelling measuring 4 x 8 metres, and an outbuilding measuring 3 x 7.8 metres which is divided into two sections: one intended for storage and the other as a sheepcote. Four dwellings have only one room of 20 square metres, and six two-room dwellings are smaller than normal (24–29 m²). Every household has the use of a *sauna,* the Finnish steam-bath cum wash-house, a separate building of about 9 square metres. In many cases, a common *sauna* is shared by two adjacent houses of a cluster. As well as the outdoor latrine, other outbuildings have been subsequently erected in many houses, such as wood-sheds, tool-sheds, hay-lofts, and outdoor cellars (fig. 24B). Buildings are constructed of timber on a concrete foundation, roofed with planks and roofing felt, and with fire-places and chimneys of brick and mortar. The original dwellings were fitted with large bread-ovens, later replaced by ordinary stoves which heat more efficiently (plates 13, 14).

Domestic groups have adapted to the basic house-plan in various ways, according to the size and structure of the group and the nature of social values attached to the house and its contents. Fig. 24A shows the interior plan of a fairly typical dwelling. The main room is an all-purpose area for indoor work, cooking, eating, talking and sleeping. Visitors are free to come and go without invitation. The side room, which can be sealed off by a door, is a more private area, which guests should enter only on invitation. If the house has a telephone, it is situated here. The side room contains the best furniture, and those fundamental symbols of household identity: the chest of drawers and family photographs. Overnight, both rooms become sleeping areas; for large families practically the whole bed and floor space may be utilized, leaving little scope for discrimination in sleeping arrangements. The sheepcote, now rarely used for its original purpose, provides an extra room in summer time. It is often made into a bedroom for teenagers of one or other sex, allowing them to come and go, receive visitors, and sleep without interference. Another setting for confidential conversation, particularly for girls, is the two-seater latrine.

Most furniture, apart from iron beds, is of simple wooden construction, much of it home-made. The fine furniture which often appears in the side room is an exception. In addition to the chest-of-drawers, this very frequently includes a set of two armchairs, settee and low coffee table of standard design. Decoration on the walls is sparse. Printed tapestries depicting classical pastoral scenes are popular in the side room. Photographs on the wall usually include portraits of sons of the house depicted in military uniform. Icons hang or rest on a shelf in each room. Letters and postcards are wedged in between the window-jamb and the wall in the main room, and exotic picture postcards from friends or relatives far away are often pinned up. Other colourful materials, magazine pictures, icon cut-outs, portraits of the president and the like, appear on the walls from time to time. Written material in Skolt homes is usually limited to newspapers, glossy magazines and strip-cartoon books. Recently, some families have succumbed to pressure from encyclopaedia salesmen, subscribing for expensive and attractive volumes in the belief that they are essential both to their children's education and as a feature of any civilized sitting-room. Most items of sitting-room material culture, including the fine furniture and tapestries, have likewise found their way to the community through a few travelling salesmen.

Every dwelling has at least one clock and a battery radio. Both punctuate, or rather *create* time: on the micro-scale by the rhythm of the music and the ticking of the clock which aurally fill the dwelling space, on the macro-scale by regular time checks on the radio and the position of hands on the clock. Erring clocks are conscientiously put right, even though knowledge of the exact time is of little or no importance in the regulation of household activity. Far more important is the reassurance that time is *passing* in an orderly and apparently controlled manner, in synchrony with the outside world.

House-repairs and enlargements

According to legislation passed in 1965 and again in 1969, grants and loans were made available for construction, enlargement or basic repairs of dwellings and *saunat.* With active encouragement from the Commune building department, work has proceeded apace. By summer 1972, seven new *saunat* and three new dwellings had been built, ten dwellings enlarged, and thirteen dwellings given basic repairs. The grants are meant to cover the costs of essential raw materials, on the understanding that household members carry out the work themselves. The many inevitable extra expenses force most builders to take out loans. Technical assistance is also required since new building methods, involving heavily insulated weatherboarding rather than solid timber, are unfamiliar to many Skolts.

According to official standards, a surface area of less than 10 m² per inhabitant within the dwelling is regarded as a criterion of overcrowding (Asp 1966: 107). By this criterion the Skolts were, and still are, grossly overcrowded. The house enlargements are intended as a remedy. The idea of a correlation between people and surface area is, however, foreign to

House structures

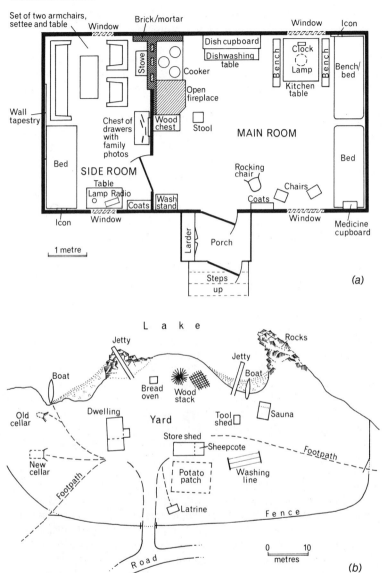

Fig. 24. A typical Skolt house. *A*, Interior plan of two-room dwelling; *B*, Sketch-map of house site.

143

Skolt values. The dwelling is basically an organizational rather than a spatial unit. So long as the organizational requirements exist for the performance of household tasks, space is a secondary problem. The pressure for building and enlargement, coming from outside sources, was accepted largely owing to the increased organizational possibilities which a four-room enlarged dwelling can give in the division of functions between rooms.

The three entirely new dwellings are all substitutes for the smallest one-room cottages: in one house the original cottage has been converted into a *sauna*. In the case of two-room cottages, the dwelling is enlarged to twice its original area by the addition of two rooms and restructuring the roof. For many domestic groups accustomed to managing on the original plan, the reallocation of functions among the four rooms of the enlarged dwelling has proved problematic. The extra space often appears under-utilized: walls and floor are bare, there is little furniture to fill the rooms, and new furniture is too expensive to buy. On the other hand, for those who aspire to modern standards of house comfort and design and have sufficient financial means, the enlarged dwelling with its single-function rooms allows scope for the realization of their ambitions.

The new look in housing: an example

One recently completed new Skolt dwelling is set apart from others by its modern sophistication, setting an example to many spectators of a style of housing that may be adopted more widely in the community. The seven-member household used to occupy a simple one-room dwelling. Many of the ambitious ideas for the new dwelling stemmed from regular contacts with the Forest Warden and his wife: relatively wealthy and influential local patrons and representatives of the culture of affluence, who had recently built an elegant dwelling of their own. These ideas could ultimately be realized through extensive charitable assistance and a regular wage income over and above the State grant.

The 60 m^2 dwelling includes a kitchen, sitting room, two bedrooms, porch and underfloor cellar, but no living room. Novel features include the indoor *sauna,* indoor flush toilet, wood-fired central heating, running water, and an all-gas cooker. Interior decoration is lavish, particularly in the sitting-room, furnished with a plush armchair and sofa set. One wall is taken up by a large bookcase and cabinet unit, although, as in other Skolt houses, there are few books to fill the shelves. Other walls are decorated with scenic landscape pictures and items left over from the material culture of grandfather's day, displayed as objects of art.

Some of the practical innovations of this dwelling, notably running water and central heating, may be readily adopted elsewhere. On the other hand, visitors have mixed opinions about the opulent interior decoration. Entering via the porch, the visitor finds himself facing what he would judge to be not a living-room but a luxurious sitting-room. He hesitates,

Plate 13. An example of the standard two-room Skolt resettlement dwelling.

Plate 14. A one-room dwelling which, until recently, housed a family of seven.

feeling that he should be invited in before proceeding further. Asked to sit, he is reluctant to soil the armchairs. If he has omitted to remove his boots at the front door, he will have to apologize for bringing dirt onto the carpet. On all accounts the visitor feels ill at ease owing to the lack of a normal living room. In the days of the one-room dwelling, the household had many visitors, and despite the shortage of space there was always somewhere to sit or lie. Today, those visitors tend to go elsewhere if they can. Even the many children of the house-cluster, who are accustomed to run in and out of all the houses in their play, are sent away. They are said to turn things upside down indoors, and bring in mud on their shoes. This attitude upsets the grandparents, who like to have their grandchildren around. They do not care for fine furniture, nor do they understand or trust the new technical gadgetry.

In sum, the enlargement and building of dwellings and the diffusion of modern housing values are leading to a new diversity of forms and interior styles of comfort and decoration, which both elaborate and constrain behaviour within the dwelling, as a few multi-function rooms are replaced by more single-function rooms. As the living-room is replaced by the sitting-room, the setting for free everyday coming and going is lost. Alternative settings are sought elsewhere, whilst the sitting-room is put on display only to select visitors. The norms of sitting-room behaviour, derived from the affluent urban milieu, are inconsistent with the articulation of multiplex local community relationships, which demand both flexibility and informality in the use of housing space.

13 The household (2): The development of domestic groups

The development cycle in Suenjel

The complete set of data on household composition given by Nickul (1948) for Suenjel in 1938 makes it possible to reconstruct a picture of the normative process of household development, as it then operated. According to the division of the *siita* into 'family areas', each household formed an independent production and consumption unit for the exploitation of its particular area, so that household composition was related to the allocation of rights of usufruct over land and water. Ultimately, these rights belonged jointly to the whole *siita* and were administered by the assembly of householders. In normal practice, they devolved from father to son, or to a daughter only if there were no male heirs, such that her sons could subsequently inherit. In the case of several male heirs, the area would be split between them as each formed an economically independent household of his own; or if area resources were deemed insufficient, an heir could apply through the assembly for some other area which, due to lack of descendents to the previous holders, had fallen out of use. Thus, a degree of balance between population and resources was maintained. The youngest male heir inherited the residual portion of the family area, along with the natal house and any moveable property that remained undivided, including the reindeer mark of his father and the remnants of his herd.

In a line with this system marriage was virilocal except in rare cases where a man might marry a sole female heir to an area uxorilocally. The couple would form a new independent household shortly after the birth of the first child. Each son would marry in turn, such that no household would include more than one married son at a time. The youngest son would take on the responsibility for the care of ageing parents. Daughters who for one reason or another did not marry, together with possible illegitimate children, remained as dependants first in their natal and later in their brothers' households.

By and large, domestic groups in the winter-village were the same as on the family areas; but an accommodation shortage apparently existed, as in four cases two family area groups shared the same winter dwelling, and in another five cases the sheepcote of a related group was used for accommodation. The incentive for housebuilding was perhaps weak since, in the winter-village, the independent dwelling was not part of a strategy of economic exploitation of immediately surrounding natural resources.

The patrilineal tendency in the mode of inheritance and division of family areas did not generate higher level corporate groups, but the spatial layout of areas tended to reflect patrilineal genealogical history. The clan was mapped out spatially as a ' fossil ' conglomerate (Dikkanen 1965). Today, the clan has acquired a new significance through its association with neighbourhood in the resettlement plan.

Household development and restricted housing

On resettlement, the authority of the assembly was undermined, and the family area system abandoned. The rationale for the normative process of household development as it operated in Suenjel was lost, to be replaced by the constraints of limited housing on the one hand and possibilities for long-distance migration and emigration on the other. The combined effect of these two factors, together with the relaxation of traditional expectations, has been to generate a wide diversity of post-resettlement developmental sequences and present-day forms of domestic group composition.

Housing were initially allocated fairly generously in accordance with the Suenjel pattern, such that even recently married couples received standard-sized dwellings of their own. However, despite the overall growth of population, no new Skolt houses have been built since resettlement. Given this restriction, only the following residence alternatives exist for a newly established couple wishing to remain in the community:

(1) Natal household of husband (patrilocal).
(2) Natal household of wife (matrilocal).
(3) Build own dwelling:
  (*a*) As a sub-dwelling on a Skolt plot (uxorilocal or virilocal).
  (*b*) By obtaining land from a local landowner, by squatting on state land, or by living permanently in the fishing cabin (neolocal).
(4) Skolt house left vacant through death or removal of original occupants (neolocal).
(5) State or Commune accommodation of non-Skolt spouse (uxorilocal or virilocal).

The first two alternatives imply that the in-marrying spouse will have to share accommodation on a more or less permanent basis with other members of the resident spouse's natal domestic group. Social and organizational rather than numerical and spatial considerations will tend to determine which alternative is adopted. In no cases do two married siblings belong to the same household. Such an arrangement, at least in the two-room house with only one kitchen and larder and at most two bedrooms, may be avoided as an organizational impossibility. If an older son, for example, has married patrilocally, his younger brother would be forced to reside neolocally or uxorilocally on marriage. In several cases of matrilocal residence, the wife's household was short of manpower for heavy work, or the daughter was required to stay at home to cook and care for an old father. In other cases, intra-household quarrels or the inability of the spouse to fit in congenially with other household members may encourage out-marriage.

As a result of patri- or matrilocal residence, structurally larger and more permanent three-generation domestic groups can be formed than was possible in Suenjel, including the parents and younger unmarried siblings of one or other partner, as well as the children, of the junior married couple. Use of the sheepcote, as formerly in Suenjel winter-village, can provide the embedded nuclear family with a degree of residential independence. A solution increasingly sought today is to construct a subdwelling on the parental plot. Three sub-dwellings have been established to date on Skolt plots to house new families: two uxorilocally and one virilocally. No grants are available for their construction, and building is permitted only on condition that the dwelling is subsidiary to the original Skolt dwelling. In one case, the sub-dwelling is little more than a bedroom, whilst cooking and eating takes place in the main dwelling. Two other dwellings of a similar type have been established. One was built on the land of a neighbouring, related ' old inhabitant '. The other is, in effect, a case of ' squatting ', since the Commune has not given permission to build, and the land still belongs to the State. However, the occupant family has lived there undisturbed since 1968, after spending the first four years of married life in the sheepcote of the husband's natal house.

One couple, after an initial six years of patrilocal residence, attempted to adopt their fishing cabin as a permanent dwelling. They lived there for two years before being compelled to move with their two children to a one-room Skolt house which fell vacant on the death of its previous occupants. However, as the house is in a neighbourhood far from the natal homes and immediate kin of the parents, they feel socially isolated in their present situation, and would prefer to be able to build in a more favourable spot. Three other families have similarly transferred to vacant houses, but within their home neighbourhoods. Like the first example, the dwelling was in each case of the smaller one-room variety. Thus, all four of the one-room dwellings, built originally to house old childless couples in the ' terminal phase ' of development, and therefore naturally the first to fall vacant, have changed hands in this way. Three of the occupant families have subsequently gone through a phase of rapid numerical expansion leading to excessively cramped conditions indoors. All three have now been able to build for themselves entirely new four-room dwellings, with government financial assistance.

Four non-Skolt women employed by the Commune have married Skolts: two are schoolteachers, the third is the school cook and the fourth the health visitor. In all these cases, the Skolt husband has settled uxorilocally in the flats provided for Commune employees in the school building complex. The flats thus house a number of small and mainly unrelated nuclear families. Apart from the necessity for the wives to be on hand for work, uxorilocal residence is dictated by the considerable difficulties any non-Skolt wife would expect to experience with her husband's family in a Skolt house. The husbands would prefer, if it were possible, to set up new houses. The converse virilocal situation is of marriage of Skolt girls with Finnish frontier patrolmen. State accommodation at the patrol station is limited, and in two cases old, empty cottages near the station have been taken up; in the third case the family shares an enlarged Skolt house with the wife's mother and brother. In the many other instances of marriage with patrolmen the family has moved away on the husband's transference to another post.

The various residence alternatives reviewed in this section have been forced on newly established families because of the impossibility, up to now, of obtaining plots of land for building. On the other hand, as formerly in the Suenjel winter-village. long-term patri- or matrilocal residence is more acceptable when the house is not located on a ' family area ', such that residence groups can be independent of the organization of primary production. It is not the procurement of livelihood, which takes place in the extra-domestic context, but the organization of activities that go on *inside* the house such as cooking, eating, sleeping and everyday maintenance tasks, which is crucial for residence decisions. Since the productive capacity of the household plot is marginal to the Skolt economy, and since any financial value the estate may have is largely theoretical when it can be neither sold nor mortgaged, the inheritance of estates is a matter only for legal speculation, and has likewise had no influence on the pattern of residence choices. Consequently, the nexus between production and consumption, depending on the allocation of rights to land and water, the ownership and management of capital assets, and the household affiliation of productive labour, is complex and variable.

Many nuclear families embedded in larger household groups aspire to residential independence. Some have applied for building plots through new legislation with varying success, and more new dwellings or sub-dwellings are planned either on Skolt plots or on land obtainable from ' old inhabitants '. The housing problem is expected to become acute as the post-war population ' bulge ' reaches maturity, even assuming that emigration from the community continues at its present level.

Dispersion and replacement

Data on the numerical size of domestic groups for various categories of dwelling are summarized in fig. 25. The mean size of groups in Skolt houses rose from 6.0 in 1938 Suenjel to 6.5 at the time of Pelto's 1958 census (Pelto 1962: 225–32), reflecting both the greater post-war infant and old-age survival rates and the impact of housing restrictions after a decade of resettlement. It has since dropped again to a 1972 figure of 5.8, a decrease which reflects the higher rate of emigration, the smaller number of local

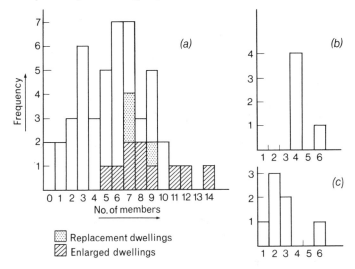

Fig. 25. The numerical size of domestic groups. *A,* Skolt houses (excluding three houses vacant since resettlement); *B,* sub-dwellings; *C,* Commune accommodation.

marriages, and the introduction of sub-dwellings and Commune accommo-dation as residence alternatives. With two exceptions, all domestic groups of four or less in Skolt houses are 'remnant groups', that is, those left at home such as old parents, bachelor sons or illegitimate children at the end of the 'dispersion phase'; whereas all groups sized between two and four in sub-dwellings and Commune accommodation are independent, recently established, nuclear families. Since any newly established nuclear family in a Skolt house must normally share accommodation with family members of one or other spouse, domestic groups in such cases include at least five members.

Most often today, it is the daughters of the household who are the first to leave on reaching maturity, attracted by opportunities for training, employment and marriage outside the community. As a result, fewer new families are generated locally, whilst more domestic groups disperse leaving only old parents and possibly one or several ageing bachelor sons at home. In those households where new nuclear families *have* been established, the group often includes older bachelor brothers of the husband or wife. In contrast, nearly all spinsters of this generation remaining permanently at home have either mental or physical disabilities, or are encumbered with illegitimate children: in both these cases the welfare income may be maximized by remaining single. If a woman with illegitimate children does leave the community, the children are usually fostered by grand-parents or mother's siblings, or they may be adopted within the community

151

by a closely related childless couple hoping for a child, preferably a son, who would care for them in old age. Alternatively, children who cannot be cared for locally are sent to the Communal children's home or adopted out of the community through an agency. In the latter case, natal links with the child are completely severed.

For the men that stay at home, it is not only the shortage of available women that limits local marriages. Premarital sexual relations are not subject to censure, whereas divorce is unknown (Pelto 1962: 147-8). Marriage often follows the birth of the first or second child, and serves merely to validate a gradual redistribution of domestic obligations leading to the establishment of a secure home and an independent family. Under contemporary conditions, however, a man can rarely offer economic security for his future wife and family, whilst he may have no better home to offer than a space in his natal dwelling or in the sheepcote. These constraints may postpone the establishment of a conjugal unit even when a potential spouse is available. Additional constraints operate on men who are particularly active in reindeer management. For them, the attachment of dependants through marriage restricts the independence, mobility and capacity for economic initiative which are nowadays essential to their success.

The institutionalized favouritism towards the youngest son that characterized ultimogeniture in Suenjel is still apparent today in a few households where the parents are now old and sons have reached adulthood. Old parents hope to keep the youngest son at home to provide for them and to carry out heavy work around the house. Today, with the decline of the traditional economy, a youngest son has little of value to expect to inherit from his parents in return, whereas, at least in theory, old people are supported through State welfare. Older sons are sent out to earn for themselves and for the household, whilst the youngest son is induced to stay at home by providing for his sometimes extravagant material requirements through the parents' pension income and for his food through their subsistence production. When older sons remain unmarried and attached to the natal household, this 'cossetting' of the youngest son can inflame already brittle relationships between adult brothers in enforced co-residence. Although sibling unity is stressed as a value antagonism between brothers may precipitate dispersion, either through uxorilocal or neolocal marriage or, where this is not possible, through periodic migration.

In contrast to the fissile bonds between brothers, the relationship between brother and sister is a close one of interdependence (Pelto 1962: 159-62). A sister resident in the community can act as a focal point for the group of siblings, maintaining connections with each of her brothers, who may themselves avoid one another. In one example, the virilocal marriage of the sole remaining sister in a large co-resident sibling group including six adult bachelors precipitated its final dispersion; whilst the sub-dwelling set up by the sister and her husband replaced the natal house as the local point of reference for the siblings. The youngest brother, accustomed to depend on his sister for domestic services, moved in with her to the sub-dwelling, as did their old father until his death shortly after. Two brothers married matrilocally into other houses in the neighbourhood. Another two left as labour migrants, but keep in touch with their sister through letters and visits. Only one of the seven siblings remains alone and isolated in the natal house. Despite the potential hostility that exists between the brothers, a sense of sibling solidarity is maintained by their common link to their sister and her household.

Old people are generally an asset to the household, on account of their pension income. Only six Skolt women from the community, aged between 54 and 83, have been relegated to the Communal old-people's home, generally owing to special circumstances such as failing health or lack of domestic help at home. However, if a replacement family is established through a patri- or matrilocal marriage, grandparents may find their position in the domestic sphere gradually eroded as the family expands, although at the same time their ability to exert influence in extra-domestic affairs may increase. One grandmother was forced by the growing pressure on space and facilities in the dwelling to reside in the sheepcote, and eventually left to join close relatives in the old people's home. Another, although provided with a room of her own in a new enlarged dwelling, is obsessed by the fear that her daughter-in-law intends to pack her off to the home, in order to be rid of an encumbrance and make room for her family.

The various forms of domestic group to be found today do not indicate different stages in a single cycle of development, as might be expected under stable environmental conditions. An irreversible change in the parameters of household development, operative from the date of resettlement, has generated a wide variety of developmental sequences. On the one hand, the limited supply of housing and restrictions on building have constrained many families established after resettlement to reside patri- or matrilocally, rather than set up a household of their own. On the other hand, with the disappearance of 'family areas', the household has lost its original corporate functions, allowing a greater degree of flexibility in domestic group composition. Consequently, there are no formal restrictions preventing a nuclear family from switching between one residence alternative and another, according to prevailing domestic circumstances. Thus, a patrilocally established family may later settle matrilocally or neolocally, or may even emigrate to Sweden if a livelihood cannot be obtained at home. Career opportunities for women outside the community have attracted away unmarried girls, setting them on a path of emigration, and leaving at home a residue of bachelors whose internal dissension may in turn trigger off periodic long-distance migration. Structural diversification in domestic group composition is therefore carried to two extremes:

of small, non-reproductive remnant groups including old parents and
confirmed bachelor sons, and of large groups including an embedded
nuclear family. Overall, fewer nuclear families are established compared
with the Suenjel norm, and more remnant groups are created.

Development phase and economic adaptation

Household economic fortunes have varied according to their developmental
phase in the traditional cycle at the time of resettlement. The household
with a maximum of nearly grown or young adult children whose labour
is as yet unspecialized and uncommitted has the greatest potential for
adaptation to new circumstances (Rudie 1969). Thus, men in the junior
generation of households which were entering the phase of dispersion on
resettlement, were well placed to benefit from changes in the reindeer
economy. Having received their training in reindeer management under
modern association conditions, and unburdened by consumption dependants, they were in a position to experiment with new techniques of
herding and to invest in risky husbandry policies. At the same time,
living members of the older generation, although now redundant in herding, are drawing an additional pension income, making them more an
asset than a liability to the domestic economy.

Those families established just before or just after resettlement, which
received houses of their own, have fared very differently. After a period of
expansion they are at present entering the phase of dispersion. The fathers
of these families are men who are still of working age today but who
received their training under Suenjel conditions. Burdened with dependants as their families grew, householders of this generation were among
the first to abandon reindeer management on the breakdown of intensive
herding in the sixties. Their sons have consequently had no opportunity
to develop herding skills. In many of these households today, both fathers
and working-age sons are on the unemployment and casual labour circuit,
whilst most daughters embark on a career of emigration after leaving
school. Generally, the household with a specialized work-force and a high
ratio of consumers to earners is thus least able to withstand environmental change calling for new techniques and investments.

14 The household (3): The organization of consumption

The division of labour in the household[1]

In line with the structural diversity of domestic groups, the organization of household activities is rather flexible. Nevertheless, a measure of normative consensus exists defining an ideal household division of labour based on the nuclear family, against which deviations may be justified by force of circumstances.

This ideal model conceptualizes a spatial distinction between the house and ' the forest ', corresponding to an organizational distinction between domestic and extra-domestic spheres of activity. Contrasting norms apply in each sphere. Within the domestic sphere, although the senior married male is theoretically the head of the household, his authority is limited. He is responsible for producing and conveying to the household the raw materials, and nowadays cash, required by his wife in order to provide the domestic group with food, clothing, warmth and light. In addition to the central task of child-rearing, the housewife is thus responsible for the organization and implementation of domestic consumption. Traditionally, too, she is responsible for the management of domestic livestock (sheep and tame deer), and for fishing in nearby waters. If the domestic group spends some time living away at the fishing cabin, the setting for domestic activity is temporarily transposed.

The extra-domestic sphere of the forest and labour sites is principally a man's world. Men are mobile; they travel extensively and may be away for weeks at a stretch, leaving their womenfolk to manage the household in their absence. Whilst away, the men may themselves have to carry out tasks preparatory to consumption: thus cooking is a skill shared by both men and women, but practised in contrasting contexts. Domestic and non-domestic consumption are separated to the extent that men leaving for the forest are expected to choose and buy their own food supplies from the shops rather than stock up from the household larder, although a man's wife or mother will pack his rucksack before he leaves.

Children are gradually socialized into this dichotomy. Daughters soon learn to help or replace their mothers in domestic tasks. Sons, however, so long as they have not achieved full economic independence, are expected to help in heavier domestic tasks such as sawing and chopping firewood, carrying water, and moving tethered deer. In households without adolescent sons, it is common to see housewives performing such tasks themselves.

155

Skolt values stress the independent nuclear family as a unit of domestic consumption. As each house has only one larder, one cooking-place, and one wood and fuel store, the consumption unit is generally congruent with the household. The domestic group therefore never includes more than one nuclear family in the same generation. In the large three-generation structures that stem from patrilocal or matrilocal residence, an element of strain may be apparent, above all between senior and junior wives; but conditions for the embedded family, though perhaps inconvenient, are not impossible. Most usually, the oldest generation is increasingly infirm and dependent, whereas attached bachelor members of the middle generation are already adult and economically active. If the older generation ' grand-mother' is still in good health, the possibility to delegate some of her domestic responsibilities to a daughter-in-law allows her to participate more widely in the management of neighbourhood or community affairs.

The junior housewife, as the integrative nucleus of the domestic consumption unit, may find herself having to care not only for her husband and children, but also for her unmarried brothers or brothers-in-law, and elderly parents or parents-in-law. In this sense, she acts as a centre of redistribution: pooling the cash and raw materials brought in often independently by the various productive members of the household, and converting them to a consumable form for redistribution to her consumption dependants. It is above all the right to receive a share of cooked food that constitutes the ultimate criterion of household membership; thus, meals are reserved for the domestic group, whereas guests are served tea or coffee.

Since ties of kinship and neighbourhood reciprocity between Skolt households generally preclude the establishment of asymmetrical service contracts, every household strives towards functional autonomy in the field of domestic maintenance. A household cannot rely on help from kin or neighbours when it lacks the requisite labour or equipment to reciprocate in the future. Apart from help frequently given to grandparents by grandchildren belonging to separate but neighbouring households, inter-household assistance in strictly domestic activities is rare, even within the cluster. Manpower shortages, often a crucial factor in post-marital residence decisions, are coped with rather through deviations from the ideal sexual division of labour than through co-operation with other households or the employment of hired help. Such deviations, increasingly frequent today, introduce a marked degree of variation in household role patterns. Thus, in remnant domestic groups whose only able-bodied members are male, men are prepared to carry out most of the domestic tasks which traditionally fall to the womenfolk. Only the baking of bread remains as a female speciality, so that all-male households have to rely either on bread baked by a female relative or on crispbread from the shops. Conversely, in households where the menfolk are absent for long periods at wage-labour sites, the housewife may take on an additional burden of fishing, and may herself attend reindeer separations in the hope of obtaining meat for domestic consumption.

Plate 15. A woman washing clothes by the lakeshore with her grand-daughter. The girl is operating a petrol-powered washing machine.

Likewise, the imperative of autonomy demands that every household should be technologically self-sufficient in the domestic sphere; whilst those that are not must rely on the services of the few available non-Skolts in the community, who remain external to the pattern of reciprocities. This may account for the proliferation of certain items of mechanical equipment to a point which appears far in excess of the number needed to carry out all the tasks for which they are required. Equipment applied towards the maintenance of the consumption unit may be regarded as a functional extension of the household, making possible or facilitating a one-way inflow of resources: their extraction from the environment, conveyance to the house, storage, and conversion to the form in which they are finally consumed. Portable or mobile extraction and conveyance equipment, which is not physically constrained to the domestic setting, is normally controlled by men; whilst stationary storage and conversion equipment within the house is operated by women. The repertoire of equipment nowadays includes a number of modern mechanical items, such as chain-saws, outboard motors, snowmobiles and cars in the first category; and cooking and heating appliances, washing and sewing machines, gas lamps and occasionally refrigerators in the second (plate 15). Many housewives are unfamiliar with innovatory gas- and petrol-powered equipment, and are forced into a greater reliance on their more mechanically-minded menfolk. Only younger generation men profess to understand the internal combustion engine. Thus, clothes-washing by machine requires the assistance of a man to start the motor, or to tinker with it when it fails to start. Further, as households become increasingly dependent on local shops for consumer goods, housewives who live more than walking distance away must rely on their menfolk for motor-transport. Only two Skolt women in the community regularly drive snowmobiles, both owing to rather exceptional domestic circumstances, though it is significant that these women are younger generation wives reacting to some extent against traditional distinctions in the sexual division of labour. As a rule, motorization has made households more reliant on their younger men, leading to new patterns of domestic co-operation and a shift in the balance of domestic sanctions.

Opportunities for housewives to break loose from the economic con-straints of domestic confinement are rather limited. One possibility is commercial sheep-rearing. A small amount of employment is available locally for married women in shops and bars, and in the primary school. In three-generation households it is possible to leave children in the care of grandparents whilst mothers go out to work. Two young working mothers employed local girls to mind their children. Although it is very common for girls to take up employment as home-helps elsewhere, this represents a new development within the community.

The raw materials of domestic consumption

The housewife can obtain the raw materials she needs for conversion into food, clothing, warmth and light from three different sources (fig. 26). Firstly, she can pool the contributions of household members derived from the direct exploitation of the natural environment. Secondly, she can

The principal materials for domestic consumption and their three different sources

Subsistence production	Exchange trade	Cash purchase
Reindeer meat	Butter	Beef, pork, processed
Fish	Margarine	sausage meat
Wildfowl	Wheat flour	Rye flour
Berries	Sugar	Dairy products
Potatoes	Tea	Fruit and vegetables
Mutton	Coffee	Bread
Wool and skins		Potatoes
Wood		Miscellaneous processed
		or semi-processed foods
		Clothing, material and
		wool
		Fuel (paraffin, oil, gas,
		petrol)

Organization of consumption

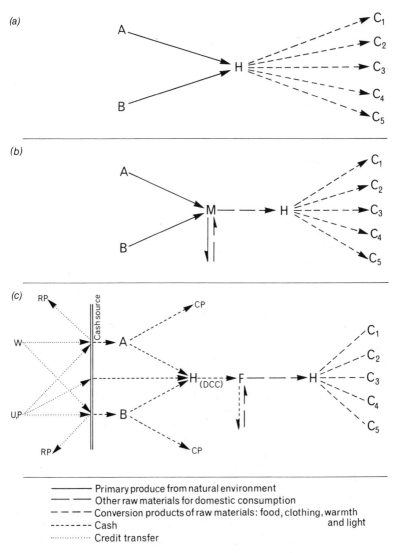

Fig. 26. Pooling, exchange, conversion and redistribution in the domestic economy. *A*, Subsistence sector. *B*, Exchange sector. *C*, Cash sector: *RP*, Regular payments at cash source; *CP*, 'Cash in the pocket' – extra-domestic consumption; *DCC*, Domestic consumption contribution; *W*, Wage income; *U*, Unemployment compensation; *P*, Pensions and child allowances. *A*, *B*, Producers contributing to domestic group; *H*, housewife of domestic group; C_{1-5}, consumers in domestic group (including *A*, *B*, *H*); *M*, Norwegian merchant; *F*, Finnish shopkeepers.

obtain supplies from the Norwegian merchant by drawing on credit accruing to the household through previous sales. Thirdly, she can use the cash at her disposal to purchase goods from local Finnish shops.

Subsistence supplies. The number of deer consumed in one winter varies according to household size, the weight and quality of the deer, and the diet. An average domestic group of around six members with a mixed diet of fish and meat consumes some six to ten deer in one winter (September–April). At one extreme are domestic groups whose productive members have entirely abandoned the reindeer economy, which may consume only one or two deer bought at separations: in the *peura* auction, or occasionally from a friend or relative on advantageous terms. At the other extreme are the households of 'big' reindeer-men, renowned for their voracious appetite for meat, in which fifteen to twenty deer may be consumed in a single season. For the household of an average small reindeer-owner, the availability of meat is perpetually problematic. If the separation or *peura*-hunt brings no result, the housewife must resort to buying highly-priced meat from the shops, when reindeer-meat supplies are exhausted. If the small-owner does find a suitable deer in the separation, ostensibly as a consequence of sheer good luck, his household is supplied with meat at no apparent cost, allowing temporary relaxation of normal constraints on consumption.

In the summer months, fish or shop-bought meat are the only alternative sources of protein. Owing to the difficulty of preserving fish in this season, and the uncertainty of catches, housewives often have to resort to buying meat. Stocks of salt-fish are built up in autumn, and many families fish throughout the winter to supplement the erratic meat supply. However among many of those younger generation Skolts who are eager to reject what they see as symptoms of primitivity or poverty, both the catching and eating of fish for subsistence have become stigmatized activities. The older generation, on the other hand, declare that they cannot eat the kind of meat, above all, sausage, sold in the shops. The taste for fish has become an important symbol of traditional identity. Thus, in one household, the old parents regularly fish as well as receiving old-age pensions. Their youngest son, who remains at home as a bachelor, refuses to eat fish, and his mother feels obliged to concede to his demands for meat. Whilst the parents continue to fish for themselves, their pension is used partly to provide the son with expensive food from the shops.

Wildfowl represents a significant seasonal addition to the meat diet of some households. Berries are important as a source of vitamins. Many households obtain a supply of potatoes for at least part of the year through their own efforts of cultivation; otherwise they are bought from the shops. Wool and skins, by-products of animal husbandry, were traditionally used for clothing. Wood still represents the principal fuel for heating. Some households are experimenting with oil, but any practical advantages of oil over wood-heating are by no means established.

Organization of consumption

Exchange goods. Credit with the Norwegian merchant at Neiden, established through sales of reindeer, berries and occasionally ptarmigan, can be converted to food supplies in the second sector which are basic additions to the diet. Whilst marketing trips to Norway used to be undertaken by men, today housewives often take the advantage of a lift or taxiride along the new road in order to make purchases themselves. Supplies are obtained in bulk, free of import duty and purchase tax, to last several months at a time.

Credit is accounted by domestic consumption units; in general, that is, by household. Thus, the merchant's books form, in a sense, a potential extension to the household larder; credit accumulates in the account according to similar principles as the pooling of raw materials destined for home consumption in the household store. The housewife retains her pivotal position as a centre of redistribution, but pooling is in the hands of the merchant who, in turn, transacts with larger wholesale firms (see fig. 26B).

Cash purchases. Shopping for domestic raw materials is always carried out by the housewife herself. The list of supplies available from local shops includes a number of items that are either new to traditional consumption patterns, or considered as luxuries. Oil, petrol and gas are all fuels introduced on a large scale only recently, along with the machinery which burns them. Ready-made clothing or material is nowadays bought almost exclusively from the shops or by mail-order, whilst traditionally a large part was home-made. In the food sector, fresh fruit, vegetables and dairy products, as well as certain processed meats, have only recently become available. Fresh meat was not available in the shops until 1971. Whereas all bread was traditionally home-baked, from a mixed dough of Norwegian wheat flour and Finnish rye flour, bread is nowadays increasingly bought ready-made. Miscellaneous items include attractive tins and packets, jams, sauces, biscuits, sweets and so on; the overall cost of which very quickly mounts up. As the proportion of cash to subsistence supplies and exchange credit which the housewife has at her disposal increases, so the diet is weighted with items from the third sector. Able to make regular visits to the shops, she buys a little at a time rather than in bulk, and buys processed food rather than basic raw materials. When she substitutes these diverse luxury and processed items for traditional items in her catering system, the costs of domestic consumption rise to an unprecedented level.

The allocation of money

In general, the proportion of financial transactions in the Skolt economy has increased considerably in recent years due firstly to the expansion of the local commodity market, facilitating both the export of produce and the import of new consumer goods, secondly to the growth of the wage-labour sector at the expense of primary production for subsistence or exchange trade, thirdly to the full penetration of the national welfare system, and fourthly to the demand for new machinery and luxury goods. Net money income accruing to household members that is not reinvested in the processes of production or extraction can be converted to a wide range of consumer items. These can be grouped into seven classes:

(1) Raw materials of domestic consumption purchased from the shops. The money allocated for this purpose will be termed the *domestic consumption contribution.*

(2) Items consumed by individuals independently of the domestic context: above all, beer, spirits and tobacco. This class should also include the redistribution of cash through gambling.

(3) Items exhibited by individuals, such as fashionable clothing, wrist-watches, etc.

(4) Items exhibited in the house: fine furniture, television, encyclo-paedias, and other cultural components of the 'sitting-room'.

(5) Modern durable storage and conversion equipment: petrol-powered washing-machines, gas-cookers and refrigerators, paraffin or gas-lights, oil-heaters.

(6) Motorized conveyance equipment: above all, purchase, running and repair costs of snowmobiles and cars. Taxi-fares can also be grouped in this category.

(7) Payment of bank-loans and interest, principally those incurred in house-building and repairs, and incumbent on the formal head of the household. About 75 per cent of all loans taken out by Skolts are for this purpose.

Raw materials in group one are normally paid by cash. Credit facilities allowed by local Finnish merchants, if extended at all, are strictly limited. Alcoholic drinks in group two similarly involve immediate cash-down payment, as do petrol costs and taxi fares in group six. Items in group four, the more costly items in group five, and cars and snowmobiles in group six, are usually obtained by hire-purchase. The initial lump-sum and subsequent instalments are paid by post- or bank-giro. Items in group three and spare parts for repairs in group six are obtained by mail order and paid through the post office. Loans and interest are paid in instal-ments at the bank.

The major sources of cash in the community are the local post office and the banks at Ivalo and Inari. The post office is managed by a local merchant family which is little trusted by the Skolts, whilst the banks have only recently begun to make an impact on the economy with the establishment of local branches and the improvement in road communi-cations. Facilities for saving and investment offered by these institutions are therefore little used: reserves are stored in nature rather than the bank. Most welfare benefit and some wages are paid through the post office, whilst the bank handles most wage payments. All expenditure excluding cash-down items and the domestic consumption contribution can be dealt with at the cash source. Cash is also available from the bank representatives at reindeer separations: profits from the sale of deer that are not allocated to settlement of the exchange account with the Norwegian merchant or arrears due to the *paliskunta* can be withdrawn as hard cash or as bank-giro slips.

Since domestic maintenance requirements present a relatively stable demand, consumption expectations are defined according to the regular component of household income. These expectations involve an estimate of the balance of income from subsistence production and exchange trade on the one hand, and from money payments, principally wages and welfare benefits, on the other. Domestic economies could be arranged along a continuum according to the proportion of total income in each sector. Three typical positions on this continuum are illustrated schematically in fig. 27. The few households of salaried employees in permanent full-time positions, which thus obtain very little of their supplies from the subsistence/exchange sector, depend on a relatively large domestic consumption contribution, negotiated as a fixed proportion of the regular money income (column C). On the other pole, active and successful reindeer-men can provide nearly all essential raw materials for domestic consumption without recourse to monetary expenditure (column A). More often, attempts to sustain the traditional subsistence/exchange economy have driven householders to enlist for unemployment benefit and casual labour, in order to raise a regular money contribution to supplement the diminished and uncertain income from *peura* hunting, fishing, gathering and trapping (column B). Although the effects of irregularities in the yield from the natural environment can, up to a point, be evened out by storage or the establishment of credit, the traditional reliance on primary production no longer accords with real returns. Domestic groups continuing to work on the assumption of a regular income in the subsistence sector often find themselves going hungry, especially during summer months, when many foods do not keep.

As a result of the overall shift towards a money economy, the domestic authority of the housewife as a centre of redistribution in the household has been undermined. Whilst the value of subsistence supplies and exchange credit can *only* be realized through their conversion by the housewife into food, clothing and warmth; the value of money can be realized in an unlimited number of ways, only some of which lie within the context of domestic consumption. A considerable proportion of total money income paid to male household members is either expended at source by credit transfer or used to purchase cash-down items for consumption in the extra-domestic context, leaving the housewife with full control only over income that is paid directly to her (fig. 26C). This accounts for the central importance attached to welfare items made out to women, such as possible pensions and child allowances, in securing a minimal fund for domestic consumption. If these welfare sources are inadequate to meet the cash costs of raw materials, the housewife must exert what authority she has in the domestic sphere to exact additional regular contributions from her menfolk. Hard cash physically located in the house and under the house-wife's control is thus never more than enough to cover her recurrent expenditure, whilst any reserves of withdrawn cash in excess of the domestic consumption contribution are carried in men's pockets. It is common for a welfare payment cashed in the post office to be spent immediately in the settlement of a short-term account in one of the local shops. A visit to the shop may drain the housewife's cash supply to the last penny, forcing her to borrow if unexpected expenses arise which must be paid before she can hope to receive a further instalment, for instance on her husband's return from the labour site or on the next payment day for welfare benefit.

Besides the domestic consumption contribution, there remain a number of regular and obligatory payments, such as interest on loans and hire-purchase instalments, which are settled at the cash source, that is, the bank or post office. In so far as these payments may cover a long time-span, they too must be taken from the regular money component of household income, leaving only the balance for the domestic consumption contri-bution. The balance may be small or negative, forcing a greater reliance on the subsistence sector and existing credit facilities, or a redefinition of income expectations: for instance by choosing work rather than deregis-tration from the unemployment lists in order to raise the regular money income component to the minimum defined by the level of unemploy-ment compensation (fig. 27B). Snowmobile hire-purchase instalments represent the greatest financial burden in this sphere, and have forced many households to a radical re-evaluation of budgetary expectations.

The contribution of unmarried productive household members is often subject to dispute. When younger generation producers are increasingly taking advantage of wage-earning opportunities rather than assisting in the subsistence sector, little control over the allocation of their earnings can be exercised on the household level. Housewives complain that their adult sons eat the food provided through the productive activities of parents without contributing any of their earnings. The youth, naturally concerned with individual rather than domestic performance, prefers to spend his earnings on items of personal display such as clothing (group three), or motor-power (group six), or on alcohol and gambling (group two). If he does contribute to household welfare, he will do so by buying 'gifts' of indivisible and durable group four and five items such as fine furniture, television, or a gas cooker by lump-sum and hire-purchase, rather than by making a regular contribution towards the costs of basic raw materials for redistribution. This procedure, stressing the element of transaction rather than incorporation, is consistent with the desire to be independent of the natal household as a consumption unit, whilst recog-nizing a continuing responsibility towards it. Labour migrants who have already achieved residential independence from the household can also contribute in this way.

Excess money that is neither expended in payments at the cash source nor transferred to the housewife's handbag or the household chest-of-drawers as the domestic consumption contribution is carried around as 'hard cash' in the mobile wallets of men. 'Cash in the pocket' conse-quently represents above all the uncertain, intermittent component of the total money income, over and above the regular component against which stable budgetary expectations are matched. It may be redistributed as stakes in games of cards, or used to buy beer, spirits and tobacco, as well as physical mobility outside the sphere of domestic obligations in the form of petrol or taxi rides. As the amount of 'cash in the pocket' limits the scale or duration of the associated activities of gambling, drinking, smoking and driving; so the resort to casual labour, which increases the 'cash in the pocket' component during periods of employment, has led to their escalation. Paradoxically, the need to meet greater household financial commitments has therefore led to increased cash consumption extraneous to the household budget, whilst for the housewife the availability of basic raw materials for provisioning the household may become problematic.

The proportion of 'cash in the pocket' to the total money income depends on the proportion of regular to intermittent income components. The difference in money allocation for a salaried employee and a casual labourer can be seen from a comparison of columns B and C in fig. 27. The former relies less on subsistence/exchange income for domestic consumption, can allocate a greater amount to expensive hire-purchase goods in groups four and five, can take out greater loans for house-building and repairs, but carries much less money around with him, and hence spends less on cash-down items, particularly those of group two. In the conventional sense, he appears more 'economical', whereas the irregular earner appears to squander a large proportion of his temporary earnings whilst maintaining his household at a relatively low standard of living as measured by domestic comfort, technological sophistication and modernity.

Unlike both the salaried earner and the casual labourer, whose money income is expended in either delayed or immediate consumption, the individual sub-contractor and owner of capital, typically the active reindeer-man with his herd and snowmobile, tends to feed money profits into further capital investment whilst maintaining the consumption profile of his household predominantly in the subsistence/exchange sector (fig. 27A). However, his profits are realized not in the form of regular instalments, but on irregular and often unpredictable occasions. That part which is realized as money accumulates as bank-giro slips or in *paliskunta* accounts, and the greater part may be reinvested without its materialization as cash. Taken as an average, the 'cash in the pocket' component of consumption is relatively small. However, on those occasions when cash is withdrawn, for example at separations or on occasional visits to the bank at Ivalo, amounts of 'cash in the pocket' may be considerable, although rapidly expended in the few days of drinking, driving and gambling which typically follow such occasions. The volume of this expenditure has increased in proportion to the availability of cash, above all through the presence of the ' bank ' on the separation site.

Two mutually contradictory paths of social and economic advancement are currently presented within the community, involving contrasting scales of value and measures of achievement. The first, embodied in the ethos of traditional pastoralism, with its emphasis on private riches and domestic parsimony, lies in the inconspicuous accumulation of physically dispersed animal wealth. The second, embodied in the system of income-based status ranking of the cosmopolitan culture of affluence, lies in the conspicuous consumption of costly items of modern design and technology, displayed principally in the domestic setting and conceptualized as the ' standard of living '. Introduced into the community by immigrant professionals, this path has been realized by a small local elite of householders having the requisite social connections and the financial security in the form of a regular salary to sustain the substantial level of recurrent payments involved.

However, for perhaps the majority of Skolts, both possibilities for advancement are more or less closed. Whatever their aspirations, neither set of values can be realized. The small-owner can no longer control the growth of his herd, whilst as a casual labourer he cannot afford the trappings of affluence. The lack of commitment to a long-term financial policy, and the consequently high level of immediate ' cash in the pocket ' expenditure, follow from his restricted possibilities for investment. Tied to an insecure compromise, he has no options available whereby temporary surpluses could be turned towards the cumulative ends of increasing either future wealth or status.

The snowmobile in the domestic economy

Since the first snowmobiles were introduced to the community, their numbers have greatly increased. By spring 1972 there were seventy-one snowmobiles in use, distributed in fifty-six of the sixty-nine households in the community. The demand for machines remains high, as they wear out or become obsolete in a period of from one to four years. New models are constantly being introduced on the market, and nearly all purchasers today are buying replacement models rather than their first machines.

Prices for new models range from 3000 to 5000 Fmk, second-hand models cost around 2000 Fmk. Owing to obsolescence and wear and tear, most buyers are faced with more or less continuous instalment payments of 100–400 Fmk per month. In addition, petrol is expensive at around 1 Fmk per litre. Repairs and spare parts add a great deal to the cost; traction belts (cost 500 Fmk) rarely last more than a winter, drive belts (cost 60 Fmk) break considerably more often, and skis (cost 100 Fmk) break with rough driving. On average, over the seven-month driving season, total costs come to some 350 Fmk per month, of which one third

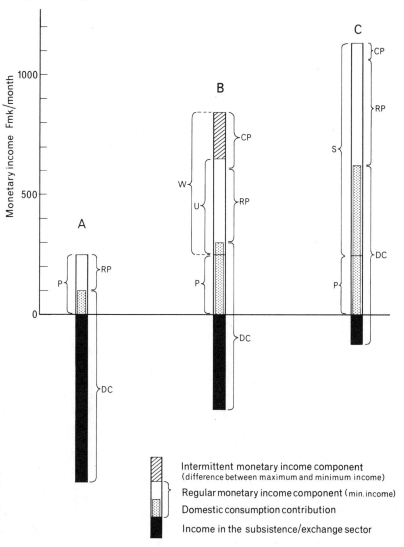

Fig. 27. The components of the household budget, represented schematically for a typical household under variable conditions of periodic income. Occasional monetary income, for example from sales of reindeer or short-term casual labour, is not indicated. Monetary income components: *P*, Regular welfare benefit (pensions + child allowance); *U*, unemployment compensation; *W*, wage income from casual labour; *S*, regular salary. Components of expenditure: *DC*, Raw materials of domestic consumption; *RP*, regular payments on loans and consumer hardware; *CP*, cash in the pocket.

is purchase/obsolescence costs, one third petrol costs, and one third repair and maintenance costs. This figure may be compared with the typical wage-labour income of 500–600 Fmk per month after tax.

The snowmobile has today almost completely replaced the draught reindeer as the principal item of household conveyance equipment. It is found to be essential in tasks such as getting to separations to extract meat, hauling timber for firewood, and visiting the shops to buy food and everyday supplies. Its adoption, though initially a matter of convenience, became a necessity as the poverty of home pastures and the increasing ubiquity of 'wild' deer and snowmobiles in the environment rendered the taming and upkeep of draught animals virtually impossible. Today, only six Skolt households still keep draught deer, which are used only occasionally for wood hauling.

Where the snowmobile is employed exclusively for the conveyance of goods destined for domestic consumption, the financial costs incurred must be met from the household money income. The machine is assigned a functional use-value, measured in terms of domestic necessity or convenience, rather than capital value as an instrument of production. Whereas the herder weighs up the costs of investment in the snowmobile against his expected resultant profits within the reindeer economy, the householder can only place the snowmobile along with other items on a scale of domestic priorities. However, the magnitude of expenditure, involving thousands rather than tens or hundreds of marks, tends to put the snowmobile in a class of its own, such that although costs and benefits of alternative models are considered in detail, they are rarely compared alongside lesser items of consumption.

Snowmobile purchase costs are generally met by instalment payments, which therefore form part of the household's regular financial commitments. Marketing agents insist on prompt payment, and will immediately reclaim possession of the machine if payment is not forthcoming, regardless of fluctuations in the financial circumstances of the household concerned. For households whose consumption requirements were obtained principally from the subsistence/exchange sector, and whose monetary outlay was previously comparatively small, the costs of acquiring a snowmobile have imposed a financial burden of a new order, multiplying money expenditure in the household budget by a factor of two to three. In order to meet this burden, many householders have been forced into casual labour, bringing about an overall shift from the traditional combination of subsistence production and exchange trade towards fuller participation in the modern market economy, and a consequent redefinition of household income expectations and consumption patterns (fig. 27B).

Within the household, different individuals may be responsible for payment and for the operation of the snowmobile. Thus, the welfare income of old parents may form the regular component allocated to snowmobile payments, whilst operation and maintenance rests in the hands of their sons, who are expected to use the snowmobile in conveyance tasks for the benefit of the household. Alternatively, a son may operate the snowmobile whilst his father is away earning wages to pay for it. A consequence of this separation of responsibilities is that the junior generation operator can manage the snowmobile without regard to cost; whilst the older generation payer, who is responsible for providing for his household yet who cannot operate the snowmobile himself for lack of competence, can exercise very little control over management, and can apply no effective sanctions in case of misuse. In one household, for example, the old pensioner parents continue to finance the snowmobile driven by their youngest son in the belief that it represents a foundation of household security, although the youth had driven five machines to a wreck in the space of five years. The snowmobile is hardly ever applied towards domestic maintenance, yet every fresh breakdown is treated as a catastrophe for the household.

It is possible to distinguish three broadly contrastive styles of snow-mobile management, depending on whether the principal operator in the household is an active reindeer herder, a senior householder no longer active in herding, or an unmarried member of the junior generation. For the first, the snowmobile figures as an essential item of capital equipment. The herder tries to make his machine last as long as possible; rapid wear and tear is a consequence of hard rather than careless use. Breakages are repaired as long as it is economically worthwhile, but since it is important always to have a working snowmobile available for use, machines are not kept after they are too worn out to be reliable.

On the other hand, the occasions on which the machine is absolutely essential for domestic conveyance tasks are relatively few. When the senior householder is also the operator of the snowmobile, the machine tends to be an old second-hand model, driven rather rarely, and semi-permanently broken down. It is kept in operation only through sporadic and makeshift repairs, which seldom prove reliable. If, however, the machine is operated by the youth of the household, whether paid for by them or by the senior generation, it tends to be the latest model, purchased brand-new and driven incessantly. Reckless driving, often on inadequate snow-cover, leads to frequent accidents, and machines rapidly break down beyond repair. In any case, they are regularly changed in order to keep up with new designs, and no attempt is made to keep old machines in working order. Whereas the senior generation is above all concerned with the snow-mobile's functions of haulage and transport, as an extension of the house-hold; the youth is concerned with its properties of power and mobility, as an extension of the individual personality.

Cash in the pocket: portability, mobility and the consumption of alcohol

Along with alcohol, tobacco and playing-cards, hard cash belongs to the cluster of commodities which are sufficiently compact and portable to be carried on the person, in a jacket pocket or under the trouser belt; and which have in common the expectation that they may be shared or given away. Tobacco or cigarettes can be offered, alcoholic drink is customarily handed around, whilst the gambling of large sums of money in games of poker is consistent with the transitory nature of hard cash. As 'pocket' items, these commodities constitute an assemblage of means for the establishment and manipulation of social relationships, which a man can carry around with him on his travels away from home. They are thus aspects of the male attribute of individual physical mobility, which, in turn, is enhanced through motorization: the attachment of the man to a snow-mobile, motor-cycle or car, driven by fuel purchased with cash. Taken together, the activities of drinking, smoking, gambling and driving involve standard patterns of behaviour for the assertion and management of identity in the extra-domestic, male-dominated environment.

The occasions and settings for these activities are typically those in which both cash and spirits are in plentiful supply. One such occasion is the aftermath of the reindeer separation, after the bank has paid out cash for reindeer sales. Similarly, when a labourer collects his cash from the bank at Ivalo, having also had an opportunity to visit the ALKO shop, the following few days may be spent in drinking and festivity, starting in the bars and restaurants of Ivalo, then in the bus on the return journey, and finally in various local settings, until cash and alcohol supplies are exhausted. The principal local settings are the bars in Sevetti and on the Norwegian frontier. Certain Skolt houses also form regular drinking and gambling settings, particularly where the domestic aspect of the household is weak due to the predominance of adult male members or the absence of an active or authoritative housewife with young children. The setting may be an outbuilding rather than the dwelling itself.

Alcohol consumption has been influenced by the opening up of new sales outlets in the area. In 1970 a new branch of ALKO opened at Ivalo (formerly the nearest source of Finnish spirits was Rovaniemi, 450 km away), and in 1971 two bars opened on the frontier, selling bottled beer. In response to this competition, a license was immediately obtained for beer sales in the Sevetti bar. Beer-consumption has rapidly reached an unprecedented level, whilst spirits are a great deal easier to obtain, whether legally from ALKO, or on the black market. Besides providing sales outlets for beer, the bars also form local settings for drinking outside the house-hold, thereby furthering the recategorization of drinking as an extra-domestic activity.

Heavy alcohol consumption is nothing new among the Skolts, nor among Lapps in general, having been a feature of five hundred years of culture contact (Aikio 1971). However, the social organization of drinking has altered significantly in recent years. Drinking customarily occurred within the domestic sphere, and the housewife herself controlled the supply. Traditional drinks were vodka, obtained during the Russian period in twenty-five litre barrels, and a mild home-brewed beer. Occasions for drinking would be a family ritual event or a welcome for guests, when the procedure would be highly formalized. In addition vodka was valued for its medicinal properties. Today, ritualized drinking in the household is uncommon: most drinking occurs in the extra-domestic sphere, where it is not regulated by formal procedures. At the same time, the mobile bachelor youth has come to form the principal consumer group. Having once defined the new style of drinking as extra-domestic, occasional drinking by girls or even married women is heavily censured by local moralists. Some are convinced that alcohol is undermining the very foundations of the community.

Excessive alcohol consumption certainly constitutes a serious social problem, but one that is general throughout northern Finland, and by no means restricted to Skolt or Lapp ethnic categories. The allocation of large sums of cash to drinking contributes to the maintenance of poverty, whilst the combined drinking of beer and spirits is physically detrimental. Skolt drinking is, however, a social activity and cannot be understood as an individual medical or psychiatric condition. There is only one case of genuine addiction, and individuals rarely drink in isolation.

The social contexts of alcohol consumption are broadly of two kinds: firstly the establishment and affirmation of transitory relationships of incorporation with a view to the sharing of strategic information; secondly, the achievement of a state of general drunkenness, in which setting strategic considerations of the real world can be transcended. Spirit bottles are the usual tender in the first context, whereas beer is held responsible for the present level of drunkenness in the community. This difference can be related to the fact that, whereas spirits can be carried on the person, the normal offering being a single mouthful, beer cannot, since it is consumed by the crate, the normal offering being a whole bottle. In practice, these contexts are not exactly separable; and the two forms of alcohol are often mixed. Spirits alone may induce drunkenness, but usually only as a very short transitory phase between sobriety and unconsciousness, whereas drunkenness induced by beer is prolonged.

Spirit bottles are usually carried in a concealed pocket. At strategic moments the bottle can be exposed, signalling an invitation for others in the immediate vicinity to drink. The drinking group, rarely including more than five people, is quite clearly defined in space, either by relative distance, physical barriers, or by tight clustering and often physical contact. The owner of the bottle nucleates and controls the composition of the group. Though transitory, the drinking group is strictly closed during its existence, and information passed between the members is private, and spoken softly.

The non-portability of beer limits its applicability in strategic contexts, and tends to restrict its consumption to public settings such as bars, dance-halls and coffee-houses, in which consumption of spirits ' from the bottle ' is theoretically prohibited by law. Drinking groups are open, and not clearly defined. Further, the speech of the drunk man is loud and rhetorical, highly repetitive, and persistent in its demands for confirmation

from the audience at large. The drunk man makes repeated moral assertions about himself and passes judgement on the characters of others by
public declaration, and insists that these be accepted, however inordinate
they may appear in practical terms. It is only in the drunken state that a
man is licensed to express himself overtly in this fashion.[2] In a sense, the
drunken world represents a second level of reality, on which the social
world appears not as a configuration of means and ends, but as a total
morality promulgated by proclamation. Drunkenness, like some forms of
ritual, lifts the setting to a plane on which covert or strategic considerations
of self-interest are no longer relevant; a state which lasts until beer and
cash supplies are exhausted.

Other activities associated with 'cash in the pocket' similarly furnish
contexts for self-assertion beyond the bounds of the strict reticence and
moderation that is expected in normal everyday behaviour (Pelto 1962:
135). The game of poker is a setting in which a man is expected to display
qualities of recklessness and aggression. The cards are slammed down on
the table with exaggerated force, to the accompaniment of a resounding
swearword. The players compete not only for the jackpot, but also for the
most powerful delivery. Similar qualities are overtly displayed in snowmobile driving, where speed and noise are of the essence. Gambling,
drinking, smoking and driving thus provide a man with channels of self-
expression in the extra-domestic sphere: the means to manipulate his
relationships with others, to give and receive tactical information, to
display the qualities of manhood, and to assert the view he has of himself
and his place in the community.

15 Youth

Youth as a social category

Youth, or 'young people', occupy a structurally transitional position, covering the gradual attainment of partial to full independence from the natal household, up to the establishment of a new domestic unit. The youth's orientations are therefore directed away from the domestic group towards the reference-group of age-mates and peers in the neighbourhood: a transition that entails an increasing degree of independent physical mobility. Entry into the category is gradual, beginning in the early teens with the onset of adolescence, usually a year or two earlier for girls than for boys. Those born in the first decade after resettlement constitute a population 'bulge' who have now reached or are reaching this stage of maturity. The community is thus loaded with a considerable youth population, without having evolved the institutional facilities to absorb it either presently or in the future. The upper age-range of male youth has been extended owing to the increasing numbers of confirmed bachelors who, even in their thirties and forties, are still incorporated in youth activities on account of their lack of formal domestic responsibility. On the other extreme, the age distribution of female youth in the community is 'truncated' as a result of emigration. Only a handful of girls remain at home beyond their teens. There is consequently a high degree of imbalance of youth numbers by sex (fig. 28).

The crystallization of an inter-generational boundary around a category of youth defined by their distinctive styles of behaviour and divergent interests reflects developments in the post-resettlement opportunity situation for young people. Traditionally, girls were largely confined to the domestic setting both before and after marriage, whilst for boys adolescence represented only a stage in the gradual accumulation of practical experience concerning adulthood. The process of growing up was not divided by significant discontinuities of experience or transition ritual (Pelto 1962: 109).

Nowadays, following from new possibilities to obtain money income, youth of both sexes can establish a greater degree of economic, and sometimes even residential, independence from the natal household. For most girls, youth is a period in which orientations are turned away from traditional domestic expectations, and set towards a future career outside the community. It is thus a preparation for departure, during which girls experiment with the styles of behaviour they believe to be appropriate according to their image of the world outside. No such clear career openings outside the community are available for boys, nor is any definite future marked out locally. Growing up into a career vacuum, the youth asserts his manhood not through demonstrating his proficiency in adult productive skills, but through extravagant extra-domestic consumption, financed by the new sources of income, and kept in check only by the finite supply of hard cash.

Age-grading and the recruitment of cliques and friends

On certain major occasions, such as dances or sports events organized by the local clubs on public holidays, all the youth of the community may be assembled in one place. The more common and everyday youth activities, generally based on the neighbourhood level, revolve around the *youth-clique* of the neighbourhood: the set of young people who regularly congregate together. The youth-clique is an entirely informal and strictly egalitarian body. It is divided into two single-sex sub-cliques, which maintain a strong separatism even in games and dances when they combine. Further subdivision may occur on the basis of relative age.

In many contexts, especially when outside the home neighbourhood, youths move in pairs of the same sex, each with his or her more or less temporary 'best friend'. In order to join in the activities of another neighbourhood, the pair must attach themselves to the margin of the local clique. The presence of a friend compensates for the insecurity of this marginal position. Youth from households outside the principal neighbourhoods find themselves in this situation for most of the time. Typically, pairs comprise first cousins, not necessarily from the same clique. Pairs are rarely siblings, as this would introduce an element of authority of older over younger sibling, incompatable with the stress on comradely equality between best friends, emphasised in mild symmetrical joking, teasing and horse-play. An older sibling can, however, help to introduce a younger sibling to youth activities, acting as a kind of sponsor, by setting an example for the other to follow, and even by loaning or sharing the motor vehicles that may be a prerequisite for participation.

Whereas the youth category is definable in terms of structural transition rather than age, a degree of age-grading is evident in the recruitment of both cliques and pairs, above all among the youngest sector of youth. This is due in part to the rapid development of physical and social maturity with age during early adolescence; since cliques and pairs operate on the assumption of equal maturity. Relatively early physical maturity is an advantage for those aspiring to clique membership. On the other hand, for the older predominantly male youth, it becomes increasingly difficult to find companions of their own age: they face either social isolation, or have to fit in with those younger than themselves by perhaps ten to fifteen years.

Further pressure towards age-grading is imposed by intrusive formal

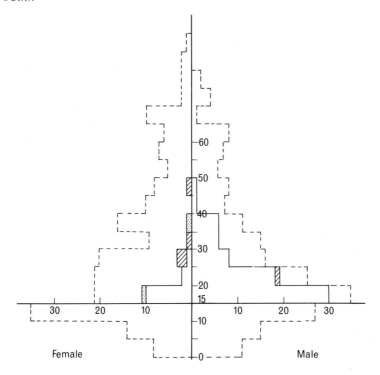

Fig. 28. Age/sex distribution of Skolt youth category, in five-year age-classes 15–19, 20–24, 25–29, etc. Solid line includes all those between the ages of 15 and 60 who are unmarried and permanently resident locally; with the exception of those with mental or physical handicaps (shaded areas) and women with illegitimate children (speckled areas). Dashed line shows the outline of the total population pyramid for Skolts (including migrants). The portion of the pyramid below the horizontal axis shows the population distribution of children aged 0–14. A population bulge is evident in the age-classes presently between 10 and 20.

institutions and regulations of Finnish society: school, military service, and the age of majority. Of these, the most important is the school system. Youth who are still at school or have recently left tend to select their friends from the same class. During their final years at the secondary schools in Inari and Ivalo, aged around thirteen to sixteen, many of the attitudes underlying later youth behaviour are formed. This is more so for girls, who respond to the sex-typing of Western mass media in their receptiveness to imported fashions, crazes and images of the outside world, propagated in the school setting and its quasi-urban environment. Boys, in contrast, continue to base their orientations on their native environment, and tend to find school both pointless and disagreeable.[1]

All young men are obliged to contribute a period of military service. Unless special circumstances intervene, a youth goes to the army at the

age of nineteen, for 9–11 months. For many, it is their first long period
away from home, and the first opportunity to meet people of the same
age from all social and geographical backgrounds. Youths usually look
forward to military service, and enjoy it despite the contrast of military
discipline to freedom at home. Military service is a transition ritual on the
national scale, and its symbolic significance in the passage from youth to
manhood is recognized among the Skolts as elsewhere. In almost every
house, framed portrait-photographs of sons in their military uniform are
exhibited.

The principal formal regulations involving age grading are the laws
stating minimum ages for buying alcoholic drinks (twenty-one for spirits,
eighteen for strong beer) and for driving (eighteen for cars, fifteen for
snowmobiles and mopeds). Though reinforcing the social definition of
these activities as exclusively adult, and thereby strengthening the
aspirations of novices to have access to them, the impact of these
regulations on the local level is largely theoretical.

Activities and settings

Youth pairs may team up for tours of the neighbourhood or more
extensive trips along the length of the community, to the international
frontier and to Norwegian social centres. Male pairs are more mobile,
whilst girls are dependent on the boys for transport. Male youth pairs
also get together for extended fishing trips: the fishing is basically for
sport, using rod and line, and the catch too small to be of economic
significance. Members of a youth-clique may gather together for a drink,
a game of cards or volley-ball, or just to talk and drive around. Larger
assemblies derived from several neighbourhoods may gather together for
organized dances and sports, ice-hole fishing contests, and snowmobile or
ski races.

Settings for intra-neighbourhood activity can be dwellings or outbuildings, the stretch of road through the neighbourhood, or a piece of
cleared ground that can serve as a pitch for games. Settings for larger
assemblies include the bars at Sevetti, on the frontier and in Norway, the
Sevetti dance-stand and sports ground, the school-halls in Norway where
dances and sometimes bingo-sessions are held, and improvised settings for
winter sports. Sevetti neighbourhood is exceptional in including both bar,
dance-stand and sports ground, which are used by the local clique as
settings for its regular activities, as well as for larger events.

In neighbourhoods other than Sevetti, the house remains an important
youth interaction setting. Youths come and go as they please among the
houses of the neighbourhood, without observing any particular formalities.
The outbuildings, particularly the sheepcote, are often used when youth
activities demand independence from the dwelling, for instance at night
when older people and children are sleeping. In the dwelling, the housewife does not expect to serve refreshments as to guests, and the youth

ignores senior household members, directing all his attention towards his peers. However, because of their mobility, youths are important carriers of information both within and between neighbourhoods. A youth doing the rounds of the neighbourhood, or a pair on their travels up and down the community, may be quizzed at length about goings-on elsewhere by the housewife, in her capacity as a selective collector, distributor and store of personal information. The youth, however, puts on the appearance of paying only cursory attention to this questioning, and answers over his shoulder, in an offhand manner.

The organization of Sevetti youth activity differs from that of other neighbourhoods in two respects. Firstly, the relatively greater concentration of youth in the neighbourhood creates a strong basis for generational solidarity. Secondly, access to extra-domestic premises for assembly, such as the bar and dance-stand, coupled with progressive exclusion from the house as the ' living room ' of the dwelling is replaced by the ' sitting room ', divorces youth activity from the household setting. In both respects, conditions exist for the emergence of a strongly bounded youth-clique and, along with this, the development of informal patterns of inter-generational avoidance. Young people refuse to address or answer older people in front of their peers, and scrupulously avoid situations which could force them to interact with the older generation of other than their own households. The older generation, already embittered by the apparent lack of traditional orientation and responsibility among young people, interprets avoidance as insult and rejection.

Physical mobility and personal display

As a boy matures and aspires towards youthful freedom from domestic authority, he becomes increasingly concerned to display the stereotyped modes of personal behaviour through which his position in the peer-group is established. At the same time, the long distances separating youth assembly points in the community make it imperative for him to have access to independent means to physical mobility if he is to break loose from the confines of the domestic setting and be along in the social activities of his fellows. In both respects, a motor vehicle is a necessary accompaniment to full participation in youth activity. Whereas for the householder, the functions of motor power are defined in relation to domestic group maintenance, for the youth its purpose lies in conferring independence from the household, as a means to both physical mobility and personal display.

Possession of a motor vehicle, above all of a snowmobile, is the greatest desire of the novice. Youngsters must at first be content to pull models on a string, to the accompaniment of appropriate noises, and their restricted mobility limits their range of movement to within the household cluster. As a boy grows older, he graduates from the bicycle, allowing a wider range of movement in the neighbourhood, to the motor-bicycle or snowmobile, with which he can cover the whole length of the community. For longer trips, particularly to the international frontier and over to Norway, the motor-car represents the only practical alternative. Youths without cars must rely on the taxi or on lifts for long-range transport beyond Sevetti, where the regular bus service terminates: indeed both the local taxi and the few cars in the community operated by youths are notorious as transporters of often drunken revellers over enormous distances (fig. 29). Fully motorized, the youth is admitted to the entire range of activities, which involve him in incessant movement between widely separated social centres. Without a machine in working order, he suffers the ignominy of domestic confinement.

Driving by youths is a form of personal prestige management. Criteria of design, power, speed and noise are of prime importance. The machine becomes an extension of the man; its deafening sound and breakneck speed form an integral part of the driver's personal performance. Snowmobile drivers learn how to wear a facial expression indicating strength and power, skill and concentration; qualities epitomized in the annual snowmobile rally, a speed event with all the motor-racing trappings from driving suits and crash-helmets to petrol advertisement stickers (plate 16). In fact the full power of the machine is mobilized by the light pull of a lever and the actual skill required to drive is remarkably little, but the

Fig. 29. The range of youth mobility. ▶

Plate 16. A group of boys gather enthusiastically around a 'Ski-doo' snowmobile during a local racing event.

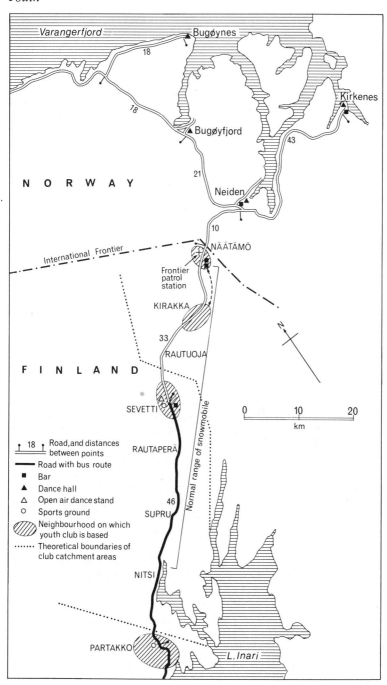

frequent failure of the machine to co-operate can cause acute loss of face. In addition to displaying technical mastery over the machine, the youth must demonstrate fluency in the language of motor-mechanics: a specialized colloquial jargon with its own vocabulary of mechanical terminology and swear-words.

Even within the neighbourhood, youths spend much of their time driving up and down the road. The shortest distances between adjacent houses may be covered by motor-bicycle or snowmobile, although, given the complexities of starting, they could be covered more quickly by foot. Points of departure and destinations within a neighbourhood, separated at most by a few hundred yards, are fixed at focal points where people are or might be expected to be gathered. During the evenings, the routes between these points can become temporary race-tracks. The driver seldom leaves his machine, but remains in the saddle; for to dismount would be to abandon his prestige-base. Physically dissociated from his source of power, mobility and independence, he would feel himself critically handicapped.

The position of the relatively few car-drivers is a particularly prestigious one. As well as being free to take advantage of distant social attractions, they become centres of attention for those seeking rides. Driving models the spectacle of the ' Arctic Rally': a yearly international motor-racing event that covers the length of the road. A car-driver, if he stops to talk, speaks through an opened window without getting out, whilst to his passengers he can offer the privilege of a share in seating space which is both mobile and exclusive, yet visible to onlookers. Thus, by having himself together with his machine observed and admired by others, the youth aims to en-hance his own personal prestige rating.

A youth with a money income of his own but who is still supported by his natal household may be able to buy a vehicle for himself. Many youths, however, operate vehicles paid for by their parents in the expectation that they will be used in support of domestic maintenance. It is difficult for a youth to fulfil these expectations without losing face amongst his peers, for it is in the peer group that values of self-reliance and independence from the household are stressed. The separation of responsibilities for payment and operation along generation lines may therefore entail the attribution to the same machine of contradictory purposes. For the householder, the motor vehicle is an indicator of domestic security, for the youth it demon-strates personal adequacy. Although this can create a situation of latent domestic conflict, satisfactory performance of the machine appears to confirm both sets of expectations for their respective adherents.

In all, the introduction of motor vehicles has swung the balance of domestic controls in favour of the youth, as well as conferring on them the means to wide-ranging physical mobility. Their liberation from domestic constraints has increased the scale of youth activities in extra-domestic contexts, resulting in the crystallization of an inter-generational boundary whose extension into the domestic domain can be a source of discord. From the point of view of the older generation, the irresponsibility of youth is evidenced by reckless driving and gross neglect of domestic obligations. From the point of view of youth, driving confers those qualities of power and independence that represent the most crucial indices of personal performance.

Youth organizations

Despite the effects of increased physical mobility in engendering a greater degree of generational solidarity among the youth of the community, attempts to bring youth activities under a formal organizational structure have met with little success. The efforts of clubs and their officials to influence the course of events are undermined by the values of independence, self-reliance and egalitarianism characteristic of youth. The wide range of club offices, from chairman and secretary to all kinds of committee positions, are purely nominal and of little practical relevance, conferring no real authority. Since it is impracticable to hold events or reserve special benefits restricted to members only, an effective contractual basis for club membership is lacking. Outside the core of officials, membership is ' floating '.

This organizational weakness is demonstrated in the recurrent failure of organized events and projects to materialize according to plan. Sports events fail because coherent teams cannot be recruited. Dances fail when, following some initiative, everyone decides to move elsewhere. Construction projects fail because of inadequate work organization and lack of effective leadership that would see them through to completion. The most effective organizers of youth clubs have tended to be adult non-Skolts who, from their socially marginal position, have been willing and able to exercise a degree of unifying authority. The frontier patrol station forms an influential centre of organization in this respect.

Two neighbouring clubs, the one based on Sevetti and theoretically embracing the whole community, the other based on the neighbouring Inari Lapp settlement of Partakko, have been in existence for some time as officially registered organizations, but the activities of both had virtually lapsed. The sudden growth of the frontier as a social centre during 1971 detracted from the influence of Sevetti neighbourhood. Partly as a result of this shift in the focus of activity, youth leaders at the frontier patrol station, including the former chairman of the Sevetti club, proceeded in the same year to set up a new club based on the frontier (fig. 29). Significantly, the catchment area of the club was defined by a boundary coinciding almost exactly with that between Näätämö and Vätsäri reindeer associations. Youth club boundaries thus came to reflect existing social and economic divisions.

This move provoked a revival of the original Sevetti club under a new leadership, and a fierce rivalry developed between them. This rivalry concerned the relative strengths of Sevetti and the frontier as social centres, each club attempting to attract maximum attendance at its own functions

whilst subverting those of the other. In practice, the range of influence of
the Sevetti club is limited to Sevetti neighbourhood, whilst that of the
frontier club is limited to the patrol station and Kirakka neighbourhood.
In both cases, the organization is based on the neighbourhood clique, from
whose members the club's officers are selected.

Whilst club officials have little control over the course of events, effective
power rests in the hands of the merchant bar proprietors as the clubs'
principal patrons. Both at Sevetti and on the frontier, bar proprietors
encouraged club developments, promising the use of their facilities for
youth functions; providing space, drink, and music from the juke-box.
For them, the establishment of one or other point as a social centre is
good for business. Thus, the dispute between the two youth clubs forms
one aspect of the commercial rivalry between Sevetti and border merchants.

Cliques and couples

Coupling between boys and girls is antithetical to the principles of clique
membership, which stress the opposition between sub-cliques of each sex.
In games, girls watch whilst boys play. In traditional hops, partners are
changed for each dance, and no overt recognition is given to any special
relationship that may exist between them. Amongst the youngest generation of youth who have not learnt traditional steps, girls have taken to
the ' twist ', which they can improvise between themselves, whilst boys
avoid dancing altogether. When not dancing, the two sexes sit separately.
Only Norwegians and other outsiders, for whom sexual prowess is an
aspect of personal prestige, flirt publicly at local dances. A Skolt couple
will restrict courting to strictly private settings, in order not to compromise relationships with peers and to avoid pressure of gossip (Pelto 1962:
147).

Marriage of a clique member leads to his or her exclusion from the
clique and a subsequent restructuring of friendship relations among
remaining members. Young married couples sometimes do attend dances
and take part in sports or other youth events. However, on such occasions
the partners separate each among their own immediate friends and kin
of the same sex. Whilst a person's married status is relevant for participation in all appropriate sectors of adult life, it is underplayed during
participation in youth activities.

Married couples of which one or both partners are immigrant professionals with a background in ' culture-Finland ' are in an exceptional
position. A non-Skolt spouse is connected kinship-wise into the community only through a marriage link with a Skolt, if connected at all. Consequently, he or she is more or less excluded from community youth events
in which the marriage link is not recognized as a basis for participation.
Conversely, for the Skolt spouse in a mixed marriage, to the extent that
he continues to activate relationships with former friends and kin at all,
his status remains more that of a youth than of a married person, whereas

it is just in the peripheral zone of elite society that the marriage constitutes a minimal requirement for participation.

When spouses isolated from the wider kinship network do take part in social functions outside their professional capacity, they accompany their partners as *couples*. This was vividly demonstrated in the formation of a 'young married set', based on the elite mixed and non-Skolt marriages of Sevetti neighbourhood, after the bar proprietor of the neighbourhood began to limit use of the bar's facilities to private parties open only to those considered sufficiently 'respectable'. Criteria of respectability included a commitment to civilized behaviour as defined by Finnish middle-class standards, and entry as a couple. Single youth were not generally admitted without partners. The remainder of the youth were left stranded and embittered outside, with nowhere particular to go and nothing particular to do. Youth-cliques were divided when older and more 'respectable' members gained admission to these exclusive events. Some found themselves having to compromise their own aspirations with clique loyalty. When leading members of the revived Sevetti youth club joined the exclusive set, the organization collapsed.

Skolts and Norwegians

The opening of the road over the frontier, connecting the Skolt community to the Norwegian road system at Neiden, initiated a new phase of inter-ethnic contact between Skolts and Norwegians or Norwegian Finns, concentrated in the youth sector. Mobile Skolts had access to Norwegian centres for entertainment, whilst the Norwegian youth began to visit Sevetti. Following the opening of the bars, youth from both sides began to meet on the frontier. The local Norwegian youth, most of them from Neiden, are of ethnically mixed composition: some are of wholly Norwegian ancestry, many are descendents of the original Finnish immigrant population or are of mixed ancestry. A few have a trace of Skolt ancestry, stemming from the remnants of the aboriginal Skolt population. 'Norwegianness' is actively cultivated, and although most youths are theoretically bilingual in Norwegian and Finnish, use of Finnish is avoided. Any traces of Skoltness are covered up altogether. In interaction with Skolts, youths present themselves as Norwegians, even to the extent of denying the existence of a common language of communication.

In comparison to the Skolts, young Norwegians give off an air of considerable affluence, and demonstrate a familiarity with western cosmopolitan youth trends. Many have travelled extensively, working periodically in southern cities or on the ships. They dress in well-tailored suits or in the best pop or boutique styles. Their tall stature makes a strong contrast to the shortness of the Skolts. In all, they appear 'well-groomed'. When visiting Sevetti, they arrive in large and expensive cars, fitted out with radio and stereo equipment which easily drowns the music supply of the Skolt youth – a small battery-powered record player.

Norwegians tend to view the Skolts as stupid and primitive, representing an altogether different and often incomprehensible kind of human being. However, for the Norwegian males who make up the bulk of the local youth, Skolt girls are desirable as objects of sexual attraction. For the Skolt girls, too, the arrival of Norwegians offers exciting prospects for sexual adventure, which are otherwise rather limited locally. On the whole, the establishment of long-term relationships is avoided. In public settings both parties can resort to 'secret' languages, Skolt or Norwegian, which the other does not understand, for communication amongst their own kind; and use of the common language, Finnish, is suppressed.

When Norwegians first began to arrive at the dances at Sevetti, they were welcomed by the local youth, since they brought with them novelty, excitement, style and music. They were viewed as catalysts in getting a party off the ground. The Norwegians' motives in coming to Sevetti were partly to escape the restrictions operative at home. Firstly there are no effective restrictions on drinking on the Finnish side, whereas rules operative on the Norwegian side are strongly prohibitionist. Secondly, there was a supply of girls which could be enjoyed independently of local political and kinship intrigue in the home community. Thirdly, the dance setting itself is entirely free of authoritative regulations and the scrutiny of the older generation to which Norwegian youth is subjected at home. On arrival at the Sevetti dance-stand, they can immediately take over the proceedings by substituting their own music supply, activating dancing, and monopolizing the girls. If nothing is happening, they can start a dance; and once news of their arrival spreads, others are sure to come. Back in their home setting in the Neiden bar, Norwegian youths boast about their conquests at Sevetti and joke about the stupidity of the Skolts.

After a year of regular social contact, initial enthusiasm has abated and been replaced even by a degree of bitterness. Skolts have become increasingly aware of Norwegian ethnic attitudes, and retaliate with derisory comments. Norwegian 'take-overs' are seen to fragment local youth-cliques and thereby to jeopardize the success of local youth activities. Skolt boys resent being left as onlookers whilst Norwegian youths monopolize the girls. The aggressive behaviour of Norwegians, leading sometimes to fights, is particularly heavily censured. The Norwegians, in turn, have found their relations with Skolts increasingly unsatisfactory.

The establishment of the bars on the frontier opened up a new setting for drinking and entertainment for the Norwegian as well as for the Skolt youth. Today, most contact between Skolt and Norwegian youth occurs on this ethnically neutral ground. The bars attract large concentrations of people from within a hundred kilometre radius, and have become notorious as scenes of extravagant drinking, and for the fights which often follow.

For the Skolts, the road connection opened up possibilities of attending Norwegian dances at Neiden, Kirkenes, Bugøyfjord and Bugøynes (fig. 29). The presence of relatively large numbers of Skolt youth at Neiden dances, as well as the regular contacts between Skolt and Neiden youth, have contributed to the hardening of specific attitudes towards the Skolt youth on the part of Neiden people. These dances are patronized by folk of all ages, and are theoretically teetotal. Skolts arriving at the dances are almost all relatively young, wildly dressed, and already drunk on arrival. Their behaviour is regarded by the older generation with disgust, by the younger generation with contempt.

Youths with the mobility and initiative to branch out to more distant destinations are in a better position to escape ethnic derogation. In the urban, but linguistically Norwegian, milieu of Kirkenes, they can merge unnoticed into the crowd. Still further afield, beyond the predominantly Lappish hamlet of Bugøyfjord, lies the tiny but almost exclusively Finnish-speaking community of Bugøynes. Skolts who reach this far experience dances with considerable pleasure. Having outdistanced the mob of Skolt youth, they are welcomed as visitors from Finland.

16 The neighbourhood

The flow of information

An individual collects and pieces together information relevant to people and activities in the community by watching and listening for the movements of others, or by talking directly or over the telephone. Generally, only information whose source lies outside the community comes by post in written form. Besides the possession of a telephone, the physical location of the house can have a considerable bearing on the degree to which household members are kept informed about movements in the community. Isolated houses or house clusters may be cut off from information by their marginality in neighbourhood activity. One measure of isolation is distance from the road, or seasonally from the winter snow-track. Houses nearest the road form the most regular stopping-off points for travellers, whereas houses separated from the road by a lake or long footpath are visited infrequently. Good views from house windows over the road enable household members to keep track of those passing by, even if they do not stop over. Alerted by the sound of a vehicle, people in a dwelling take up positions by the windows in order to spot it. The individual driver may not be visible from a distance, but his identity can usually be inferred from the colour and brand of his vehicle. The observers then attempt to reconstruct the purpose of the traveller's journey, and draw conclusions accordingly.

Local information may be seen to have two possible but contrasting kinds of content. The one is action-specific, telling about past or future events or about the deployment of political or economic resources that may have a bearing on the receiver's decision-making in particular action contexts. The other relates to specific persons and their relationships with others, enabling the receiver to build up a cumulative picture of individuals as moral personalities, and to make value assessments of character and behaviour. Any item of information may include content of both kinds, the difference lies in the way the receiver interprets it and links it with previous knowledge. An item telling of certain characters engaged in a certain activity will in the former case be sifted for the additional information it gives about that activity, and will be linked to previous knowledge on the subject; in the latter case it will be sifted for hints on the characters' personalities and the state of their social relationships, and linked to previous knowledge concerning their individual histories.

This content distinction corresponds with differences in the kinds of settings in relation to which one or other interpretation is relevant. The most fundamental distinction is that between domestic and extra-domestic spheres of activity. Extra-domestic settings are action-specific. Whether or not they are marked out by permanent physical structures, people gather there for the purpose of engaging in a particular activity, and leave when it is complete. The domestic unit possesses a continuity independent of the diverse activities that go on within it, being associated with the long-term process of socialization – the creation of moral persons. The uniqueness of each unit is defined in terms of the sum of the life-histories or personal identities of domestic group members. Thus, the relevance of action-specific interpretations lies above all in relation to the extra-domestic context, that of person-specific interpretations in relation to the domestic context.

The principal concerns of adult men and youths are with extra-domestic affairs, although these may be to some extent an aspect of their responsibilities towards the household. Typical topics of information are observations of reindeer movements,[1] news of separations, recent luck in fishing, latest price movements, and imminent employment prospects; for youth, news of dances, parties and sports events. Information relevant to these affairs can be picked up in both domestic and extra-domestic settings. When at home, a man may receive information from, say, the arrival of a visitor carrying news, or a telephone call. He may, however, actively seek out information by visiting other households, attending events and frequenting settings where he expects people to be gathered.

It may be necessary to prevent action-specific information of strategic value from being overheard by others in the vicinity. In the dwelling, the side room can be used as a private setting for the exchange of tactical information, and the telephone is always situated in this room for the same reason. In large, extra-domestic gatherings, for example reindeer separations and dances, privacy must be established by other means such as whispering or the setting up of closed drinking groups.

In contrast to men and youth active in extra-domestic contexts, the housewife, in her role as the focus of domestic organization, is principally concerned with ' person-specific' information. This concern stems from a perspective rooted in the domestic context, insulated from the political and economic affairs of the community. Based on the tasks involved in child-rearing and the implementation of domestic consumption, it is a perspective emphasizing moral order and routine, rather than individual strategy and choice. The housewife acts as a monitor of social morality. From the information she receives, often indirectly, she constructs the characters of others, evaluates their faults and their virtues, and judges their actions. Virtues are upheld through moral criticism of others; thus an individual may be censured for drinking, gossip, laziness, irresponsibility, neglect of kinship obligations, or for evil intent.

This last form of criticism, resembling classic forms of witchcraft accusation, is invariably propagated by women, usually against other women though in clear cases of deviance it may be directed towards men. If the virulence of criticism exceeds a reasonable level, the housewife may find it rebounding on herself. This points to a certain role dilemma, for whilst acting as a moral critic, the housewife is ideally expected to be reticent and tolerant rather than outspoken and malicious.

As the housewife is largely confined to the domestic setting, much of the information she gathers comes in from visitors to the household. The most frequent visitors are drawn from those who are most mobile, above all, youths with motor transport. During conversation with a visitor, information of relevance to both parties may be exchanged, though handled in contrasting frameworks of interpretation. Indeed, the visitor's main reason for calling may be to elicit information, but this aim is indicated only indirectly or in passing, or may be subtly concealed by phrasing questions as open-ended comments which guide the conversation in the required direction. The housewife may actively interrogate her guest, but the replies of the latter are characteristically oblique statements of qualified ignorance, leaving the housewife to form her own conclusions. Matters are raised directly only if the express purpose of the visit is the conveyance of a message or the transaction of business, rather than the affirmation of neighbourhood. Within the household cluster, young children are often sent as messengers from household to household under instructions from their parents, but may still be questioned for what additional information they can produce.

The only direct channel of communication between housewives who are not immediate neighbours is provided by the telephone network. Over the telephone, women can talk with one another without leaving the confines of the domestic setting. The main substance of their conversations consists of the protracted discussion of 'person-specific' information and dissemination of moral viewpoints that constitute gossip. The introduction of the telephone therefore greatly accelerates the ramification of gossip. Moral caricatures, based on a combination of hearsay and invention, are exaggerated and reinforced, thus aggravating personal hostilities between the promulgators of gossip and their victims. However, to be linked into the gossip chain the housewife must have access to a telephone in her own home. Since the recent renovation of the network, more than half of the households in the community have their own telephones, though some of these are officially for public use.

Certain women are rather more mobile than the normal housewife, making regular visits to households within the neighbourhood and to relatives in other neighbourhoods, given the availability of transport. These women belong to the oldest generation of 'grandmothers', whose children are adult and who can delegate domestic responsibilities as necessary to a daughter or daughter-in-law. Mobile grandmothers see themselves as guardians of community morality, making regular attendance at church, keeping an eye on children, checking that mothers are managing their families and households correctly, commenting on the behaviour of youth and menfolk, and never failing to pass censure when it is felt to be required. Criticism, often laced with wry humour, if not addressed directly to the individuals concerned, is raised in discussion with other women and thereby fed into a gossip chain which, as it ramifies, sooner or later reaches their attention. Those under criticism maintain a tactful distance from their critics, which can amount to rigid avoidance. Open quarrelling very rarely breaks out.

Social visiting, marginality and hostility in the neighbourhood

Inter-household visiting by adults is the most important means of affirming kinship and neighbourhood relations. Deliberate neglect of visiting is interpreted as a sign of avoidance, and hence of hostility. It is enough that the visitor sits for some time in the host's dwelling and drinks tea or coffee served by the hostess; he is not obliged to make conversation. Most social visiting of this kind is reserved for Sundays. No invitation is necessary, and arrival formalities are limited to a word of greeting and a handshake. Although it is customary to knock before entering, the visitor himself opens the door, whilst the host gives only passive acknowledgement to his arrival, merely inviting him to sit. The effect of this procedure is that the relationship of visitor to host is activated entirely by the former.

Ideally, the network of social visiting should be complete, linking all those bound by the fact of common neighbourhood. In practice, owing to specific anomalies in the resettlement plan, of which the neighbourhood itself is a product, certain households may be placed in a somewhat marginal position in relation to this network. They may be cut off by relative physical isolation, or may lack ties of immediate kinship or common clanship with other households of the neighbourhood. However, even between households which are fully incorporated both physically and kinship-wise into the neighbourhood, contacts may be deliberately avoided. Such avoidances represent both an indication of interpersonal hostility, and a means by which conflict within the neighbourhood is contained.

Owing to the Skolts' explicit abhorrence of openly aggressive confrontation (Pelto 1962: 100-1, 135-40), mutually hostile parties are not normally called upon to muster support through the mobilization of wider loyalties. Rather enmities persist on the interpersonal level as a perpetual undercurrent to the regular flow of social interaction, reaching neither overt expression nor resolution. There are two particularly potent sources of intra-neighbourhood antagonism: the one between men, the other between women. Firstly, conflict between brothers, a factor which catalyses domestic dispersal, may persist if they are forced to remain resident as near neighbours. Secondly, housewives bent on the collection and dissemination of gossip can rarely tolerate one another as neighbours. In order to illustrate the configuration of division and exclusion that can arise within the neighbourhood from a combination of resettlement anomalies, sibling rivalries and malicious gossip, we shall examine the pattern of social relationships within a particular neighbourhood in some detail.

Suova:[2] *kinship and households*

Suova comprised seven households on resettlement, scattered around the shore of a single, rather large lake of that name. There were three clusters of two houses each (II + III, VI + VII, VIII + IX) and one house (X) isolated on the opposite side of the lake from the others (fig. 30). In addition, an old Lappish house (V) was incorporated into the neighbourhood. The dominant clan, *U,* was represented by three brothers (E, F, R) and their half-sister (T), in households II, III, VIII and IX respectively. The father of these siblings lived in household IX until his death, and his surviving second wife is now living at the old-people's home.

Members of households VI and VII were both connected matrilaterally to the dominant clan, and therefore bore ' foreign' clan names. It was one of the anomalies of resettlement that these two immediately neighbouring households shared no closer kinship connection than the distant clanship link. Since close relations have never existed between them, the house-cluster VI + VII is not considered to constitute a household cluster. However, ties of immediate patrilateral kinship have been maintained between VI and II, and between VII and VIII. The physically isolated household X was another anomaly kinship-wise, but since close ties have, over the years, been established between its members and their nearest neighbours and kin in VIII and IX, reinforced by a marriage in the junior generation, the three households VIII, IX and X may be regarded as a single household cluster.

The most striking feature in the development of the neighbourhood since resettlement has been the dispersion of the large group of siblings, representing clan *W,* from household VI. Members have married into households IX(S), II(B) and most recently VII(Q), and have established families in the first two cases. Two of the siblings have left as labour migrants. The youngest (A) joined his sister (B) when she and her husband set up a sub-dwelling, household I. The dwelling was built on State land about a kilometre from the parent house II, and marks the southernmost extremity of the neighbourhood. Following this dispersion, only a single bachelor (P) remains in the siblings' parental house VI.

The junior sibling group from household III has also dispersed. L married the sole Lappish heir to the nearby household V shortly after resettlement, and has reared a large family. J is married in another neighbourhood. His youngest sister married a Finn who built a sub-dwelling (IV) on land belonging to house V; but the family was for much of the time resident at Ivalo, where the husband had work. Together, III,

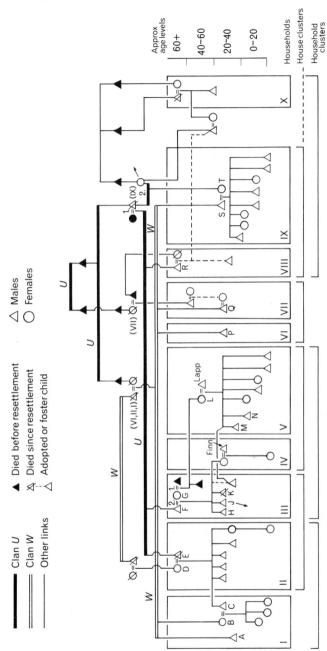

Fig. 30. Key genealogy for Suova neighbourhood. Emigrant and deceased individuals not relevant to the structure or the text are omitted. Capital letters and roman numerals refer respectively to individuals and households mentioned in the text of ch. 16 only. Households are arranged and numbered in the order they appear 'on the ground'.

Social relations of resettlement

IV and V constitute a household cluster. However, since specific relationships of avoidance exist between members of these households and those of households I and II, the latter are combined in a household cluster on their own.

Avoidance relationships

Quarrelling brothers (E and F). The lifelong dispute between the brothers E (household II, now deceased) and F (household III) appears to have arisen in connection with partition of the family area amongst the siblings in pre-war Suenjel. This was solved at the time by a reallotment of areas, but on resettlement the quarrelling brothers found themselves again as near-neighbours. In economic activities they consequently allied themselves to different sets of relatives: thus in the days of intensive herding, E joined affinal relatives of clan W (household VI) in the herding coalition, whilst F allied with his clan U siblings.

Under normal circumstances, the quarrel remains on an interpersonal level. The neighbouring 'grandmothers' D and G are on speaking terms, whilst H often accompanies his cousins on hunting and fishing trips. Nevertheless, contacts are considerably less frequent than is usual between members of contiguous households. F himself occasionally visits household II to fetch his post, but feels uneasy there. He claims to have fulfilled his share of fraternal obligations, but that his brother unreasonably and consistently failed to reciprocate. He has transferred this antagonism to his brother's five sons, whom he regards as both incompetent and amoral. The decline of their herds compared with the outstanding success of his own sons, H and J, as reindeer-men is taken as evidence of incompetence; heavy drinking and alleged fighting in household II as evidence of amorality. As a man, F takes an unusually firm moral stand, but unlike his wife, he keeps his views to himself.

Gossiping housewives (B and L). With the exception of S (household IX), a negative stigma is assigned to all the W siblings coming from household VI, particularly by the U members of households III and V. Some of the empirical justification for stigmatization is found in outstanding personality features of the siblings, who all display a marked nervous intensity, sometimes rigorously repressed, but occasionally vented in aggressive outbursts. The principal victims of stigmatization are the recluse (P) and the housewife (B) of household I, the focus for the siblings since their dispersion from household VI.

B accounts for the stigmatization of her sibling group by reference to their minority position as W's in the neighbourhood, stressing the element of clan solidarity. The U clan people, she says, want to make it clear that Suova is a U neighbourhood in which W's are not welcome. She draws the list of those people she professes to like and to emulate exclusively from clan relatives, including those from outside the neighbourhood. She

192

characterizes these people according to approved norms as quiet, peaceful and friendly. Her own behaviour deviates strongly from this ideal. She is a strong and often vicious talker, and is widely criticized in the community as a disseminator of malicious gossip, and as a heavy drinker and smoker.

Between her and the housewife L of household V, there exists a relationship of intense hostility. Like B, L is a strong gossip, and a compulsive collector of news. Her household is the information hub of the neighbourhood, receiving more incoming visitors than any other. Not coincidentally, it houses the only public telephone in the neighbourhood. The house, like house I, stands immediately beside the road, and forms a regular stopping-off point for passers-by from other neighbourhoods. Hardly a vehicle passes unobserved. As well as soliciting information from visitors, L encourages her son N to visit other households in the neighbourhood, and interrogates him on his return. Both B and P shut their doors to N on account of his suspected espionage.

Both housewives make abundant use of the telephone to collect and disseminate stories about the other, though very rarely moving outside their homes. For B, the necessity to avoid members of households III and V keeps her at home. She is not prepared to walk along the road past their households except in the dark, nor does she visit there, for fear of meeting L. She justifies domestic confinement by painting an idealized picture of happy family life in her household, contrasting this to stories of tumultuous domestic upheaval in household V. She values the opportunity to escape from neighbourhood gossip by moving seasonally to the fishing cabin, which is used fairly intensively. Avoidance factors have also influenced the situation of the sub-dwelling, within reach of the parent home II, but well outside the ambit of those from households III and V.

The recluse (P). Household VII is the most marginal in the pattern of kinship and neighbourhood relations, and rarely receives any visitors. The only immediate cognatic kin of its original members are found in household VIII. The recent uxorilocal marriage of Q, the oldest of the siblings from the contiguous household VI, has done little to integrate household VII into the neighbourhood. His marriage was made possible by the lack of close kinship between the two households, and represented a means to escape from intolerable inter-sibling tensions, above all with his brother P, during the final throes of dispersion in household VI. Since his marriage he has involved himself as little as possible with his siblings, and makes few appearances in the neighbourhood. However, during his prolonged absences as a labourer on construction sites, his childless wife passes the time with rounds of social visiting which include her new affines. This liberty has been conferred as a consequence of marriage, since under the authority of her foster-parents she had been largely confined to the household.

Q was the most recent of the siblings from household VI to leave the old parental house. Following this transfer of residence, only the bachelor P remains in VI. P's inability to get on with his brothers contributed towards his present isolation. He cuts himself off from contact in the neighbourhood with all except members of his sister's household I, on which he occasionally has to rely for help, support and information. He takes very little part in productive activities, living parsimoniously, supported principally by money contributions sent by an older brother, a migrant labourer.

The odd behaviour of the recluse naturally arouses suspicions in the neighbourhood. His waking and sleeping times, affected by drugs prescribed for a nervous disorder, are erratic. Whilst it is usual for house doors to be open when people are at home, P locks his door as a protection against supposedly threatening neighbours. His personal appearance is also unusual: he has grown long hair and a bushy beard, regarded by others as extremely ugly.

P's symptomatically paranoid perception of his own situation, although elaborated to bizarre proportions, takes its cues from a highly sensitive assessment of the intentions of others, and accurately reflects the wider pattern of moral segmentation and exclusion in the neighbourhood. He believes that his enemies are plotting either to murder him or to have him removed from the community on grounds of insanity. The master-minds of this plot are the brothers H and J from household III. Both made their fortunes in reindeer during the 1960s, and are now the biggest reindeer-men of the *paliskunta*. It is widely held that the brothers built up their herds through extensive theft, partly from the herds of the former alliance based on clan *W*. P believes that he holds vital evidence that would prove the brothers guilty, and that they, realizing this, wish to remove him. The assumed conspiracy is not limited to reindeer affairs, but includes sub-plots involving sexual competition and the liquor trade.

Whilst avoiding household III, P used to call regularly at household V in order to keep up on information and use the telephone. On one such occasion, J called in at V whilst P was sitting there. A violent quarrel between the two men ensued. The youth A(I), P's brother, was passing by at the time and meant to look in, but went away on hearing the row, to avoid a compromising situation. Subsequently the housewife L began to circulate rumours that P had become insane. It was reported that he had been seen lurking in the moonlight, carrying a very long knife, and threatening small children. L went so far as to telephone the authorities at Ivalo, claiming that P was a danger to the community and should be sent to a mental hospital. The police visited and made inquiries. No grounds for suspicion against P were found, and he was advised to avoid household V in the future, to prevent further quarrelling.

Since this incident, P has rigidly avoided both households III and V. This has caused him some inconvenience. In order to use the telephone or to pick up information he has to walk or cycle some way to his sister's house I. He frequently misses reindeer separations since news does not reach him in time. In order to benefit from the mobile shop, which stops outside V but not by house VI or VII, he has to arrange for his sister to buy for him. Further, since the road to I passes right beside house V, P has had to take to travelling at night so that his movements should not be seen. This only increases local suspicions.

Reactions to crisis

In normal everyday life, neighbourhood antagonisms appear as more or less unconnected affairs, without wider repercussions beyond those directly involved. However, situations of crisis whose immediate causes may be wholly accidental call for demonstrations of moral support and personalized explanation. Repercussions ramify throughout the network, to align and polarize the whole neighbourhood. On such occasions, the pattern of schism and alliance in the neighbourhood stands out as a unified, coherent and persistent structure which forms a basis for the moral generalizations involved in the response to crisis. The course of an observed crisis in Suova neighbourhood is traced below, as an illustration.

One of the *W* siblings from household VI, a migrant labourer, had returned home to be married to a Finnish girl. After the wedding, his sister (B) arranged a party at the Sevetti bar. Family members, clan relatives, and a number of Sevetti friends were invited. Among the guests were J from household III, who was married and living uxorilocally at Sevetti. By the end of the party almost everyone was drunk. J set off by snowmobile along the road to Suova, carrying two passengers, both immediate kin of the *W* siblings. The snowmobile veered off the road and hit a tree. J received severe head injuries. His passengers were unhurt, but were too drunk to realize what had happened. The accident was first noticed by M(V). J was rushed to hospital and was in a coma for several days. He survived, but suffered permanent brain damage which has affected his memory.

The *W* siblings were shocked and upset by the news of the accident, which one of the passengers brought to household I a day later. The circumstances were discussed at length, every new detail was taken up in an attempt to circumvent the facts, which obstinately remained. No personal allocation of blame was made, and the accident was put down to drunken driving.

The news was brought to household III by M. The drunken driving explanation was rejected, J was not known as a heavy drinker. Blame was put entirely on the ' *W* crowd', and above all on the housewife (B). First, it was argued that B had caused the accident by inviting J to the party. If he had not gone, nothing would have happened. Secondly, backseat passengers affect the steering by taking the weight off the skis in front of the snowmobile. Since J would never take passengers under normal circumstances for this reason, he must have been forced on this occasion, again by members of the ' *W* crowd'. Thirdly, the fact that none of the ' *W* crowd ' visited household III, neither bringing news nor expressing condolence, was interpreted as a tacit admission of guilt.

In household III, the accident was connected with the circumstances surrounding the drowning of J's brother (K) some years earlier. The drowning had occurred within earshot of household II. At that time, B and her family still lived at II, prior to the establishment of the sub-dwelling. It was argued that members of household II must have been able to hear K's shouts and go to rescue, but they had done nothing.

In the weeks following the accident, rigid avoidance was maintained between members of cluster III-V and those of cluster I-II. Avoidance directly contravenes the norm whereby neighbours should express condolence and provide moral support on such occasions. From households I and II only the grandmother D attempted to express sympathy to G in household III. G's bitter and incriminatory retort was to ask why all five of D's sons had survived whereas of her four, two had died and one was now seriously injured.

The generalized pattern of accusation and expression of support in this case indicates a structural rift in Suova neighbourhood, of which the quarrel between E and F, the antagonism between B and L, and the ostracism of P are particular isolated aspects. On the one side are the socially allied households of cluster I-II and stigmatized *W* siblings from VI, linked in the senior generation through the marriage of E to D, and again in the junior generation through that of C to B. On the other side are the households of cluster III-V which have no affinal links with the *W* siblings. Households of cluster VIII-X, maintaining links with both sides, are in an equivocal position.

The idioms in which this rift is expressed closely resemble the classic idioms of witchcraft. Thus, the *W* siblings from household VI are said to possess an evil quality that runs in the family, and that may even be be generalized to include more distant clan relatives ('the *W* crowd'). The siblings in household II are reputed to fight among themselves in the dwelling, a sign of total moral perversion. The housewife B is held to cause misfortune through evil intent, whilst the recluse P is said to threaten children at night. These witchcraft-like expressions of anti-social behaviour apply specifically *within* the neighbourhood as a field of everyday social interaction, and are thus a product of the structure of resettlement. This may account for the lack of a more standardized idiom for witchcraft beliefs. Since the resettlement structure is rather inflexible, and since the response to accusation is avoidance rather than confrontation, basic animosities are extremely persistent.

The structure of the neighbourhood

According to the idealized resettlement model, the neighbourhood comprises a number of household clusters based on senior generation sibling groups. Outside the cluster, neighbourhood relationships are

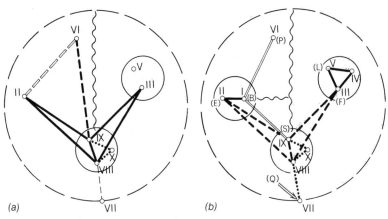

Link based on sibling bond in senior living generation:

     ▬ ▬ ▬ *U* clan
     ▭ ▭ ▭ *W* clan
     – – – Other

Link based on sibling bond in junior living generation:

     ▬▬▬ *U* clan
     ══ *W* clan

Link based on more distant kinship ••••••••
Rift separating opposed siblings ∿∿∿
Outer circle—neighbourhood boundary
Inner circles—household cluster boundaries

Fig. 31. The development of Suova neighbourhood structure: 1949–72.
A, Resettlement – 1949; *B*, today – 1972.

dichotomized into further links of immediate bilateral kinship resulting
from the extension of sibling groups beyond the cluster range, and more
distant kinship connections. Through the association of clan and neighbourhood, the latter tend to be patrilineal clanship links. 'Foreign' clan
surnames may be introduced through uxorilocal resettlement such that a
senior generation man lives in the neighbourhood of his wife's natal clan,
or joins a cluster with her siblings. The building blocks of neighbourhood
structure are thus household units and sibling groups, superimposed on a
diffuse and undifferentiated field of clanship relations mapping out a
potentially complete network. Sibling groups are linked in households
in the same generation through marriage, across generations through
filiation. Conversely, households are linked by sibling groups as members
disperse and marry into other households.

Ideally, siblinghood is a morally binding relationship. In practice, it is
subject to intra-familial tensions, which reach their peak during the phase
of domestic dispersion, above all among brothers. As long as the siblings
remain resident in the neighbourhood, tensions may persist after dis-

persion. The moral severity of breach of siblinghood bonds is equivalent to their ideal strength: such a breach can only be deliberate and highly charged. Relations are either close and intact, or broken and negated through the exercise of avoidance, but never indifferent. Thus, it is the very power of siblinghood as a binding force that makes it a potential source of rupture within the neighbourhood. Whether it unites or divides is very much a function of the individual personalities of the siblings themselves. The structure of the neighbourhood cannot therefore be predicted from the kinship map alone.

In Suova, the breach between E and F forms the basis for wider structural divisions through ramification along chains of sibling support, which are given overt expression in the moral idioms of housewives at opposing poles in the structure. Only those households linked equally to the divided parties adopt a neutral stance. The network of bonds at the time of resettlement is presented schematically in fig. 31A. Prior to the dispersal of the *W* siblings from VI, households II and VI were linked in the senior generation. When S married T(IX) uxorilocally, he established close relationships with members of cluster III–V, adopting rather than compromising the set of relationships recognized by his spouse and her immediate kin. He is the only member of the siblings to have done so, and has escaped stigmatization as a result. He was able to 'carry over' links with household II, which were already recognized by households VIII and IX. When B married C virilocally in household II, links between VI and II, and between IX and II, were compounded in the junior generation, but were transferred to I when the new sub-dwelling was established. At the same time, the direct link between VI and IX disappeared with the passing of the most senior generation in the two households.

Figure 31B shows the neighbourhood structure as it exists today, a full generation after resettlement. Though the brothers P and S maintain links with their sister's household, they avoid one another. P's isolation in household VI is partly a consequence of his being the only remaining member of a household occupying one extremity in a charged structure of schism and alliance, doubly excluded through the wider pattern of friction stemming from the break between II and III, and through internal divisions within the *W* siblings themselves. This is reflected in his own behaviour and in the accusations directed against him. The relative isolation of household VII is of a different kind. Lying largely outside the structure and without close bonds to other households in the neighbourhood, it is not subject to structural tensions. Through marriage into household VII, Q broke off relations with his siblings, 'opting out' of his position in the neighbourhood.

The internal structure of the neighbourhood can be expressed as a network of inter-household links of immediate bilateral kinship which can be either strongly positive or negative. Households not linked by immediate kinship are marginally placed with respect to this network. In everyday life, structural rifts appear only in the form of specific personal avoidances, but in times of crisis they back moral generalizations expressed in witchcraft-like idioms. The network subsumes patterns of neighbourhood interaction with the exception of the activities of youth, who are not subject to structural constraints based on kinship and household affiliation and who therefore act as important carriers of information between mutually antagonistic parties. The total neighbourhood as a field of social interaction, marked out physically but conceptualized in terms of clanship, as well as its initial configuration of schism and alliance, stem from features of the original structure of resettlement. As new generations mature and disperse, and as old bonds of siblinghood fade into the field of distant kinship, the configuration may gradually shift, but abrupt change is inhibited by the continuing perceptions of the older generation.

17 The central village

Sevetti households

In the layout of its ten Skolt resettlement houses, situated in clusters along a stretch of lakeshore, Sevetti constitutes a neighbourhood much like any other. However, the neighbourhood is also a centre for local community services including the shops, bar, post-office, school, health-clinic and church. It is the presence of these services that makes Sevetti not just a neighbourhood but a village. The category ' village ' (Fin. *kylä*) is defined as a place where people go visiting or to conduct business. The actual location of the village within the three kilometre long neighbourhood therefore varies according to a man's purpose, or where the greatest concentration of people is to be found at a particular time. When the mail-bus arrives, the village is centred on the post-office; but when people go for a drink, it shifts a kilometre down the road to the bar.

The concentration of services in Sevetti brings visitors from throughout the community. On certain occasions, many Skolt households may be packed with guests. Such occasions are weekends when church services are held, periodic visits of the doctor to the health-clinic, assembly meeting at the school, and major sports or entertainments events. Nearly every non-Sevetti Skolt household in the community recognizes ties of immediate kinship with at least one Sevetti household, from which it can expect hospitality. Inter-neighbourhood links of immediate kinship are thus activated a great deal more frequently with Sevetti households than between other neighbourhoods. Since the provision of hospitality is a source of prestige on both neighbourhood and community level, some Sevetti households are counted among the most influential in the community.

Besides attracting visitors, however, local services support an occupational elite whose members have exercised a profound influence in shaping the life of the village through the projection of a scale of stratificatory values wholly antithetical to traditional patterns of hospitality and of kinship and neighbourhood reciprocity. The core of the Sevetti elite is marginal to the neighbourhood of Skolt households, and indeed to the community as a whole. Its members - professionals, salaried employees and merchants - are mainly immigrant, but a few Skolts are incorporated through ties of occupation or affinity. The domestic groups of the elite are generally small nuclear families, related neither to each

other nor to the Skolt neighbourhood genealogy. Professional accommodation includes the six school flats and the health clinic. The Forest
Warden was originally provided with a large house, but has built a new
dwelling along with the shop, bar and tourist centre managed by his wife,
to which they moved on its completion. The house was later occupied by
the family of the Finnish road maintenance engineer and his Skolt wife.
The shop of the second merchant, the post-office run by his wife, and
their family dwelling make up another house complex. Taken together,
the residents of these households make up almost a third of the Sevetti
population. Their position as representatives of the 'new elite' will be
considered more fully in the following paragraphs.

Commune Point: a microcosm of urban society

The complex of school buildings and the health clinic are grouped apart
from other neighbourhood settlement on a small peninsula which has been
dubbed 'Commune Point'. It forms in many respects a world of its own;
the social organization of its residents based on principles diametrically
opposed to those applying in the traditional Skolt neighbourhood. The
complex includes seven households: two teachers' flats in the school
building, the third teacher's flat and those of the caretaker, cook and
matron in the boarding house, and the accommodation of the health
visitor in the clinic building. All accommodation is provided by the
Commune. The teachers, matron and health visitor are immigrants with
a background in so-called 'culture-Finland', representing the values of
the professional bourgeoisie. All three teachers and the health visitor
married locally. The caretaker's wife is an immigrant, bringing in a
zealous adherence to the Pentecostal Church, whilst her converted
husband is a son of one of the local Lappish 'old inhabitant' families.
The cook is the daughter of another 'old inhabitant' family, but is
married to a Skolt. Domestic groups are small and atomistic, only two
being linked by kinship through in-marrying Skolt husbands, both from
Sevetti neighbourhood.

Residents of Commune Point who remain on good terms keep up a
certain amount of social contact outside their strictly professional
capacities, but in many cases relationships are strained by status rivalries.
Social visiting is not unrestricted, often based on invitation communi-
cated by telephone. The visitor has to pass through several doors, which
may be locked, and ring a bell before gaining admission; whilst inside the
comfortably furnished flat his behaviour is circumscribed by formal
etiquette.

Social contacts between Commune Point and the Skolt neighbourhood
are even more limited. Only Skolt men who have married into Commune
Point interact freely with their fellows in the neighbourhood, but rarely in
the company of their wives. It is common to see an immigrant wife
waiting outside in the car or on the sledge whilst her husband calls indoors

a Skolt house. For the immigrants of Commune Point, their lack of a common background of shared assumptions blocks successful interaction in Skolt households. When they do visit, both they and their hosts are consequently nervous and restrained. Only when visiting in their professional capacities, for example in the rounds of the health visitor, can the social context be defined in a way that is unambiguous and mutually acceptable. Relations are thus restricted to those of a single-stranded character. Outside Commune Point, the identity of the immigrant professional is normally defined in terms of his or her occupation alone.

The inhabitants of Commune Point are far from satisfied with their accommodation. Spouses in mixed marriages have actively campaigned for building plots, basing their claims on special Skolt privileges attributed to the husbands. Paradoxically, it is the immigrant elite, without a pressing need for new housing and with careers outside the traditional economy, who support most vigorously the campaign on behalf of Skolt rights to land for housing seen as a basis for the *preservation* of the traditional economy. This represents one respect in which the elite claims a share in Skolt culture as an asset in the pursuit of extra-cultural goals. One couple has been able to purchase a plot from a nearby ' old inhabitant ', and plans a house on a more extravagant scale than any other in the community, well outside the financial means of any Skolt household.

The households of Commune Point are organized around an imported system of two linked scales of value. One is based on occupational status, the other on personal conduct and consumption profiles. Since opportunities for occupational promotion do not exist locally, those low in the hierarchy strive to deny the relevance of professional qualifications, articulating rival claims in the idiom of conduct and bearing. As defined from above, the occupational hierarchy is divided into two main levels, but within each of these the order may vary:

Headmaster   Teachers   Health visitor

Matron   Caretaker   Cook

Behavioural aspects of the ' conduct and bearing' scale include linguistic hypercorrection, abstention from drinking, and personal cleanliness, dress and grooming. In terms of consumption profiles, all Commune Point households are, by local standards, well equipped with mechanical gadgetry. One family is even able to boast a package holiday to Sicily.

The endemic status rivalries of Commune Point can be highlighted by an illustration concerning the use of electric washing machines. The complex is provided with an electricity supply from a generator. Though intended primarily for institutional needs, the families of Commune Point also use it for private consumption. Despite warnings from the caretaker, who is responsible for the supply, two of the teachers acquired expensive fully automatic washing machines, which use so much power that the school lighting occasionally fades, and so much water that the pumps are periodically overloaded. In the opinion of the caretaker, this is proof of the selfishness of the teachers. More concerned with their own aggrandizement than with communal welfare, they consider themselves too fine to wash their clothes like everyone else. Pending an official inquiry which, he hoped, would lead to a ban on the use of the machines, the caretaker proposed to take direct action. Although the teachers may wash their clothes behind locked doors, the caretaker can see what is happening from his meters, and can cut the supply to the flats at will.

The caretaker is intensely jealous of the teachers. He considers himself a pillar of respectability and a man of affairs of some standing, prominent in local politics. Relative to the wider community his high-ranking position is assured, being one of the very few enjoying a permanent salaried post. However, in terms of the hierarchy of Commune Point, his occupational status is menial, and he feels slighted by the teachers' assertions of professional superiority. These touch him at his weakest spot, since he himself subscribes to the very set of values he finds himself having to condemn in the teachers, in order to safeguard his own status claims.

In its internal organization, Commune Point appears as a small, isolated outpost of ' culture-Finland ', a microcosm of urban society, and at the same time a centre from which this cultural influence spreads to the surrounding neighbourhood. Its urban character is defined by flat-type accommodation, atomistic and unrelated domestic groups, closely circumscribed social interaction, stratified occupational differentiation and intense status rivalry based on bourgeois aspirations. The internal organization of households is characterized by independently earning wives and a more flexible division of labour in which many of the usual menial tasks of household maintenance such as heating, lighting, washing and water-collecting are relegated either to private machines or communally provided services managed by salaried employees. In all these respects, life in Commune Point is in complete contrast to that of the Skolt neighbourhood.

Sevetti merchants: commercial power and professional status

The commercial history of Sevetti merchant enterprises was sketched in chapter 8. The manageress of the ' Trading Centre ' has established a fragile position of dominance through partnership with the Forest Warden, but is threatened by competition from the border. Eclipsed by the expansion of this enterprise, the ' general stores ' continues only on the strength of its connection with the post-office and consequent control over the cash supply. In addition to the two merchants, the school caretaker operates on the side as a petty entrepreneur, providing a tractor haulage and unofficial taxi service, and acting as the local sales representative for a prominent snowmobile marketing firm.

Although pursuing a style of life comparable with the Commune Point elite, the two merchants' relationships with each other and with the

Skolts of the neighbourhood rest on different principles. The position of the merchant is defined not through a professional status qualification but through the exercise of commercial power over a body of customers. Whilst the professional receives the financial support to pursue his style of life indirectly, through a State- or Commune-paid salary, and has obtained his qualifications outside the local community, the merchant's income is derived directly from commercial exploitation of the local populace. Values of kinship and neighbourhood reciprocity are incompatible with the commercial relationship. Consequently, the marginal position of the merchant has a transactional basis, rather than stemming solely from differences of values and background; and unlike the immigrants of Commune Point, the merchant can make no claim to ethnic incorporation into 'Skolt Culture', remaining as a broker on the periphery.

On the other hand, as the basis of their business, merchants regularly engage in transactions with local clients, and are therefore intricately involved in the political and economic affairs of the community. However, transactions take place on their own terms and on their own premises; merchants never visit Skolt households. Both merchants and the school caretaker have repeatedly stood for election to the Commune council, attempting to set up as brokers of political as well as economic resources. In contrast, residents of Commune Point, with the exception of the caretaker, have few dealings with local people, and have shown no propensities along these lines.

The same difference is evident in forms of competition. The two merchants are engaged in harsh commercial rivalry, reinforced by personal avoidance. Rivals compete for economic and political clients, and resulting gains or losses can be very real in terms of possibilities to continue the enterprise. In contrast, the rivals of Commune Point dispute status claims independently of local support within a fixed, imposed hierarchical structure, in which continuity is assured but advancement is not possible within the confines of the local arena. Gains achieved through conduct and display are not cumulative but must be constantly validated. The rivals are thus tied to an indefinite oscillation around their starting positions.

The merchants and immigrant professionals regard each other with mutual suspicion. Whilst the former may criticize the latter for their neglect of community welfare, the latter accuse the former of dishonesty, exploitation and pretence. Within Commune Point, the same contradiction is evident in the situation of the school caretaker-cum-entrepreneur.

Patronage and brokerage at the 'Trading Centre'

The dominant entrepreneurial concern in Sevetti, the 'Trading Centre', is founded on a business partnership between the Forest Warden and his wife. As the local representative of the massive Forestry Authority bureaucracy, the Warden places himself at the apex of benevolent authority in the community, a view shared by his clients, although in fact he occupies the lowest grade of the overall bureaucratic hierarchy. The extent of his patronage is limited by the quantity of assets attached to his administrative post that are available for distribution, and by the range over which he can exert direct personal influence. In practice, the majority of clients are from the neighbourhood of Sevetti. They are recruited through the arrangement of casual employment and through occasional acts of charity, all of which are expressed as personal favours but designed to put the client in a relationship of dependency on the business concern. Thus, whereas in other neighbourhoods most casual work is obtained through the State Employment Agency, in Sevetti only one man is regularly on the register, whilst ten are intermittently employed by or through the Forest Warden or his wife. The personal element in the patron–client relationship is apparent in the mutual use of first names, and in the free passage of the client to the 'backstage' living quarters of the shop and bar complex. Service is expressed as loyalty rather than as a formal contract: thus a willing client who helped out in the bar at a time of peak demand was rewarded not with pay at a fixed rate, but with a box of chocolates.

Where the Warden can act as a patron on account of his administrative authority, his wife is free to act as a broker since she is not constrained by the regulations of office. In partnership, they have been able to combine aspects of both patronage and brokerage. For the broker, the maximum quantity of resources that can be made available for distribution is not independently fixed, but is variable and dependent on the level of custom. Outside the range of patronage, the merchant may have any number of customers, but without the resources to withstand sufficient extension of credit, their loyalty cannot be secured in the face of competition. In the absence of a patron–client tie, credit is normally strictly limited and short-term, inducing no more than a weak commitment on the part of customers to buy from the creditor. Through partnership with her husband, the manageress of the 'Trading Centre' has established a virtual monopoly in brokerage within Sevetti neighbourhood. Outside the range of patronage, the appearance of merchant competitors has rendered her position extremely fragile.

Patrons have the power to circulate innovatory resources of their own choosing on their own terms (Paine 1971b), and are in a position to exert considerable personal influence over their clients. Thus, the Forest Warden and his wife have played a significant part in the importation and distribution of resources appropriate to new status values, and hence in the diffusion of those values themselves. Sevetti Skolt households in which new status symbols are most evident are those whose members are established clients of the 'Trading Centre'. The proximity of shops in Sevetti encourages their daily use by local households and leads the domestic economy towards a greater reliance on the cash sector. Consequently, some Sevetti households were among the first to abandon the traditional pattern of subsistence production and exchange trade in favour of a

205

predominantly monetary economy with its associated scales of value. This is not, however, by any means true of all Skolt households in the neighbourhood.

The Skolt elite: living standards and education

Amongst those of other neighbourhoods, certain Sevetti Skolts have a reputation for being ' finer ' than other people. This generalization may represent positive approval or negative criticism. It implies a distaste for ' dirty ' subsistence tasks, and relative success in the pursuance of status values based on material consumption and display. Though a minority of Sevetti Skolts actually conform to this image, those that do often regard non-Sevetti people – even immediate kin – as rather rustic backwoodsmen. A precondition for the realization of elite aspirations is access to a regular salary, whilst only through marriage and the formation of a local domestic unit can status claims be manifested as a ' standard of living ' on the household level. According to these criteria of income and marital status, the native Skolt elite comprises, besides spouses in mixed marriages with immigrant professionals, only three families of the junior generation. All three are major clients of the ' Trading Centre ', and all have frequent contact with Commune Point as a result either of employment or kinship with Skolt residents. A distinctive characteristic of all elite couples is the full- or part-time employment of the wife, who may even be the principal earner.

Paradoxically, the concentration of services at Sevetti, whilst increasing the scope for the realization of traditional values through the attraction of visitors, has also supported an elite whose influence has been to undermine these values. This paradox appears in radically contrasting patterns of domestic life not only between one household and another within the neighbourhood, but even between generations in the same household. Staunchly traditional grandparents may find themselves powerless to prevent dwelling space once freely laid open to visitors from being taken up by untouchable furniture and incomprehensible gadgetry acquired by a junior generation anxious to improve its material standard of living. Former visitors, daunted by such finery, go elsewhere when they come to the village.

Elite households possess a relatively complete repertoire of locally available items of consumer hardware, including televisions, gas-fuelled lights, cookers and refrigerators, oil-fired heating installations and washing machines. Although some of these items are more widely distributed, elite households stand out as centres of diffusion for new imports, always searching for innovations as previous items become generally adopted. The elite is thus concerned with the status implications of new equipment, whilst those that follow on base their acquisition decisions more on any practical advantages that the innovation might be observed to have. Nevertheless, almost two-thirds of the households in the community remain without any of the items listed above.

Besides these domestic gadgets, motor vehicles – cars and snowmobiles – constitute important display items which were introduced into the community through the local elite. Today, the 'family car' carries greater weight in validating status claims on the level of the domestic group than the one-man snowmobile, which confers prestige on its operator rather than status on his household. Whereas car ownership is still largely restricted to the elite, the snowmobile has achieved almost universal distribution, such that virtuosity in operation replaces the mere fact of possession as a criterion of differentiation.

Another indicator of elite values is a concern that children should be brought up correctly, cultivate good taste and manners, and above all, be successful at school. Elite housewives are adamant in their criticism of the 'negligent' upbringing of children in the large families of more 'backward' neighbourhoods, also favouring the restriction of family size through birth control. This contrasts with traditional norms which favour large families and liberal upbringing, and according to which school education is not regarded as a positive endowment.

The performance of Sevetti children now between their fifth and ninth years of school is compared with the overall Skolt performance from the community in Table 3. On completing their fourth year at primary school,

Table 3. *School attendance between the fifth and ninth years*

	Primary + Civic School	Middle School	Total
Sevetti pupils	5	10	15
Non-Sevetti pupils	32	3	35
Total	37	13	50

pupils either continue to a five-year 'middle-school' at Ivalo, or spend two more years at primary school and continue to 'civic-school' at Inari, lasting two or three years. The middle-school is more academic, giving access to 'senior-school' and eventually to higher education, whilst civic-school emphasizes practical subjects.[1] In both cases, education is financed by the Commune. In 1971–2, 26 per cent of pupils in these years from the community had achieved a place in middle-school: an extremely low proportion by normal standards. However, of the Sevetti pupils, ten out of fifteen had reached middle-school, compared with only three out of thirty-five from the rest of the community.

This striking difference stems partly from parental encouragement in Sevetti elite households and partly from the lack of disjunction between school and home environments in Sevetti neighbourhood, where pupils can attend primary school without having to board. Sevetti parents have more contact with the teachers, and take an active part in school affairs. The children of the elite experience a smaller value discrepancy between what they are taught at home and at school. In contrast, for boarding pupils from the more traditional households in other neighbourhoods, home and school form two entirely separate and often contradictory worlds: behaviour approved in one is censured in the other, parents attach little value to children's education, and their contacts with teachers are minimal.

The performance of pupils after they have reached middle-school is often a disappointment to their parents. Many 'stay down' year after year, break off altogether, or are transferred to civic-school. Far from home, cut off from most of their comrades, and thrown into a quasi-urban and predominantly Finnish environment, they experience considerable initial problems of adjustment. The years at Ivalo lead to a gradual estrangement from home and an exaggerated adoption of manners and habits picked up from the outside world. For the majority who go later on to the civic-school at Inari, where the intake is predominantly of Lappish pupils from comparable backgrounds, this disjunction is much smaller.

On their return home, Sevetti pupils from middle-school bring with them the styles and values they have learnt at Ivalo, and confirm in the junior generation the image of the neighbourhood as a place for 'city folk', with value orientations which, in the view of more traditionally-minded critics, are wholly inappropriate in the local environment.

The centralization of settlement

When the original resettlement plan was drawn up, scattered settlement was held to be necessary on economic grounds, allowing each household access to fishing waters and lichen pastures in the immediate surroundings. These economic constraints have since fallen away. Reindeer are no longer tended by individual households or groups of households, whilst the economic significance of fish stocks in home waters has declined considerably. The snowmobile puts distant waters or pastures within easy reach, whilst in summer fishing cabins can be used as a base for productive activities.

The increasing demand for new building plots has given rise to a good deal of discussion, both locally in meetings of the community assembly and in administrative circles, concerning the form that the plan for future settlement should take. Three alternatives are available. The first, linear scattered settlement, would mean a continuation of the present arrangement, but with the qualification that all houses should in future lie near the road as well as by a lakeshore. The importance of road access is the only point on which Skolts and officials are in more or less unanimous agreement. The second alternative, centralized settlement at Sevetti, would involve the establishment of a number of small, adjacent plots of between half and one hectare in the heart of the neighbourhood. The third alternative is a compromise: the localization of settlement in around three to five neighbourhood centres.

The administration favours centralization on logistic grounds, since the provision of communal services to a scattered population is costly. In some respects, such as school dormitory accommodation, this argument is valid. In others, services are considered essential in terms of urban standard-of-living assumptions which are locally inappropriate. Thus, a village-wide piped water and sewage system is quite unnecessary as long as settlement is *not* densely concentrated. Many forms of communal service, such as post, bus and telephone, are ' linear '; becoming no more costly if houses are scattered along the road. Electrification admits a partially ' linear ' solution, but requires a degree of grouping of houses, as in the localized settlement alternative.

Skolt opinions cover the whole spectrum of alternatives. However, outside Sevetti the majority is decisively opposed to centralization. This opposition rests largely on interpretations of the observed social character of present-day Sevetti neighbourhood: the urban pretensions of the elite, the degeneration of the youth, rowdiness and drinking stemming from the proximity of the bar and the position of Sevetti as an entertainments centre, and the dependency on local shopkeepers. Many feel the idea of living bunched up on tiny plots under the constant scrutiny of immediate neighbours to be inconceivable. Most Sevetti people, on the other hand, have no objection to centralization. They have come to rely on institutions and services located in the village, and centralization would not mean a move on their part. Opposition to centralization in other neighbourhoods is put down to the reluctance to move away from the natal neighbourhood, where an individual is surrounded by kin and clansmen, to one where he might be regarded as an intruding stranger.

The arguments put forward by the advocates of centralization do not rest on logistic grounds alone. The administration holds that centralization promotes social integration, and hence the achievement of a better organized society with a more co-operative spirit. To bolster this argument, it is observed that the solution being proposed – concentrated permanent dwellings and dispersed fishing cabins – comes close to the traditional settlement pattern of Suenjel.

In contrast, the objectors to centralization maintain that it would exacerbate conflict rather than promote integration. They wish to live in peace and quiet, away from the interference and gossip of troublesome or malicious neighbours. Significantly, those who speak most vigorously in support of scattered settlement are those such as B in Suova household I, who are already the objects of exclusion and surrounded by avoidances. They fear that greater concentration would only intensify intra-neighbourhood tensions, whilst the impossibility of maintaining personal avoidance under dense settlement conditions would produce intolerable conflict. With scattered settlement, on the other hand, one can live outside the range of accusation, and keep on good terms with everyone.

Social relations of resettlement

One can speculate as to the effects that planned centralization might have on the pattern of social organization. Compared with the present-sized neighbourhood, a larger population would allow the individual to be more selective in his everyday relationships. The significance of kinship ties would be reduced as extra-domestic, action-specific institutions replace the household as interaction settings.[2] The greater freedom of the individual to activate and manipulate his own relationships, coupled with more 'associational' bases for interaction would therefore reduce rather than exacerbate neighbourhood tensions based on kinship bonds and avoidances of the kind described for Suova neighbourhood. Along with increasing differentiation and stratification, tensions would be transferred to the field of status rivalries and jealousies, exemplified in Commune Point. In Sevetti today, two extremes of social organization are found side by side: the traditional households of the Skolt neighbourhood, and the immigrant elite of Commune Point. Skolts from traditional backgrounds adopting immigrant models connect the two worlds, and give an indication of the form future social developments might take.

Part III The minority culture

18 Leap-frog politics (1): The headmanship

The Skolt assembly

Throughout Tsarist times, the affairs of Suenjel *siita* continued to be regulated along traditional lines by the assembly of householders, presided over by an elected headman, that met annually in the winter-village. The assembly was authorized to administer the division or reallotment of the constituent 'family areas' of the *siita* territory, and to arbitrate internal cases of theft, poaching, adultery and disorderly conduct. It also appointed delegates empowered to treat with neighbouring *siita* communities over the administration of flexible 'condominium' frontiers, and the securement of access to such valuable natural assets as salmon-runs and coastal fishing sites located on 'foreign' ground, in return for usufruct concessions on home territory (Nickul 1973). These diplomatic relations between Suenjel and its neighbours were either broken off or curtailed as a result of the disruptions and border closures that followed the First World War and the Russian Revolution, but the assembly's function as a monitor of internal affairs persisted until Suenjel itself was lost in the aftermath of the Second World War (Pelto 1962: 84–5).

It was in a meeting of the assembly, reconvened after the war, that the Skolts registered their overwhelming acceptance of plans for resettlement in Finland. The effect of resettlement, however, was to strip the assembly of most of its remaining functions. Lands and waters are no longer divided into 'family areas'. Applications for fishing-cabin plots and for logging and hay-cutting sites, although sometimes brought before the assembly, have ultimately to be approved by the State Forestry Authority. Local officials of the Authority hold an annual meeting to which all residents of the resettlement area are invited, to discuss the utilization of State-controlled land and water resources within the area. All reindeer-management business is handled separately by the *paliskunta* associations. The original judicial functions of the *siita* assembly have been transferred entirely to the Finnish courts. In the structure of local administration, the assembly has no more than an informal, advisory status.

Today, the purpose of the assembly is no longer to settle internal differences but to advance the common interests of the Skolts, defined as a *resettled* population covered by special legislation, through the framing of demands to be brought by the headman[1] to the attention of officials at higher levels of government. These demands have been largely concerned with improvements in local communications and services, various claims for economic compensation and support, future settlement planning, and legislative reform. ' Old inhabitants ' are admitted to assembly meetings, which are conducted in the Finnish language, and have actively contributed, if only to complain of inadequate representation. They are, however, separately represented on the local landowners' association (*manttaalikunta*); and have from time to time registered their opposition to assembly proposals through this channel, for example on the question of the division of Muddusjärvi *paliskunta*.

The headman

In the years after resettlement, meetings of the community assembly appear to have been convened infrequently, largely on account of the growing infirmity of the ageing headman. This man, J, first assumed responsibility for the affairs of the community shortly before the collapse of Suenjel in 1938, taking over from his brother K who, until his terminal illness, had combined the roles of headman and local policeman. Though embodying all those qualities traditionally expected of the headman – conservatism, balanced judgement and intimate knowledge of his people – J was not well equipped to deal with the new problems of the post-resettlement period, which demanded expertise in written bureaucratic procedure rather than wisdom in arbitration.

A more vigorous campaigner on behalf of Skolt interests has been K's eldest son, J's nephew, M. He was born in Suenjel in 1924. As a youth, he helped to manage the family herds, in particular during the evacuation period of the Winter War in 1939–40. He was subsequently called up on active military service. After the war, he applied and was admitted to a teachers' training college, but after less than a year he had to abandon the course owing to financial difficulties. Returning north, he joined many of his fellow Skolts as a construction worker on the Soviet hydroelectricity project, and in 1949 moved with his family to their new home at Sevetti-järvi. Three years later, he left for Helsinki to attend a two-year course at the Labour Academy, an opportunity afforded through the patronage of an academic prominent in Lapp affairs and sympathetic towards the Skolts. He married a Finnish girl in 1953, and the couple returned the following year to live at Ivalo, where M took employment with the State Roads Department. They have lived there ever since.

Joining the Social Democratic Party, M was elected to the council of Inari Commune in 1957, a seat which he held until the 1972 elections. From this vantage point he has sought to exert influence at higher levels of officialdom, as well as in the Lappish minority movement, as a spokesman on Skolt affairs; on the grounds of being the only native Skolt with the qualifications and experience to do so. The culmination of his career came in 1969, when, following the resignation of his uncle, he put himself forward as a successor to the headmanship. His accession, accompanied by a denunciation of his predecessor, was accepted in the community by passive consent. As no other candidates were forthcoming, he could claim unanimous election. Later in the same year, he became secretary of the newly founded Näätämö *paliskunta.*

M's rather pompous and aggressive style is in direct contrast to the reticent and unobtrusive leadership of his predecessors. The exaggerated importance which he attaches to the headmanship, and his overt pursuit of public power, contradict the values of the local community, which accord neither rank nor formal authority to its elected representatives. M is an innovator who has carved out a political role for himself according to his own specifications. As a broker between the Skolts and the government bureaucracy, he is equally concerned to invent ' Skolt demands' as to press for their implementation, in order to increase the volume of his business and his stock of political capital. His strength lies in his relative familiarity with official procedure and party political manoeuvre; his weakness in his own decreasing familiarity with the people he claims to represent for, living and working outside the community, he is largely out of touch with its everyday affairs.

Whilst directing his performance towards the outside world, M has taken great pains to camouflage this critical flaw to his credibility as the mouthpiece of his people. His success has very much depended on his ability to control the outflow of information about the community. He is consulted for every statement that is required on Skolt affairs, and finds a place on every committee on which Skolt representation is considered necessary. His is the only Skolt name known outside the local region, through frequent press and radio appearances. In a number of speeches, articles and pamphlets on the Skolt predicament, he has been mainly concerned to declare the depths of his own cultural roots in Suenjel, presenting himself as a man who not only speaks Skolt, but thinks and feels Skolt. His professed identification with his people is taken to the point of total confusion: ' the Skolts' *are* M, and ' Skolt problems' *are* M's problems. Thus, many of his statements turn out to be lengthy autobiographies, but written pseudo-anonymously in the third person with scarcely hidden conceit. This is how, in an article entitled ' What it is to be Skolt ', he fabricates his ' election' to the headmanship: ' The choice came to this new headman as such a surprise that at first he quite lost his words; and then asked: " Isn't there any other person who could fill this office?" – to which the people shouted with one voice: " You alone are the right man for the job! We have no-one else so iron-fisted as you, whom we have now chosen as headman!" '

Most Skolts, in fact, feel that they are frequently misrepresented by M, and many disapprove of his tendency to act, in the name of the Skolts but without the backing of a Skolt mandate, in pursuance of political ends at odds with local values. His independently concocted ' demands' have, on occasion, caused consternation when revealed locally in the press. As a person, he is much disliked. It is therefore something of an enigma that he should be tolerated as headman. There are two reasons for this: the absence of competitors, and the indispensability of his services.

M's career is one that is not possible within the narrow political horizons of the local community, and his unique opportunity to study at Helsinki leaves him without rivals from among the Skolts of his generation. As long as his interpretation of the headmanship remains unchallenged, any competitor could only be a Skolt who had embarked on similar objectives. As it stands, the job is not one that inspires envy; for the price of political advancement is alienation from the community. At the same time, few would deny that in his capacity as a political broker, M has brought real material improvements to the community, albeit at considerable profit to himself. His ability to negotiate with agencies of the national bureaucracy represents an asset which cannot lightly be discarded, as long as no-one else is willing or in a position to take his place. The widespread assumption that leadership potential is in some sense hereditary cannot be discounted as an additional factor behind M's acceptability. This assumption has only been strengthened by the emergence of his younger brother, A, as a challenger in the arena of local party politics.

The meeting

After the long period of incumbency of his uncle, during which the community assembly had been allowed to fade into obscurity, M set about the restitution of the assembly as a backdrop to the management of his own public image. Meetings, formerly infrequent, are nowadays convened several times a year, on his own initiative. They are held in a classroom of the primary school. Every participant has to find a seat by one of the desks, which are arranged in neat rows. The headman, who invariably takes the chair, sits facing the ' audience' in the teacher's place, flanked by a secretary elected by the meeting to keep the minutes. Local people may be outnumbered by observers – officials, journalists and radio-men – who, being usually the first to arrive, occupy prominent positions at the front of the class. Those arriving later are relegated to the few remaining seats along the back of the room. A prohibition on smoking inside the classroom obliges those who wish to smoke and chat to leave to the corridor.

The effect of these arrangements is to impose an element of rigidity on the meeting. The seating plan introduces a marked separation between headman and rank-and-file, and necessitates a rather formal style of address. The presence of observers and recording equipment acts as a deterrent to spontaneous contributions from the floor, whilst from their position at the back of the class, only the most articulate local people can make themselves heard. Consequently, contributions from ordinary members of the assembly are rare. If a man is unsure what to say and when to speak, he will rather keep silent; if called upon to speak, he may confuse his words. Many Skolts find it hard, or make little effort, to follow what is being said; and spontaneous contributions seldom bear any relation to the item of the agenda supposedly under discussion. If people wish to discuss a point amongst themselves, they have to leave the room, since the inflexible seating and the prohibition on smoking inhibit the free flow of conversation ' on the floor '.

The agenda for the meeting is prepared and circulated in advance by the headman himself, and generally includes a number of ' Skolt demands ' of his own invention. He begins the meeting with a long, rather formal, opening address, read from a typescript, in which he outlines past achievements and current issues. Local people, little concerned with punctuality, keep on arriving throughout the speech, creating so much disturbance that few pay any attention to it. The principal items of the agenda seldom arouse interest. In the absence of comment from the floor, the demands are duly recorded as having received ' unanimous ' approval, and are later given extensive publicity in the press. Other items, less newsworthy but of greater practical concern, are accorded scant coverage.

The relegation of local people to the status of a non-participant audience allows the headman to take advantage of the situation as an occasion to make a public demonstration of his claim to speak, unopposed, for the Skolts; and to impress any outside observers with his political stature and the degree of apparent support for his policies. For observers, attendance at the meeting provides an opportunity for them to familiarize themselves with Skolt circumstances and opinions ' on the spot ', although these are rarely voiced by others besides the headman himself. Local attendance at meetings is extremely variable, depending largely on the availability of transport and whether they can be timed to coincide with other events that would draw people to the village. Many latecomers merely take a ' look in ', and leave on finding little to interest them in the proceedings. Others drift off early to chat in the corridor. As attendance dwindles, the headman is forced to save face by bringing the meeting hurriedly to a formal close before it collapses of its own accord.

Compared with these meetings of the community assembly, the twice-yearly general meetings of the reindeer association present a complete contrast. Association meetings take place within the cramped confines of a local cottage or forest cabin. People sit around on the floor, beds, benches, crates, or whatever else comes to hand. No outside observers are present. These meetings have the informal quality of a moot: protracted discussion goes on against the background of a continual hubbub of conversation. The chairman, separated from others only by his papers, makes no effort to intervene in the flow of discussion; and meetings, as a result, can last all day, until everyone has had the opportunity to speak his fill.

In meetings of the newly formed Näätämö *paliskunta,* M, as secretary, takes little part except to keep the minutes. His job is to promote the interests of the ' Skolt *paliskunta* ' at higher levels of government, and not to meddle in the technicalities of the association's internal affairs, with which he is not entirely acquainted. On the other hand, for the elders of the association, its meetings have taken on something of the likeness of the old *siita* assembly as it operated in Suenjel; the association chairman displaying many of the qualities of the traditional headman. The contrast with present-day meetings of the community assembly illustrates the degree to which M has turned the headmanship towards his political advantage in the wider society.

The problem of legitimacy

The problem that leads M to erect such an elaborate facade of publicity, in assembly meetings and in the mass media, is a familiar one for those who choose to insert themselves as middlemen in the process of integration of small, peripheral minorities into the structure of nationwide politics and administration. This problem is a fundamental contradiction in the bases of his legitimacy. From the point of view of the community, where Skolt ancestry is not a scarce resource, he is accepted in office on account of his negotiating skills, despite the motive of self-interest that is said to govern his actions. The establishment of political indispensability on the local level thus entails the acceptance of social marginality: to negotiate he must go *outside* the moral and physical limitations of the traditional order, accepting the prevailing ethics of competition for public power; at the same time relating back to the community from a position of brokerage, trading benefits won from the administration for local support.

On the other hand, from the point of view of those with whom he negotiates, in departments of the bureaucracy and on the many committees of which he is a member, his uniqueness lies not in his personal abilities but in his native Skolt ancestry, by virtue of which his utterances are accepted as authentic, unbiased reflections of Skolt sentiment. The use of ethnic identity as an asset for political advancement thus rests on the assumption, among his political patrons, that he is an *insider*, fully incorporated, both socially and culturally, into his native community. It is naturally this view of himself that M wishes to project. For this reason, he has time and again found occasion to defend publicly the purity of his ethnic sentiment and deny charges of self-interest levelled against him.

M's uncle, J, was remarkable for his total commitment to the values and way of life of his people, a quality that has won him admiration and respect both within the community and outside. However, during his long period ' in office ' he became little more than a figurehead. He was ill-equipped to deal with bureaucratic procedure, and achieved little in the way of improvements for the Skolts. In the end, his retirement from office and denunciation by his nephew were greeted without a word of protest. As man he was respected, as a leader he was entirely dispensable. M went to the opposite extreme. Having sacrificed his membership of the community for the sake of political expediency, he is forced to legitimate his activities by fabricating a picture of cultural incorporation. The fact that he finds it necessary to do so itself casts doubts on his integrity, and has indeed earned him hostility and even ridicule from many quarters.

The particular strategy that generates this kind of problem could be characterized as one of 'leap-frog' politics: the attempt to negotiate directly with those in the higher echelons of power on the strength of representing a small underprivileged minority, whilst bypassing political competition within the local arena. At either end of the 'leap', the politician must apply different assets and cultivate a different view of himself, erecting barriers to prevent the emergence of contradictions between the two. In general, the smaller the minority, and the weaker its voting strength, the greater is its propensity to throw up leaders of this kind. Further, the bigger the 'leap', the more favourably the politician may be expected to be received, for sympathy for the 'minority cultures' increases with distance from them, whereas information about their real situation proportionately decreases.

As M never tires of pointing out, a great deal of his time is spent on high-level committees, as well as talking with officials in provincial and national capitals, and even abroad. On the other hand, he is notably silent on the Commune council, and makes little attempt to defend local interests through it. This strategy generates an inflated sense of his own self-importance, which does not help him to achieve a convincing performance in the eyes of either his political superiors or the Skolts themselves. His greatest weaknesses are exposed on the local level where information cannot be tightly controlled, and where expertise specific to ethnic ancestry counts for little. His rivals in the arena of Commune party politics, principally the two merchants and the salesman-cum-caretaker from Sevetti, brokers like himself but with neither the advantage nor the embarrassment of a claim to Skolt identity, ridicule his propensity to magnify 'Skolt problems' in the mass media rather than to make a determined effort to solve them through the proper channels of local government. On the other hand, local professionals such as the Sevetti schoolteachers, whilst having no wish to become involved in what they see as the ignominious business of politics, are themselves concerned to lay claims to Skolt cultural incorporation; at the same time casting public doubts on M's authenticity, above all in the crucial area of linguistic competence.

The issue of M's competence erupted in 1972, when a primer in Skolt was constructed for experimental use in Sevettijärvi school. M, who regards the custodianship of the Skolt language as an important aspect of his responsibilities as headman, had spoken often of a Skolt dictionary supposedly in preparation, employing an orthography of his own invention. Nobody else had ever seen the work. The primer, however, was devised by an academic linguist with advice from one of the Sevetti schoolteachers and her Skolt husband. M was predictably furious at having been bypassed. His orthography was not used, nor was he even consulted. In a series of newspaper articles he launched a bitter attack on the primer and its makers, claiming them to be mere dilettantes in the Skolt language who had mutilated it to the point of obscenity. Why, he asked, had they not sought the advice of a ' real Skolt'? The acrimonious controversy that followed was given much publicity in the national press, which did much to harm M's credibility, although the culture-snatching activities of professionals and academics also came in for some criticism. Within the community, most parents remained largely unconcerned about the whole question. Hardly able to oppose the primer in principle, M eventually compromised by setting up a local ' language board', with himself as chairman, in order to discuss ways in which it could be improved.

The regularization of the headmanship

Until recently, the Skolt headmanship had received no formal recognition in the categories of administration. Officials with responsibilities covering the resettlement area were obliged neither to invite nor to listen to the views of the community assembly. Ever since he ' took office', M had pressed for the regularization of the headmanship, demanding that the post should be rewarded by a modest State salary. In this, he had received the backing of the Nordic Lapp Council, the mouthpiece of the pan-Lappish minority movement, and of Finnish academics active in the promotion of ' Lapp Culture', who were concerned that the assembly and headmanship should be preserved as the sole survivals of a once universal indigenous Lappish institution.

M brought the matter up as one of prime importance on the agenda of several assembly meetings throughout 1971 and 1972. He declared that the remuneration of the headman would represent a major step forward in Skolt history. Skolt reaction at the meetings was sceptical and apathetic. The financial benefits, after all, were to go to M and not to them, and the suspicion of self-interest on his part was unavoidable. Further, M had read his proposal for the regulations of office from a paper at such a speed that few were able to catch the details, which were embedded in a morass of numbered sections and subsections. The muted reaction was, as usually, recorded as ' unanimous approval', and the proposal received much publicity under the umbrella of the Lappish Movement. It was eventually ratified by the government, to take effect from October 1972.

The new post comes under the aegis of the ' Lapp Affairs Advisory Committee' (*Saamelaisasiain Neuvottelukunta* – SANK), a small appointed body of senior civil servants and experts on Lapp questions, which was set up in 1960 to inform the government on matters of policy affecting the Lappish population. According to the regulations, the headman must himself be a Skolt who can speak the language. He is responsible for convening meetings of the community assembly at least once a year, and has the right to attend all the meetings of SANK, on which he is bound to represent the views of the community. He receives a salary of 700 Fmk a month.

By according a special position to the Skolt headmanship, M's leap-frog strategy has received official acknowledgement. Instead of going through the usual tortuous channels of political representation, Skolt interests can be brought directly to government attention through the agency of SANK. However the contradiction between the criteria of legitimacy applied at either end of the 'leap', a contradiction inherent in such a strategy, was not removed by its regularization. At one end, the headman is regarded as a broker, at the other as an authentic representative of his culture. This dilemma reappeared as one between the principles of election and appointment in the selection of office-holders. Whilst it was naturally assumed that, at least in theory, the headman should be chosen by the community assembly, the government insisted that, as a salaried official under the civil service, the incumbent should be *appointed* by SANK on the basis of his personal and cultural qualifications. If, in the future, the community were to select an alternative candidate, the terms of the appointment would have to be reviewed in the light of the candidate's suitability.

M, the only Skolt known in higher administrative circles, was automatically appointed. The appointment caused understandable confusion in the meeting of the community assembly held to ratify the new regulations. It appeared that the Skolts were called upon to elect a headman who had already been appointed. Further, the regulations paid no more than lip-service to the principle of election, having nothing to say on voting procedure or the period of office. M, not a little embarrassed by the exposure of this deliberate ambiguity, explained that the office had to remain appointive until the regulations were finally ratified, allowing elections to take place. However, M's adaptation of the headmanship was to such an extent self-styled, that few Skolts made any distinction between the office and its incumbent. In the absence of any serious challenge, M was able to declare himself 'unanimously elected' at the next assembly meeting after the regulations were ratified.

M's appointment as a salaried official under SANK assured him a place in the higher administrative structure, at a time when his popularity in the arena of local party politics was rapidly crumbling. Secure in office, he is no longer answerable to those he supposedly represents. Despite the preservationist intentions of those who lent their backing to the regularization of the headmanship, its realization marks the conclusion of a process whereby the headmanship has been drawn initially from the centre to the periphery and finally removed altogether from the bounds of Skolt society.

19 Leap-frog politics (2): Legislation

Resettlement compensation

An essential element in the leap-frog procedure is the exceptional position of the Skolts as laid down in the 'Skolt Law' of 1955, which defined the resettlement area and the conditions of tenure for the houses and plots of land granted to them within it (SA 1955: 273). This legislation was basically intended to compensate the Skolts for the loss of their homes and *siita* territories in Petsamo. As a part of its obligations towards the support of the resettled community, the State was committed, under a clause in the law, to finance and carry out all improvements necessary 'to protect and promote reindeer management, fishing, communications, and the conditions of livelihood of the Skolts' in the resettlement area. It is on the basis of this undertaking that the demands of the community have been accorded special priority by provincial and national administrations, at the expense of other groups not so favoured whose needs would appear equally urgent.

Since he assumed responsibilities for representing the community, M has repeatedly used the ploy of compensation for losses in Suenjel, and the promise of government support, to win significant benefits from above. Indeed the community has largely come to rely on this situation of privileged dependency, assuming that all material improvements are to be gained through direct, and preferably personal, representations to the relevant government ministry. The success of the leap-frog tactic has been put succinctly by M himself, in his own idiosyncratic style: 'Not until 1957 did the Skolts get a Sevettijärvi man (*sic*) on Inari Commune Council. This councillor set to work and reminded the high officials of what they had promised the Skolts, what had become of these promises; and suggested that it was about time they were carried out. As a result of this Skolt-councillor's efforts, Sevetti has got a road, a telephone network, Näätämö *paliskunta*, etc.'

Many of these benefits have undoubtedly advanced the Skolts' material welfare. Others, such as the formation of Näätämö *paliskunta*, are more contentious. In this particular example, the ethnically biassed presentation of the case for division through the community assembly in terms of the obligation 'to protect and promote Skolt reindeer management' was used with striking success to the advantage of a limited section of the community at the expense of its neighbours. M has even suggested that Näätämö might be able to claim its coveted border-fence with Muddusjärvi as compensation for several miles of reindeer fence which were left behind in Suenjel. Resettlement compensation from above may thus be converted into an ethnic asset to be applied in ecological competition on the local level. In the long term, however, the future of the Skolts' traditional livelihood depends not on such competitive advantage but on the regeneration of natural resources: a factor that demands a rationalization of systems of production rather than direct financial aid.

Skolt land tenure: the principles of normalization and reservation

The special legal provision made for the Skolts, as opposed to other elements of the displaced Petsamo population, derived from the fact that all but a very few Skolts of Pattsvei and Peättsam *siidat,* who had acquired plots of their own, had possessed no formal title to land in their *siita* territories. Although the Skolts' customary rights to exploit the resources of their *siidat* had been fully recognized, the land was technically regarded as State property. Consequently, they were not able to apply for resettlement plots on the basis of the general land dispensation law, introduced after the war for the benefit of the large displaced population from the eastern border regions, which compensated only for the loss of titled lands. The few Skolts who had owned land in Petsamo, and who were therefore qualified for plots under the land dispensation law, were excluded from the terms of the Skolt Law, and therefore also from the benefits, such as grants for home improvements, which it guaranteed.

Besides the undertaking of State support for the resettled community, the 1955 Law incorporated two major components. The first, enshrined in the principal clauses of the law itself, laid down the provisions under which 'Skolt estates' were conveyed to the occupants of resettlement houses at the time of enactment. This part of the law was intended as a ' once only ' measure, applying solely to the generation that had suffered resettlement, and its provisions regarding the sale and mortgage of estates remain in force for a limited period of fifty years. The purpose of granting estates was to put the Skolts on a similar footing with other elements of the population as regards land tenure, so that Skolts of future generations would be in a position to inherit shares in their parental estates, or to obtain plots of their own by rent or purchase, on the same basis as any other Finnish citizen. Official policy has been to regard the Skolt Law as a step towards normalization, such that it would automatically be ' phased out ' over time.

The second aspect of the Law is spelt out in the accompanying ordinance, which defined the geographical boundaries of the Sevettijärvi and Nellim resettlement areas, and the privileges granted to the Skolts to exploit the natural resources within them. The intention behind the delineation of these ' reservations ' was rather different from, and in some ways contradictory to, the principles applied to the formation of individual ' Skolt estates '. Where the latter aimed to bring Skolt land tenure into line with that of the rest of the population, the former aimed to preserve to perpetuity at least some semblance of the traditional *siita,* regarding the resettlement area privileges as replacing the customary usufruct to which the Skolts had been entitled in their original territory. It is on the basis of this ' reservation principle ' that some of the more articulate Skolts, as well as observers sympathetic to the idea of cultural conservation, have chosen to regard the Skolt Law, in its *entirety,* as a kind of ethnic charter, laying down ' traditional rights' to which all those with a claim to Skolt identity, whether through descent or marriage, should be entitled.

In accordance with its compensatory nature, that part of the Skolt Law relating to estates made no specific provision for future generations, though there was nothing to prevent a young Skolt applying for a building plot under the general land-use regulations. However, plots are available only in the neighbourhood of settlement centres on land that has been designated and reserved for building by the Commune planning department. Pending the preparation of a future settlement plan for the Sevettijärvi area, whose form is currently under discussion, the Commune administration has frozen all applications from Skolts for plots in the area. As a result, there has been no new building, except of sub-dwellings built on Skolt plots or on land obtained privately.

An alternative means of obtaining land was made available through the enactment, in 1969, of the ' Reindeer Estate Law ', a major piece of legislation with implications for the whole reindeer-management area of northern Finland (SA 1969: 590). This law entitles those whose principal source of livelihood is in reindeer management to apply for land holdings of their own totalling at most four hectares of cultivable fields and as much forest as is necessary to satisfy domestic building and fuel requirements. In the far North, this forest area would amount to some 150–200 hectares. In addition, the holder would be entitled to substantial building grants and loans. The law was aimed to give pastoralists, who were not traditionally concerned with the establishment of private landholdings, the same rights as are enjoyed by those who had earlier benefited from the favourable terms offered to settlers in the era of land colonization during the last century. It represented a further attempt to normalize the position of the indigenous population, subject to a universal legislative framework anchored on the concept of real estate – a concept of dubious applicability in the northern wilderness.

The Reindeer Estate Law has run into considerable difficulties in its application, and is taking several years to put into effect. No estates are yet formed. The implications of this complex law are widely misunderstood, and there have been calls for substantial modifications. The eligibility test, that reindeer management forms a principle livelihood, is difficult to apply, because tax records do not show the important element of domestic income from subsistence production. At the close of 1972, 310 out of 380 applications had been accepted. The law applies equally to younger generation Skolts who do not own land under the original ' Skolt Law '; but few today can claim reindeer management to be a principal source of livelihood. To date, there have been only five applications from the Sevettijärvi area.

To coincide with the enactment of the Reindeer Estate Law, a further piece of legislation known as the 'Skolt Land Regulation Law' was introduced to apply specifically to the holders of 'Skolt estates', or of shares in them (SA 1969: 593). This law laid down provisions under which the estates or shares could be either converted into, or exchanged for, a reindeer estate. The conversion could be effected by the addition of a large area of private forest to the original estate. At the same time, usufruct privileges formerly enjoyed within the resettlement area would be forfeited. The law likewise enables the holder of part or whole of a Skolt estate to exchange it for a building plot granted under the general land-use regulations, again at the cost of forfeiting resettlement privileges.

The intentions of the Skolt Land Regulation Law were two-fold: firstly to speed up the 'phasing out' of original Skolt estates by bringing them under provisions applying generally elsewhere; secondly to ease the strain on Skolt settlement conditions and allow more building. Its practical impact has been negligible: to date only one application has been received. The reason may lie in the incomprehensibility of the legislation itself, which has perplexed even the Land Department officials. It may equally lie in the reluctance of Skolts to forfeit what they regard as 'traditional' usufruct privileges. For the main part, however, the need for building plots exists amongst Skolts of the younger generation who, at the present time, hold neither Skolt estates nor shares in them, and who are not therefore eligible under the terms of the new law.
are not therefore eligible under the terms of the new law.

In 1972, a number of Skolts signed a petition requesting an alteration in the law such that 'young Skolts can obtain building plots in the resettlement area, in order that they can practise reindeer management and other traditional forms of livelihood, and establish families'. The move was a characteristic one; rather than identifying the causes of the building freeze in local government inertia, appeal was made through the ombudsman to the national legislature, for consideration as a minority having a special claim in law to protection and support. The leading voices behind the petition were, in fact, immigrant spouses in elite mixed marriages whose livelihood is *not* based on traditional economic pursuits, but who were concerned to use their claim to ethnic incorporation in order to improve their own material housing standards.

A major element in their argument was that the impossibility of obtaining building plots is forcing young couples to seek a home and livelihood elsewhere, through emigration from the community; and that the future of the Skolts as a cultural group is thereby being placed in jeopardy. This argument has no empirical foundation. Most young girls leave the community before marriage, for reasons quite other than those of housing, and it is this exodus that ultimately limits the number of local marriages. Most male migrants are single, and only one couple emigrated after attempting to set up in a Skolt house, owing to the failure of the traditional sector to provide an adequate livelihood. No amount of new building will compensate for this inadequacy, nor for the paucity of strictly local opportunities for young Skolts in the *non*-traditional sector. Nevertheless, of those Skolts who *have* remained and married within the community, many have been forced by housing restrictions to reside patri- or matrilocally and, as their families grow are anxious to be able to establish dwellings of their own.

A State committee including a senior civil servant, three members of parliament for Lapland province, and M as Skolt representative, was appointed in 1972 to look into the situation and make any necessary proposals for legislative reform. The committee was sympathetic towards the Skolt viewpoint, taking the position that the benefits accorded by the original Skolt Law - not only usufruct privileges, but also plots, buildings and financial grants - are not to be limited to those who lost their homes in Petsamo, but are to be regarded as a lasting ethnic entitlement for which all those of Skolt descent are eligible, regardless of whether or not they presently hold land under the provisions of the Law. Thus, it was recommended that the Skolt Land Regulation Law be changed such that *any* Skolt could apply for a building plot within the resettlement area; that applicants would be entitled to building grants; that the normal ruling which limits the situation of plots to the vicinity of settlement centres would be waived; and that those who obtain plots would not forfeit 'traditional' usufruct rights as a result. The committee's report, submitted in 1973 (KM 1973, 69), represented an endorsement of the 'reservation principle' and the view of the Skolt Law as an enduring ethnic charter; and a reversal of the previous official line which had treated the Law as a compensation measure to be phased out over time.[1]

The implementation of these proposals would eliminate the wholly artificial scarcity of building land that has resulted partly from the literal application of rules derived from urban and agricultural contexts, in which private land represents a real investment, to one in which its only value is as a base for a house. There is no conceivable reason why families should be living in cramped conditions when an abundance of potential building sites exists on otherwise worthless land. On the other hand, there are dangers inherent in the strategy of overcoming bureaucratic friction by resort to special legal dispensation. The principles of normalization and reservation, placed side by side in the original Skolt Law, do not readily co-exist, as the subsequent history of legislative confusion has amply demonstrated. To protect one narrow section of the population whilst bringing other, equally disadvantaged, categories into line with the prevailing norm is to introduce artificial divisions which may act as sources of discord and injustice in the future. Thus the application of the Reindeer Estate Law and the revised Skolt Land Regulation Law to the same population in the same territory would merely add to the present disparity between 'colonist' landowners, with private holdings of up to 200 hectares, and Skolts with plots of only three hectares. The only difference would

be that some Skolts would become big landowners whilst others would
be forced further afield to enjoy their customary rights of usufruct.

The perpetutation of dependency

Although the 'leap-frog' strategy has paid off in the short term, it only
reinforces the status of the Skolt community as a handicapped 'special
case' on the periphery of Finnish national society, dependent for its
welfare on State assistance, and therefore equally vulnerable if and when
such assistance fails to materialize. Rather than opening up the political
horizons of the community to expand the breadth of local representation
and participation in intermediate levels of government, its boundaries are
tightly drawn by special legal provisions, stretching the hierarchical and
administrative distance between makers and subjects of policy, and thereby
placing the representation of community interests in the hands of a broker
who, by the very nature of his task, operates outside the local milieu. In
the legal codification of the 'reservation principle' and the appointment of
the headman as a salaried official, the two complementary components of
the leap-frog procedure have gained official recognition. By endorsing the
regularization of this procedure, the Skolts may in fact be making themselves party to a system that is practically unworkable, holding benefits
only for those middlemen who depend on the perpetuation of 'minority
problems' for their own advancement.

The practical weakness of the system was well illustrated in the case of
the State committee appointed to investigate the Skolt housing and settlement problem. The three members of parliament on the committee had
never visited the community except occasionally to collect votes at election
time. They were understandably ignorant of local conditions, and their
parliamentary duties left them little time to devote to Skolt problems.
The appointment of M as the sole Skolt representative was automatic. The
community was given a chance to express its views to the committee in an
assembly meeting at the school, but the event was a fiasco. The non-Skolt
committee members, who had not even seen a map of the area, were quite
unable to focus down on the practical aspects of the problem. The Skolts,
on the other hand, were not prepared to present their case in a form
sufficiently coherent or comprehensive to be understandable to the
committee. Instead, they took the advantage of a rare opportunity to
give voice to a multitude of grievances covering everything from reindeer
fences to badly fitting window frames. The MPs flew back to Helsinki as
suddenly as they had arrived, and no wiser for their visit.

The strategy of direct appeal to the legislature thus places responsibility
for the formulation of Skolt policy in the hands of bureaucrats and politicians so remote as to possess only the most rudimentary grasp of the
practical problems they are dealing with. The result does no more than
compound the string of misunderstandings and anomalies that have plagued
officials concerned with the implementation of Skolt policy since the days

of resettlement. The burden on the bureaucracy created by such special cases may be enough to delay indefinitely the arrival of the promised 'cargo' of government aid, leading to yet further appeals for reform. The remoteness of decision-making places the entire onus of Skolt representation on the present headman, who maintains his monopoly of brokerage by ensuring that the politico-jural boundaries of the community remain intact. This, in turn, inhibits the emergence of truly representative political leadership on the local level, and creates a dearth of expertise in the procedures of local government, binding the community in a vicious circle of self-reinforcing dependency on distant benefactors, intermediaries and profit-seekers.

20 Party politics

Political parties and the electoral system

Every Finnish citizen over the age of twenty is entitled to vote in the election of members to the national parliament, and of councillors to his local Commune. In both cases, a system of proportional representation is employed. For parliamentary elections, the country is divided into a number of electoral districts, whose boundaries normally coincide with those of the province. Each district has a certain quota of members to be elected. The numbers chosen from each party are weighted in proportion to the totals of votes cast for candidates of those respective parties within the district. It is therefore possible in borderline cases for candidates representing strong parties to be elected despite receiving fewer votes than others who are excluded on the grounds of insufficient support for their party as a whole.

Elections to the Commune council are held every four years. The numbers of councillors from each party are similarly weighted in proportion to party support, but there is no internal subdivision of the Commune into electoral wards: every elector is presented with the full list of candidates from which to choose. Formally, therefore, no particular councillor can claim to represent any particular region within the Commune. As in parliamentary elections, the voter can choose only one candidate from the the list.

The effect of the proportional system is to generate a multitude of political parties to cater for every ..inority interest. The four major parties are, from Left to Right, the mainly communist People's Democratic League (SKDL), the Social Democratic Party (SDP), the Agrarian or 'Centre' Party (Keskusta), and the Conservative Coalition (Kokoomus). Smaller parties include the Rural Party (SMP - a recent breakaway from the Agrarian movement), the ethnically based Swedish People's Party, the Liberal Party, and the Christian League. Other fringe parties are for ever in the process of formation and fragmentation. The sheer number of parties on the Finnish political scene has made it very difficult for any government to hold office for more than a year at a stretch.

The last parliamentary elections were held in January 1972. The nine members for Lapland province include three from SKDL, three from Keskusta, and one from each of Kokoomus, SMP and SDP. The support for SKDL comes principally from workers concentrated around the big pulp mills in the south of the province, and on logging sites throughout the forest zone. The Centre Party, Keskusta, has traditionally represented the interests of the agricultural sector, as well as those of reindeer management; though many of its former supporters, particularly in poorer, peripheral regions, have now switched their allegiance to the Rural Party, SMP.

The council of Inari Commune has twenty-three elected members. SKDL and Keskusta are again the two strongest parties, having gained seven and five seats respectively in the 1972 elections. SMP follows with four seats. Support for SKDL is concentrated in and around the main population centre of Ivalo, whereas Keskusta and SMP find the bulk of their support from agriculturalists and pastoralists in areas outside the limits of commercial forestry. Support for SMP is nowhere stronger than in the Sevettijärvi area. Kokoomus, traditionally the party of the merchant and professional bourgeoisie, holds three seats on the council, as do the Social Democrats. The one remaining seat is held by a Liberal.

The issues of party politics seldom reach the Skolt community except at election times. In parliamentary elections, Skolt voting follows a predictable pattern, unaffected by preferences for any particular candidate over another. Until the establishment of SMP the majority of votes went to Keskusta, the only party with a claim to uphold the interests of reindeer management. A minority who have long been involved in casual labour, and who therefore see themselves as part of the rural proletariat, regularly vote for left-wing parties, principally SKDL. Some older Skolts, unfamilar with the different parties and unable to read the candidate lists, vote more or less at random.

Parliamentary and Communal elections

Few of the fifty-seven parliamentary candidates from Lapland province put up for election in 1972 were even slightly known locally, and only a handful considered it worth their while to tour such a remote and sparsely populated area to canvass support. Election meetings were usually held on the premises of one or other of the Sevetti merchants. They were poorly attended, attracting audiences of from one to at most a dozen people, many of whom were passers-by finding themselves at the meeting quite by chance. Some stayed out of curiosity, others went about their business, blandly ignoring the speaker.

Despite candidates' attempts to discover in advance a little about local issues in order to add relevance and a smattering of concrete promises to their speeches, they often misfired. Thus, politicians of every complexion pledged that they had the interests of Näätämö *paliskunta* at heart, and would see that a border fence were built if returned to power. One Kokoomus candidate, however, addressing himself specifically to his ' Sevettijärvi friends ', did not realize that all but one of his meagre audience were in fact Muddusjärvi Lapps visiting the village for a reindeer separation. Other candidates were bewildered to find their audiences sharply divided on what should be done to solve local problems; and finding it impossible to fit such issues into their generalized party dogmas, were unable to promise anything specific at all.

Skolt audiences remained as much mystified about broader issues of national party politics as the speakers were about local disputes. Many of these issues, concerned as they are with such macroeconomic problems as wages and prices, unemployment, industrial nationalization, and agricultural policy, do not directly relate to local circumstances where there is neither industry nor agriculture, where unemployment can be beneficial, where subsistence production still provides an important element of income, and where much of what is bought comes from Norway. The only issue to which audiences infallibly responded was the universal grumble of excessive taxation.

In Communal elections, there is no such barrier to understanding between candidate and voter. Rather, many candidates have themselves only a hazy notion of the national policies propounded by their respective parties, or of the ideologies behind them. The number of candidates for one election may be enormous: in 1972 there were 166 within Inari Commune alone, or one for every twenty-six voters. The majority of candidates have no real political ambitions, and are fielded by their local parties merely in order to gather extra votes from their immediate circles of friends and relations who might otherwise remain uncommitted. Only prominent local personalities who can draw on a wider range of influence have much chance of election, although a large kinship network can be a significant asset. Thus, party divisions demonstrated in parliamentary elections may be distorted on the Communal level by the presence of enduring social relationships between candidates and voters, by the personal standing of particular candidates on the local scene, and by the sides they take on local issues that have little to do with national political debate. However, since every vote for an individual is also a vote for his party, the element of party factionalism remains strong even on this local level.

Though six Skolts resident in the Sevettijärvi area have at various times stood for election to the Commune council, the Skolts in general are noticeably less active in local party politics than the 'old inhabitants' of the region. Their first contacts with the procedures of modern representative government did not come until their resettlement as citizens of Inari. For many Skolts, the Commune administration remains a somewhat alien entity, staffed by officials who can only be influenced through intermediaries rather than controlled from above through direct participation in local government. To the extent that they continue to identify their needs and interests as distinct from other citizens of the Commune this view is reinforced, and leads to the vesting of responsibilities for representation of the community in the hands of external brokers considered qualified to negotiate with officialdom.

The rise of the Rural Party

SMP was formed in 1966, as a breakaway movement from the Centre Party (Keskusta). Its representation in Parliament has since risen to eighteen members.[1] In the parliamentary elections of 1972, SMP received only 9 per cent of the national vote, but 22 per cent of the vote from Inari Commune In the three neighbouring communities of Kaamanen, Partakko and Sevettijärvi, SMP's share of the vote rose to between 40 and 50 per cent. This sudden surge of interest and enthusiasm for a minority party is all the more remarkable among the Skolts, who were not formerly noted for political activism, and calls for some explanation.

SMP claims to represent the interests of peasant smallholders and petty entrepreneurs struggling to make a livelihood by their own efforts. It has taken issue with the major parties of both Left and Right over the infringement by big business, whether private or State-controlled, on individual constitutional freedoms. The party leader, Veikko Vennamo, has presented himself as the prophet of a new social order, destined to free the righteous from the yoke of monopolistic oppression. His tirades in Parliament have verged on the fanatical, and have on occasion led to his ejection from the House, a martyrdom which he has greatly relished. His supporters follow him like disciples of a faith, his more numerous opponents regard his outbursts with derision.

SMP derives most of its support from the most marginal areas of Finland, outside the principal regions of agricultural and industrial production. The far North is no exception, and Skolt small-men in particular found that through SMP their long-felt frustrations could at last receive overt expression at the highest levels of power. Vennamo presented action and drama, whilst the major parties appeared engrossed in invisible and apparently fruitless machinations. The number of local adherents grew rapidly, not least owing to the efforts of the regular post-bus driver, an ardent SMP man, who spread the new gospel on his daily journeys up and down the length of the road between Kaamanen, Partakko and Sevettijärvi. In 1971 he was able to set up a local branch of the party, the first of its kind in the area.

The first Skolt SMP candidate ran for election in 1968. This man, A, was a younger brother of M, the only Skolt holding a seat on the council at the time. A person of extraordinary vitality, he was a popular local figure, and polled more votes from Sevettijärvi than any other candidate, including his brother. Nevertheless, he narrowly failed to obtain a seat, whereas his brother was returned to power. The result caused a certain amount of bitterness, and it was only through the exertion of considerable psychological pressure by the new local branch of the party that A was persuaded to stand again in 1972. Despite M's appeals, addressed to the community assembly, for a concerted vote behind his own Social Democratic Party, A won an overwhelming majority and gained a seat on the council, whilst M lost the seat he had held continuously for sixteen years.

Councillor and headman

Notwithstanding the shortcomings of SMP doctrine, and the party's bizarre parliamentary record, the political activism that it generated on the local level has brought many Skolts to a greater awareness of their interests not merely as members of an isolated community, but as citizens of the Commune. Such a redefinition of political boundaries implies that the institutions of the Commune cease to be regarded as agencies of an alien authority, coming to be viewed instead as integral parts of the local social and political order. Likewise, the relationship of the electorate to local government is transformed from one of dependency on distant and all-powerful officials to one of democratic participation: the elected councillor is thus no longer a broker chosen to negotiate with officialdom but a representative member of a body responsible for the formulation of policy, to which local officials are held directly accountable.

From the former perspective there was little to distinguish M's activities as headman from the role he had already assumed as what he liked to call the 'Skolt councillor': the one was merely an extension of the other, providing him with an additional title with which to impress his political patrons. The Skolts accepted him as headman for the same reasons that they had voted for him as councillor: he was an experienced negotiator who could turn his ethnic identity to advantage. In this he had the edge over his party political rivals who, although themselves experienced brokers, could not aim so high in the world of officialdom, where only the voice of the native is given credence. Thus, although M's Social Democratic Party received little local support in Parliamentary elections, he could secure the largest share of the Skolt vote in Communal elections on account of his personal credentials.

Today, however, as Skolts are increasingly drawn into the affairs of the Commune, they wish to see their own political opinions as citizens and ratepayers represented on the council. As political horizons expand, so the field of operations of the traditional broker is progressively curtailed. With the election of A to the council, the roles of councillor and headman, formerly merged under M, became vested in separate individuals of very different political complexion and background. Both the community and its leaders were called upon to define the scope of the restyled headmanship *as distinct from* the responsibilities of the councillor: to separate, in other words, their unique interests as members of a resettled community from their common concerns as citizens of the Commune.

An indication of this impending problem was given on the occasion of an assembly meeting a few months before the 1972 Communal elections. M used his opening address to make what was, in effect, an electioneering speech, in which he outlined his personal achievements as headman-cum-councillor, as well as the virtues of the Social Democratic Party. Of all people, he claimed to be the most experienced and qualified to handle the special concerns of the community. The speech was strongly resented by the more politically articulate Skolts, especially the supporters of SMP, who felt that the introduction of party politics into the supposedly neutral community assembly was wholly illegitimate. Their objection did not rest merely on their opposition to Social Democracy; for the real enemies of SMP are held to be the communists of the more left-wing SKDL. Rather, the separation of Communal party-politics from ethnic leap-frog politics was felt to be a matter of principle: to the extent that interests are identified with those of the Party, they lie outside the portfolio of the headmanship, whatever the political opinions of its incumbent.

The aim of party activists is certainly not to abolish the headmanship altogether, but to restrict its scope to those fields in which the community is covered by special legislative provision. M's status as a broker with high officials of the provincial and national administrations remains unchallenged; it is only his authority to deal with *all* matters pertaining to the community that has been undermined. Nevertheless, this breach of monopoly is, for him, a severe embarrassment, since it weakens his claims to legitimacy at higher levels. The election result makes it all too clear that M is not the 'man of his people' that his patrons had been led to imagine.

Indeed, M's attempt to combine his party career with the headmanship at a time of growing political consciousness among the Skolt electorate was a tactical blunder of some magnitude. Had he not stood for re-election, the erosion of his support would never have been revealed. In the event, he was defeated at the polls by the very image of himself that he had been led to fabricate in order to justify his dealings with high officials: an image so demonstrably false to all familiar with the local scene as to dispel any credibility he may have retained as a representative. Party politics and leap-frog politics are thus basically incompatible: the one destroys the premises of the other.

M's career was saved only in the nick of time by the regularization of the headmanship and his subsequent appointment. Although ousted from the council, his formal status provides shelter from which he can gaze towards the heights of power without running the risk of exposure. Having had his foothold removed from beneath him, he remains suspended from a rung of the national bureaucracy: he may go up, but there is no way down. Thus, as the headmanship was drawn outside the bounds of Skolt society, so the role of the councillor, in contrary progression, has been encompassed within them. The two offices, having merged for a time on the boundary during the period of M's dual incumbency, are now irrevocably separated, their positions in relation to the community reversed from those obtaining at the commencement of its political integration into the structure of modern government, when the councillor was alien to Skolt society and the headman at its core.

21 The Lappish Movement

The minority question

In the Nordic countries of Norway, Sweden and Finland, the Lapps form today a minority population of around 36 000. They live intermixed with Scandinavians, with whom they have had contacts over many centuries. As the North was peopled by colonists and drawn into the broad sweep of modernization, Lappish groups came under heavy pressure towards cultural uniformity with the main population. Their fate has become a cause for serious concern, particularly among academics and the small educated Lappish elite, and the years before and immediately following the last war saw the founding of a number of organizations in all three countries to promote Lappish interests and save ' Lapp Culture ' from apparently imminent destruction. Co-operation between these organizations led to the establishment of a ' Nordic Lapp Council ', under whose direction international ' pan-Lappish ' conferences have been held every three years since 1953.

From these organizational developments has emerged the ' Lappish movement ', whose aim is to mobilize the Lapps around an ideology of ethnic pluralism, stressing the unity of the Lappish people across national frontiers, and their complementary relationship with other Scandinavian peoples (Eidheim 1971). Politically, the movement contains an uneasy alliance between conservatives concerned with the preservation of Lapp culture and radicals who talk of neocolonialism, linking the fate of the Lapps with that of other oppressed minorities around the northern circumpolar belt under the banner of the ' Fourth World ' (Homme 1969, Küng 1970, Otnes 1970, Valkeapää 1971, Paltto 1973). The grand inter-Nordic or even global conceptions of the movement have tended to ignore the more mundane problems of everyday life in remote Lappish communities, and it has therefore had some difficulty in making its views relevant on the local level.

A major concern for the movement has been to arrive at a coherent definition of the status of the Lappish minority that could form a basis for its constitutional recognition, and that would be acceptable both to national governments and to the Lappish people themselves. Discussions on this question tend to become locked in an intractable paradox with regard to the articulation of the ethnic boundary. On the one hand, there is a desire to maintain the ' true standards ' of a distinctively Lappish way of life, on the other hand boundaries are to be kept open such that Lapps can partake on an equal footing with other groups in a plural form of society. To add to this difficulty is the awkward realization that ethnic identification is a subjective matter, and that a person will not present himself as a Lapp merely because he has been defined as one on the basis of purely ascriptive criteria. These problems have acted as a stumbling block for the ideologues of the Lappish movement throughout its history, and a wealth of devious verbal attempts to surmount it are to be found in the chronicles of debate on the minority question.[1] Two central concerns in this debate have been the adequacy of language as a definitive criterion, and the place of the reindeer economy in traditional culture.

Any legally acceptable definition of minority status must begin with a precise answer to the question: 'Who is a Lapp?'; an enigma which has sorely taxed the ingenuity of the movement's ideologues. The 1971 Finnish State Commission on Lapp affairs began its draft of a prototype 'Lappish Constitution' with the following clause: 'A Lapp is a person who, or of whose parents or grandparents at least one, has learnt Lappish as his/her first language, according to the survey conducted in 1962 by the Nordic Lapp Council. A Lapp is also a person of whose parents or grandparents at least one is a Lapp according to the above.' (KM 1973, 46: 185, trans.)

The NLC survey, the most accurate count of Finnish Lapps to date, recorded a total of 3582, on the criteria of the first sentence of the above definition. However, of these only 3001 considered themselves to be Lapps, and only 2789 could actually speak some form of Lappish (E. Nickul 1968, Asp 1966). In future generations this last number is expected to diminish, whereas the total number of 'Lapps' would, according to the second sentence of the definition, multiply through bilateral transmission, irrespective of language use.

The definition proposed by the Commission, which follows a widely accepted formula, is thus self-contradictory, cloaking the inevitable paradox between ethnic purity and pluralism. The Lapps are presented as a linguistic minority, yet some 25 per cent of the population so defined cannot today speak the language, and an even greater proportion never use it. The purpose of the definition is evidently to 'renationalize' the large and increasing numbers who have left the exclusively Lappish milieu to enjoy the benefits of participation in the wider society, together with their descendants, on the basis of the linguistic competence of their ancestors (von Bonsdorff *in* Hill and Nickul 1969: 33-4).

The movement is likewise concerned that, as part of the process of what is called 'active readjustment' to the modern era, Lapps should be admitted to the entire range of occupations on which modern society depends for its functioning. As one learned Norwegian ethnologist put it, in a comment that aptly illustrates the plane of reified abstraction on which the debate is conducted: 'According to the second law of thermodynamics, Lappish Culture will die if it is restricted to reindeer husbandry.' (Hill and Nickul 1969: 105). Nevertheless, discussions of the minority question have always had a tendency to become 'hooked' on the subject of reindeer pastoralism: a fact that has often puzzled and even embarrassed the ideologues themselves. They have found it necessary to make repeated assertions to the effect that reindeer pastoralism is a rock foundation without which the whole monument of 'Lapp Culture' would collapse, whilst at the same time advocating occupational diversity. This is all the more remarkable when ample evidence exists to demonstrate that pastoralism in fact originated only a few centuries ago as a response to the pressure of colonization, and that today it represents a principal source of livelihood for at most 20 per cent of the Lappish population, broadly defined.

The reasons for the exaggerated significance attached to reindeer pastoralism, though nowhere made explicit, are not hard to identify. For one thing, it is the only economic adaptation that has ever been *exclusive* to the indigenous population, whereas hunting, gathering, fishing and farming have been commonly practised by other groups as well as by the Lapps themselves, and extend over a far greater territory than that covered by the Lappish population. Exploitation of the reindeer has therefore formed the basis for a distinctively Lappish way of life, together with a host of items of material culture including dwellings, clothing, and all kinds of everyday hardware, which constitute an invaluable pool of items for those in search of ethnic symbols. Without reindeer pastoralism, the pool would simply dry up, and the Lappish movement would be put out of business.

Besides, the present habitat of the reindeer corresponds more closely than that of any other animal or plant species of primary economic value to the territory with which Lapps are associated as the indigenous population. Thus, through the reindeer, a connection may be established between population and territory. Through language, a connection is established between population and culture; and again through the reindeer, the culture is provided with an economic and territorial foundation. Together, these two crucial elements, the Lappish language and the reindeer economy, bind together the three components of population, culture and environment on the level of theory into the kind of quasi-autonomous system that the Lappish movement aims to realize in practice. Remove either of these elements, and this whole conceptual construct, on which the rest of pan-Lappish ideology is built, falls apart.

For these reasons, therefore, the movement has found it necessary to present the Lapps as a linguistic minority although a large proportion do not speak the language, and to assert that 'Lapp Culture' rests on reindeer management although the majority do not practise it. Combined, these two basic contradictions define a core of genuinely 'traditional Lapps': pastoralists occupying aboriginal territory, speaking only Lappish, and practising an assortment of culture traits such as wearing Lapp costume, living in tents and turf huts, drinking reindeer milk, and singing traditional songs. Whether such culturally fossilized characters actually exist is beside the point. What the ideology attempts is to nurture a vision of 'pure

The minority culture

Lappishness', and then, by reference back to the past, to ' pick up ' the large number of those of Lappish descent doing none of these traditional things, providing them with an identity anchored on this vision. Thus, Lapps can participate fully in the wider society, whilst at the same time being able to claim cultural incorporation. It is of course for the ideologues of the Lappish movement themselves, many of whom are successful practitioners in education, law, commerce and administration, that the establishment of such a claim is most important.

The role of the protagonist

Right from the start, a disjunction has existed between the ideological constructs of the Lappish movement and the perceptions of people ' on the ground ' in local communities: between theories of culture and the day-to-day business of living it out. The ideologues, with established careers outside the local context, are able to look back on it from a holistic and generalized external perspective: a view which is not obtainable for the less privileged whose lives are constrained within this context. Indeed, the projection of the Lapps as constituting a ' minority culture ' systematically distorts their actual experience as members of local communities. The search for minority problems has thus become the self-fulfilling pre-occupation of an expanding body of commentators occupying a peripheral zone enclosing Lappish societies but insulated from them by an ideological barrier to penetration.

Moreover, the contradictions and reifications inherent in pan-Lappish idioms defy practical application. The codification of these idioms takes place through a confusion of underlying assumptions and nominal definitions with objective fact. ' Lapps ' and ' Lapp Culture ' appear to take on an existence independent of the assertions made about them, and are then held to provide empirical foundation for these assertions. In other words, statements are incorporated in the jargon of debate on the minority question at the point when their logic becomes tautologous. From then on, the whole pan-Lappish ideology, like a balloon, can support itself, and rise to ever more rarified heights of abstraction, without further reference to the ' facts '.

Given this initial disjunction between local level experience and the constructs of ideology, the latter have a natural tendency to expand in generality. The Lappish movement attempts to justify its demands for minority recognition by reference to moral principles to which national governments are said to have paid only lip service (Eidheim 1971: 48). Such moral principles, by their very nature, cannot be justified by resort to ' facts ', but only by reference to a yet more generalized level. Thus, frequent reference is made to the Charter of the United Nations, to which the Nordic governments supposedly subscribe, and in particular to Article 73 of this charter, which pledges nations to work towards the cultural, social, political and economic advancement of dependant peoples of territories they control; and to develop institutions of self-government for these peoples (United Nations 1945: XI, 23–4). Moral principles of world-wide application and great ambiguity are thereby brought to bear on a problem that referred originally only to northern Scandinavia.

At the same time, new concepts such as ' Third World ' and ' Neocolonialism ' crop up in the argument; the Lapp Question is connected with the fate of American Indians, the Negro problem, and Black Africa's struggle against colonial domination. Fashionable ' big-names ', from Jomo Kenyatta to Claude Lévi-Strauss, are dropped with increasing frequency (Nordiska Udredningsserie 1969: 141, 157). The academic world, not least social anthropology, provides a wealth of tricky general concepts which are eagerly absorbed: culture, ethnicity, pluralism, identity, assimilation, stigma, complementarity, marginality. Even the development of ' cognitive anthropology ' in the United States is hailed as ' proving ' that Lapps are not culturally inferior to other Europeans.

In this manner, the jargon of the Lappish movement becomes increasingly theoretical and decreasingly meaningful in the local context, advancing along this continuum by absorbing ever more general items which may be of wholly unconnected derivation. A niche is in this way cut out for a kind of middleman whose task it is to bring pan-Lappish ideology down to the people ' on the ground ', and to translate it into concepts more familiar to local experience. I call this middleman a *protagonist,* and the activity in which he engages I call *focusing* (Ingold 1974a). The more ' out of focus ' the ideology becomes, the more formidable is his task, but the greater is his latitude of interpretation.

The protagonist's calling is in many ways a thankless one. The 'apathy' and ' passivity ' of Lapps in local communities is an oft-heard refrain: a sure indication of loss of focus and translation failure. Regarded by dominant sectors of society as ' bungling products of culture contact ' (Eidheim 1971: 42), and frequently suffering from identity crises of their own, Lappish protagonists have found themselves misunderstood and distrusted by their own people. Many have been led to cloak their failure behind a facade of publicity; as the protagonist who, on a television programme, arranged for a ' genuine ' Lapp, apparently unable to express himself in the majority language, to deliver a prepared speech in Lappish concerning minority rights and the United Nations Charter, which was then ' interpreted ', word for word, for the benefit of the audience. In this, as in countless similar examples, an ideology projected from above was presented in the media as a spontaneous reaction from below.

The double-inversion effect

Despite a certain lack of realism, the impact of the Lappish movement in Finland in recent years has been considerable, and its claims have attracted widespread sympathy. Minority cultures have become a fashionable subject of liberal debate. A succession of ' cultural ' events, seminars and conferences have been accorded a great deal of publicity on radio and television, and in both provincial and national newspapers. The favourable reception given to the report of the State Commission on Lappish Education (KM 1971, B63) was regarded as a major achievement for the movement, as was the establishment in 1971 of a commission to look into the whole constitutional, economic and social position of Lapps in Finland. A ' Lappish Culture Week ' was held at Rovaniemi early in the same year as a prelude to the formation of the first ' central organization ' of Finnish Lapps (Suoma Samii Riihkaseärvi – SSRS), whose aim was to co-ordinate all organizations in Finland with a predominantly Lappish membership, including the northernmost reindeer associations and the Skolt assembly. Despite the big build-up of publicity, the impact of SSRS was spoilt by internal factionalism, and it never really got off the ground. On the inter-Nordic level, attention was drawn to the seventh pan-Lappish conference held at Gällivare, Sweden, in August 1971, and to plans to set up a Lappish Institute in the Norwegian Lapp centre of Kautokeino, to co-ordinate research and development and act as an information centre for the entire Lappish population.

Regular and profuse reports of this activity reached almost every Skolt household through extensive press and radio coverage; but despite the prominence given to the subject in the mass media, the Skolt reaction was almost entirely negative. Most professed ignorance of what it was all about, some declared that it had nothing to do with them, others complained that the ' big names' in the minority movement were merely using the Lapps as fodder for their political ambitions. The movement had brought no tangible benefits for the Skolts, and they did not expect any. Evidently, attempts to focus down onto the Skolt community have singularly failed. The reasons for this failure lie partly in the personal leadership style of the self-appointed Skolt protagonist, who is of course M, the headman; and partly in the limited extent to which the Skolts consider themselves to be Lapps at all.

No politician can hope to establish a base of local support solely through his activities as a protagonist. If he is already securely established in some office of the wider society, grass-roots apathy may be of no consequence; whilst claims to successful focusing validated through the mass media may enhance his reputation in the more comprehensive framework of the Lappish movement. For the less well-founded, however, protagonistic ideals must be compromised by an element of political brokerage which can be seen to bring positive local benefits. Support so gained may provide the politician with a foothold from which to project an image of his role as a protagonist in the service of the Lappish movement.

This, in effect, is what M has done, above all through his management of the community assembly. His prepared agendas for assembly meetings tend to be a mixed bag of pragmatic items concerning negotiations with the bureaucracy and more theoretical notions carried back from the Lappish movement. Thus, in a rather poorly attended meeting in 1971, the local audience was not at all interested in hearing a report from their headman on the Nordic Lapp Conference at Gällivare, nor about the

founding of SSRS (to which a non-Skolt was appointed as a delegate),
nor even about the report of the State Commission on Lappish Education.
On the other hand, more concrete matters such as electrification, settlement planning and tourism raised vigorous discussion.

Likewise, many of the 'Skolt demands' which M brings up in meetings
of the assembly are scaled-down versions of pan-Lappish ideology with
'Skolt' substituted for Lapp. The general lack of interest in these demands
is invariably registered as 'unanimous approval' in the minute-book, and
in the press. Since M is known locally as a political operator in the external
field, no more credibility is accorded to his 'demands' than to his widely
promulgated autobiographies of cultural authenticity. It is assumed that
his public statements are motivated by self-interest rather than missionary
zeal. The necessity to obtain local support through brokerage has therefore
undermined his effectiveness as a protagonist.

However, the problem goes deeper than this, owing to the special position
of the Skolts as members of a resettled community. This has brought them
simultaneously into a relationship of dependency on the Finnish government,
and into one of opposition to their immediate Lappish neighbours in the
strictly local arena of reindeer politics. As in the formation of Näätämö
paliskunta, an advantage gained from the former may be applied with effect
in the latter. In his capacity as a broker with Finnish officials, M therefore
represents the absolute opposition between Skolt and Lappish interests.
The Lappish movement, however, includes the Skolts as a sub-category of
Lapps on the basis of cultural similarity, and tends to make appeal not
directly to national governments but to international opinion, even to the
United Nations. In other words, whereas from the internal perspective, in
terms of which ethnic boundaries demarcate competing interest groups, the
Skolt/Lapp distinction is absolute; from the external perspective, in terms
of which ethnic boundaries are those of culture, the distinction is only a
relative one. Therefore in his capacity as a protagonist, M is led to equate
the Skolt predicament with that of the Lapps in general.

This triple contradiction in M's position, as a peripheral broker in the
eyes of the community, as an authentic representative carrying Skolt
opinion 'upwards' in the eyes of officialdom, and as a protagonist focusing
the pan-Lappish ideology 'downwards' in the eyes of the minority movement, was nowhere better illustrated than in a meeting of the community
assembly in 1972, in which he proposed that Skolts should cease to be
called by that name but by their own term in the native language: *Sääem.*
He explained that studies in linguistic history had revealed the origins of
the word Skolt (Fin. *koltta*) as a term of abuse, with roots in Norwegian
and English. Skolts, he said, should have the right to call themselves by
their own name. This is an exact translation of a widely accepted item of
pan-Lappish ideology which states that *Lapp* is a word of abuse and should
be replaced by the native term, *Sami.*

At first, M's suggestion was greeted by silence: much of his audience
was paying no attention at the time. Then, one younger and fairly artic-

ulate Skolt pointed out that the term *koltta* had been used for a long time with no apparent abusive connotation. He thought the proposal would generate confusion since the Skolt *Sääem* and Lapp *Sami* would be mixed up. Indeed, *Sääem* and *Sami* are equivalent words in the two closely related languages, both referring, in effect, to ' our people ', as opposed to outsiders. Despite the objection, the resolution was carried ' unanimously ', and head-lines in the provincial newspaper the next day declared: ' The word " Skolt " does not tell the truth – SÄÄEM in its place. Skolt headman M has demon-strated this in connection with language research.'

Several Skolts who remained silent or inattentive at the meeting were angry to read the headline. For them it was equivalent to eliminating the distinction between Skolts and Lapps: a symbolic denial of the separate existence of a Skolt community, which would prejudice its special relation-ship with the authorities and play into the hands of its Lappish adversaries. M's attempt to translate pan-Lappish ideology was interpreted as a sell-out. The attempt, and others like it, was thus subverted by what could be called a double-inversion effect. The Skolts form a minority *within* a minority: for every Skolt there are ten Finnish Lapps and ten thousand Finns. In order to protect itself from immediate domination, the Skolt community appeals to the very agency that the Lappish movement is appealing against: namely, national government.

The Lapp Parliament

One of the immediate tasks of the Finnish State Commission on Lapp Affairs was to devise a parallel system of representation for the Lappish population. The idea of a Lapp Parliament was first mentioned shortly after the commission was instituted in summer 1971, and trial elections, organized under the commission's direction, were planned for October 1972. The parliament was to have twenty elected members, with a mini-mum of three from each of the three northernmost communes of Inari, Utsjoki and Enontekiö, and from Vuotso parish in the north of Sodankylä Commune, which together constitute the ' Lapp Area ' of Finland (Ingold 1973: 810). All adult Lapps, as defined by the criterion of linguistic ancestry, were entitled to vote, as were their spouses if not Lappish. The electorate comprised 2549 persons, so defined. Voting was to take place by post, in order to overcome the problem of scattered and remote settle-ment. There was to be no reference to political parties, candidates being elected entirely on the basis of popularity ranking.

The commission went to enormous trouble to publicize the forthcoming election: yet even immediately beforehand a large part of the electorate, including many Skolts, knew nothing about it. In the event, however, 82 per cent voted: a remarkably high proportion for any election. Four of the forty-three candidates were Skolts, including the headman M and the recently elected councillor A. All four were elected, putting the Skolts in a strong position on the parliament. It was remarkable that A, who had recently polled so well in the Commune elections, received relatively few votes, whereas M came second only in overall popularity.

Although the electoral procedure has been satisfactorily tested, the formal capacity of the parliament remains somewhat unclear. In its report, submitted in 1973 (KM 1973, 46), the commission proposed that besides monitoring the general social, economic and cultural affairs of the Lappish population, the parliament would be empowered to control the usufruct of all renewable natural resources on State-owned land and water within the Lapp Area. These resources would be reserved for the Lapps, and 'outsiders' would be allowed to benefit from them only by permission of the parliament. In view of the many non-Lappish interests in the area, both public and private, this proposal is unlikely to pass without considerable opposition.

In some respects, the commission's proposals resemble the leap-frog strategy writ large. The parliament would come directly under central government, and would bypass decision-making at Commune level on matters specifically connected with the legal protection of the minority, defined *outside* the field of party politics. Likewise, the 'Lapp Area' resembles an enormous reservation in which usufruct privileges would be reserved for the Lappish population. The overwhelming vote for characters such as M, reputed for negotiating ability rather than representativeness, suggests that the electorate shared this impression. On the other hand, as a decision-making body itself, the parliament would go a long way towards increasing the overall representativeness of Lappish politics, providing a forum in which Lappish communities could settle their internal differences, whilst bringing the Lappish movement as a whole into rather more close touch with reality.

The idea of a separate Lappish constitution raises in acute form the whole question of the extent to which it is possible by legislative means to bring a historically disadvantaged minority onto a level of equality with other sectors of society, without automatically granting outright privileges. On a much smaller scale, this problem has already become apparent in the special treatment accorded to the Skolt community. In this case, legislation aimed at equalization was interpreted as a charter of ethnic privilege. Similarly, a constitution designed to protect Lappish interests within a defined territory would, in effect, turn the remaining inhabitants of this territory, who constitute a majority of 70 per cent of its population, into second-class citizens, Though admittedly of colonist origin, the Finnish inhabitants of the 'Lapp Area' are often no better provided for than the Lapps themselves, and are subject to many of the same problems of economic hardship, inadequate service provision and physical isolation. Indeed, there is virtually no congruence today between the boundaries of disadvantage and of Lappish linguistic ancestry. The latter, applied in practice, would create quite arbitrary divisions, since it bears no relation to occupational or residential criteria, nor even to that of present-day language use.

It could moreover be argued that the disadvantages from which Lapps have suffered in the past are social and economic handicaps most of which, given sufficient political will, can be put right within the existing constitutional framework, and in such a way as to reach all and only those citizens so handicapped, regardless of linguistic ancestry. If the existence of a minority is defined in terms of a particular problem or problems from which that minority suffers, then is not the constitutional enshrinement of minority status a formula for the perpetuation of these problems, benefitting only those who make it their business to alleviate them? To the extent that such problems are curable, the legitimacy of including 'minority cultures' as a part of the social order envisaged for the future is highly debatable.

22 Culture and community

Culture and community

The minority culture and the cultural minority

It is generally assumed that where there exists a minority, there must, logically, exist a majority in opposition to which the minority is defined. Yet those who speak of ' Lapp (or Skolt) Culture ', whilst in no doubt about the identity of the minority in question, are surprisingly vague when it comes to the specification of the majority. This elusive entity has, on various occasions, passed as ' Finnish ' (or ' Norwegian ' or ' Swedish '), ' Scandinavian ', ' European' and ' Western '. As a rule, the identity of the majority appears both irrelevant to the argument and too obvious to require precise definition. In this section, I shall show that far from having any objective existence in contraposition to a majority, the source of the ' minority culture ' lies in the minds of a rather small elite who can establish some connection with the Lappish milieu but whose values, couched in terms of extreme generality, are of wholly external derivation. What the ' minority culture ' presupposes, then, is not a majority culture, but a collection of individuals for whom the pursuit of culture forms an important criterion of personal achievement: the ' cultural minority '.

To begin, let us examine the meaning of the term ' culture ' more closely. Our concern is not with the many and various connotations of the term to be found in the literature of scholarly research, but with its implicit significance as a fundamental criterion of bourgeois discourse. Few terms on this level of abstraction can have diffused so effectively into the working vocabularies of wealthy, educated elites of practically every nation in the modern world, and few can be employed with such remarkable consistency in contexts so heterogeneous. In everyday usage, ' culture ' may refer to one of three things. Of individuals, it signifies ' the training and refinement of mind, tastes and manners' (OED): one of the most important criteria of rank among the middle-classes. Of civilization, it signifies the cumulative store of expressive works preserved in the form of literature, art, music, and so on. Of a people, it signifies a conception of their way of life viewed *from the outside* as an integrated totality, including a catalogue of diverse traits from traditional or ancient customs and beliefs to food, shelter, and bits and pieces of material equipment. These latter two meanings share in common the audience or observer perspective.

Now these apparently divergent usages are in fact closely related, for a man may invest himself with culture in the first sense by establishing claims to culture in the second or third senses. In other words, culture refers both to a goal – social refinement – and to the assets which may be applied to achieve that goal. An artist does not perceive his creativity as 'culture', nor does a people employ any such concept through which to view its everyday activities and aspirations. Culture is generated only when the principles expressed in everyday life are disconnected from the living processes of creation, and are reduced by an external projection to objects of value. It is through a reduction of this kind that the products of human creativity, discarded by their makers once they have served their practical or expressive purpose, enter the salerooms of collectors. In order to effect such a reduction, the culture-seeker must himself be dissociated from the creative process, distinguishing his own personal values and ambitions from those of the people whose activity he observes. A man cannot command that of which he is a part: thus he cannot possess culture so long as he himself is 'living' it. Having placed himself outside the way of life to which he refers, he can, as it were, seal it within a shell so that it may be regarded objectively as a unit entity, a thing that can be possessed. He does not belong to the culture, but the culture belongs to him.

Made to refer to a way of life, 'culture' conjures up a world from which the subjective, purposeful aspect of behaviour has been extracted. It is a world in which people, if they exist at all, are the unwitting slaves of custom and habit. As in the tourist's photograph, time and motion stand still. As action, consciousness and will are abstracted away, the values and principles that guide everyday life collapse into a residue of redundant skeletal remains in the form of a miscellany of objects and customs which are then available for collection by the connoisseurs of culture. Their concern for 'cultural preservation' follows automatically, for a skeleton from which the driving force has been extracted cannot support itself. Thus, the deliberate promotion of culture appears as a pursuit for outsiders and implies a degree of alienation at the cultural source itself.

The culture-seeker, almost by definition, belongs nowhere: he is for ever an observer looking in, one of a mass of individuals 'floating' in the interstices between more solidly anchored groups, attaching themselves first to one, then to another, and spreading the concept of culture as they go. Lacking, or having rejected, primordial attachments to any place or community, he is faced with an incessant quest for individual achievement measured in terms of abstract and indeterminate qualities of universal applicability. Having no tradition of his own, he is led into a parasitic existence, finding the means to self-expression by feeding off the symbols of others. No wonder, then, that he seeks to perpetuate them, for he is dependent on cultural continuity for his source of assets.

Briefly: those that 'live' culture, being encompassed within it, do not objectively perceive it as such; those that espouse culture reify it, make it their property, but do not live by its premises. Thus, the culture-concept has no place, and no equivalent, in the collective representations of local communities. Its origin lies among the cosmopolitan bourgeoisie, from where it reaches only as far as the 'border zone' of the local professional elites, a zone occupied by other outsiders from the same source who appear from time to time on the local scene: mass-media reporters in search of 'minority problems' or cultural exotica, politicians of the minority movement, casual researchers, charitable emissaries and tourists. For all these people, the culture represents a source of assets which can be applied in the pursuit of extra-cultural goals, be they occupational, political, educational, spiritual or recreational. Through culture-spectacles, they can observe and comprehend life 'on the ground' from the safety of their own preconceptions. Arriving with its bearers from outside, the minority-culture ideology rebounds from the periphery without penetrating the surface of community life.

Why, then, is 'way of life' culture invariably viewed in the minority? Clearly, in the absence of an objectively defined majority, this cannot be a mere matter of numbers. A clue is to be found in the characteristics of externality and generality epitomized in the concept of culture itself. The value perspective of the bourgeoisie, belonging nowhere, knows no frontiers. Given a view of such cosmopolitan dimensions, any way of life which is seen to be grounded in a limited environment will appear as a minority, on the basis of scale alone. Moreover, the idea of a minority suggests enclosure or encapsulation, indeed it reflects the very cognitive process whereby 'culture' is generated: the dissociation of the culture seeker's values from those of the people he observes, and the comprehension of the latter in the terms of the former. Finally, minority implies dependency: the dependency of peripheral communities on the modern system of administration and welfare, which has brought with it a host of professional statuses alien to the traditional order. It is above all the incumbents of these statuses who constitute the local culture-elites. Thus, the creation of minorities goes hand in hand with the spread of the formal apparatus of the State. In the next section, the position of the Skolt culture-elite, the professionals of Commune Point first introduced in chapter 17, will be examined more closely.

The ethnic affiliation of the local elite

It is possible to distinguish three kinds of social boundary which, given a history of population movement, may be attributed with an ethnic quality. In the first, the boundary demarcates a rigidly hierarchical distribution of ascribed power according to one or more of the major principles around which the society is organized. The existence of ethnic stratification on these lines is formally denied in Finland; although some Lappish spokesmen, acting in pursuit of political goals defined in the framework of the wider society, claim the real situation to be of this kind.[1] The second kind of boundary stems not from hierarchical division but from balanced segmental competition in which strategic ecological resources are differentially

distributed between competing groups. Here too, the element of competition implies at least one common principle which specifies the crucial
criterion for the determination of group membership. This is illustrated
locally by the disputes over pasture access in which the Skolts of Näätämö
paliskunta are continually involved with their Muddusjärvi-Lappish neighbours, representing ecological competition within a commonly accepted
framework of associational reindeer management. Boundaries are those of
associational territories, envisaged in the concrete form of the reindeer
fence; whilst historical differences recognized by the disputing parties
are significant as sources of ideological support rather than divergent
aspirations.

The third kind of boundary stems from the *absence* of shared principles
or scales of value: the inability to establish common assumptions restricts
interaction across the boundary to narrowly defined asymmetrical transactions, and thereby contributes to its maintenance.[2] This has become
evident within the Skolt community through the importation of an entirely
new set of values, defining a style of life which in its most prominent
aspects represents an exclusive alternative to the traditional. For example,
income-based status-ranking is incompatible with the ethos of traditional
pastoralism, whilst the elite style of Commune Point residents has been
shown to represent the point for point opposite of that of the Skolt neighbourhood. The importers belong to the professional bourgeoisie, those who
typically follow ' spiralist ' careers according to which occupational promotion entails residential mobility. The values they hold and the professions
they represent are therefore distributed on a nation-wide scale, but have
their origins in the relatively affluent and cosmopolitan South. Their arrival
in the community marks the practical extension of the ' Welfare State ' to
its most remote territorial margins.

Owing to the absence of shared values and common assumptions, contacts between immigrants and Skolts tend to be limited to those in which
the former are involved in a strictly professional capacity. A social boundary
is clearly evident here, but the extent to which it can be considered to be
ethnic is problematic. The Skolts themselves regard immigrants – both
professionals and merchants – as an assortment of individuals, distinguished
from one another on personal and occupational grounds, rather than
designating them as representatives of a particular ethnic category. In the
case of the merchants, exclusion follows from the operation of brokerage.
For professionals, the situation is different. Formally, professional status
is ethnically neutral. Access is not denied to the Skolts, nor are there any
rules specifying or limiting those statuses which Skolts could occupy. In
practice, owing to linguistically and regionally differential access to
educational resources, the majority are occupied by immigrants of Finnish
background. However, of these immigrants, some are self-consciously
seeking Skolt ethnic incorporation; for example through marriage with
Skolts, attempts to learn the Skolt language, and the adoption of Skolt
handicraft techniques. In the contrary direction, Skolt aspirants to bour-

geois values appear to be able to adopt them in place of the traditional
without rejection of ethnic identity. In the former case, immigrants retain
their values but seek to adopt a new ethnic identity; in the latter case,
members of the native Skolt elite aspire to new values, but retain their
ethnic identity. In both instances, the attempt to effect a transfer leads
to an explicit espousal of 'Skoltness', expressed not in the traditional form
of support in opposition to Lappish rivals in the local field of reindeer
politics, but from an external perspective in terms of Lappish cultural
affiliation.

The achievement of the elite is to have established Skolt or Lapp
'culture' on an equivalent and comparable level with Finnish ethnic
symbols, themselves derived in a similar fashion from the traditional
rural background. Everyday utensils are classified as arts and crafts,
beliefs once viewed as superstitions are valued as folklore, fishing-cabins
become summer-cottages. This re-evaluation is an example of what
Eidheim (1971: 79) calls *idiomatic complementarization,* through which
Lappish ethnic symbols are allowed to qualify as 'culture' alongside their
Finnish equivalents. The establishment of complementarity is a product of
the political campaign on behalf of 'minority cultures', and has reached
general acceptance only in the last few years.

In order to invest in culture, the individual whose own value perspective
is of external derivation must establish a connection with it. 'Culture' in
the form of art, literature and so on may be bought and sold on the
market. 'Way-of-life' culture may also be purchased, for example through
handicraft sales. Such transactions do not, however, form a basis for
cultural *membership.* An exclusive entitlement to the extraction and use
of cultural material may be established in only two possible ways: through
links of descent from, or marriage to, human subjects of the culture-source
itself.

Lack of educational prerequisites has so far prevented those of native
Skolt descent from reaching all but the lower echelons of occupational
status. For this reason, intermarriages between Skolts and immigrant
professionals form the basis of the local culture-elite. In these marriages,
it is the immigrant spouse who is concerned to gain access to the culture-
resource, and who is therefore most self-consciously explicit in the adoption and display of cultural symbols, encouraging the Skolt partner to
present himself, especially in extra-community contexts, in a suitably
genuine fashion. For the Skolt spouse, who is well aware of the realities
and limitations of life in the 'traditional' community, marriage to
professionals gives access to other bourgeois value resources, which are
not otherwise available on the local level. Mixed marriage represents one
solution to a basic dilemma facing the Skolt youth, presented on the one
hand with an image of the social refinement of 'culture-Finland', desirable
but locally inaccessible, and on the other hand with a strong attachment
to home.

It is not an easy solution for either party. The immigrant spouse may expect to meet disapproval from own kin hoping for a marriage on the same or on a higher status level and perhaps holding ethnic prejudices, whilst relations with Skolt in-laws are strained by the lack of common value understandings. Similarly, the Skolt spouse may be spurned by his kin, for although local, the match represents an outmarriage and a negation of community values. Moving into Commune Point, he becomes socially marginal and residentially separate. However, the transfer remains only partial: the Skolt neighbourhood remains as a backstage to which he may retreat as though he were an unmarried youth. Thus, he feels most intensely the strain of divided loyalties and the ambivalence of a commitment to two quite different sets of values demanding strongly contrastive styles of self-presentation. This strain is also indicative of the contrary aspirations of the marriage partners: the immigrant seeking entry into what is perceived as a culture without giving up imported value scales, the Skolt seeking a way out of the limitations of local community values without entirely being able or prepared to reject them.

The position of the culture-elite entails one further anomaly. Traditionally, in the days of hunting and fishing, Skolt values were strongly egalitarian. Unlike the wealthy nomadic Lappish pastoralists, they did not accumulate riches in the form of articles of cloth, gold and silver. Consequently, there is a dearth of symbolic material whereby elite status may be expressed in native cultural idioms. For those seeking cultural incorporation, the only alternative is to adopt complementarized high-status nomad-Lapp symbols in place of Finnish equivalents. Thus, on special occasions, the Skolt culture-elite dresses in the traditional nomad costume, although posing as Skolts, not Lapps. In two mixed marriages, the costume was worn by both bride and groom for the wedding, the costly ornaments having been purchased from Norwegian shops. This use of symbols, though inappropriate from a locally-centred perspective, is however entirely consistent with the external, cultural approach, according to which Skolt culture is only a variation on a Lappish theme.

It is revealing to compare the local culture-elite with their polar opposites, periodic labour migrants. The value orientations of the migrant remain rooted in the local community perspective, but he has to leave in order to collect the resources necessary to realize these values. Living from a suitcase in barrack accommodation, he entertains a dream of enjoying the fruits of his labours at home, even though he may never return. The two worlds of home and work-place, the former the locus of values, the latter the locus of resources, are kept strictly apart. Outwardly, he would appear wholly 'assimilated' into the urban proletariat, yet on his return home he is instantly incorporated into the community, as though he had never left. Likewise for the culture-elite, the loci of values and resources are exactly separate; but whereas their values are of external derivation, the resources on which they depend, including a regular salary and access to 'Skolt Culture', are available locally. Whilst displaying ethnic symbols as a strategy for the management of identity, they remain socially marginal to the community.

The Skolts: minority culture or peripheral community?

Throughout this study I have referred to the Skolts as members of a community rather than as representatives of a culture. This follows from an approach emphasising action alternatives recognized by the Skolts themselves in their daily lives rather than cognitive traditions which, after the upheavals of the last few decades, have lost both meaning and coherence, remaining as nostalgic memories of times past. The present-day Skolt approaches the world empirically, pragmatically and independently, each free to find his own solutions in his own way. The result is an enormous variety of attitudes and responses to changing environmental conditions.

If, as has been the general trend in contemporary discussions of the ' Lapp Question ', it had been assumed as an initial premise that the Skolts constitute a ' minority culture ', problems of social change would have been posed in a different form, requiring a different kind of answer. Rather than viewing the individual as an independent decision-maker coping with relatively mundane but often demanding situations of life in a marginal, physically isolated and unproductive region, he is seen as the victim of the attack of an aggressive dominant culture on a weak, sensitive minority. As the active forces are lifted to the plane of culture, so the problems are embedded on the psychological level: the individual is faced not with situations of conscious choice but with largely unformulated crises of identity.

For the understanding of certain linguistic and social psychological aspects of assimilation, particularly in the field of education, this perspective may be valid. However, it is a perspective which denies the relevance of actor models, leading to a concentration on unperceived (subconscious) problems in terms of an unperceived (culture) framework. The results are therefore liable to be no more than a projection of the researcher's own external ideology. Applied to the field of social and economic action, the minority culture perspective would assume that social change amongst the Skolts differs fundamentally in kind from that among similarly peripheral communities of the majority population. This is by no means entirely the case. With respect to many aspects of social change covered in this study, developments in the Skolt community reflect a pattern typical of northern and eastern Finland, which stems not from the ethnic diferences but from regional underdevelopment following from the concentration of political and economic power in the South. The Skolts may represent an extreme case; owing to their prolonged isolation they are experiencing in a few decades developments that in other parts have taken nearer a century. The difference, however, is one of degree, not of kind.

For example, patterns of migration are related to the distribution of employment and welfare, which applies to members of peripheral communities whatever their ethnic affiliation. In this respect Skolts differ only in being educationally disadvantaged, not having received schooling in their mother-tongue. The transition from traditional to modern exhibited in new material equipment, styles of life and value horizons is everywhere evident, though this transition has been relatively more abrupt among the Skolts. To attach different cultural labels to the old and the new and to regard modernization consequently as acculturation would be to affirm the view of culture as an entirely static tradition and to deny that similar developments are taking place *within* the majority population itself.

Further, many of the developments which have crucially affected Skolt fortunes stem from internal processes, catalysed perhaps by resource or value inputs from outside, but hardly brought about through direct external interference. Thus, the transformation of the Skolt reindeer economy, which has parallels in other parts of Lapland under comparable environmental conditions, was a result of the mounting contradiction between the social relations of pastoralism and its ecological foundations. The shift to a money economy, attested by the commercialization of reindeer management, the adoption of the snowmobile, and the resort to casual labour and welfare, though bringing a greater dependence on the institutions of the wider society, may be related to this internal transformation.

To the extent that social change cannot be understood as a process of culture-contact, solutions to the practical problems thrown up by change cannot be found in culturally specific policy. To allocate resources differentially on ethnic grounds would be to put the recipient group into even greater welfare dependence on remote bureaucratic organs; diminishing its political bargaining strength in competition for local resources and aggravating inter-ethnic tensions on the local level where the immediate impact of such policy would be felt. Local disputes hinder the united presentation of demands to the administration and guarantee the persistence of under-development (Brox 1972, Ingold 1973).

The future of an exclusively Skolt community is threatened not so much by acculturation, as by coldly logistic viability factors. At all levels of inclusion, demographic and resource factors set upper and lower limits to the scale of operation of social institutions specific to particular levels. In many crucial respects, the size of the Skolt community, in terms of the population and the resources under its control, lies below the critical level for institutional autonomy. Thus, the Skolts do not control a sufficiently large and diversified pasture range to form a viable reindeer-management unit. Demographically, even allowing for a reversal in migration patterns, the community is too small to form an endogamous unit under modern conditions of increasing mobility and free choice. Mixed marriages, in turn, threaten linguistic continuity. There are not enough school-children to justify a separate school beyond the primary level, and its future may even be called into question if the child population continues to drop during the next decade or two. On logistic grounds, the future of the Skolt community therefore appears unpromising. Autonomy can be bought only at the expense of resource dependence on higher levels through a leap-frog strategy, which ultimately impedes development by placing the community at a handicap in its relations with the wider society.

Apart from the possible loss of ethnic exclusiveness, future developments are scarcely possible to predict. Seen from the perspective of a small and marginal community, events witnessed on higher levels as minor aspects of a larger, gradually evolving design may appear on the local level as sporadic parametric alterations in the premises of local life. The oscillations of the East–West pendulum of European politics, the development of technology and the expansion of the communications network appear on the local level in the form of evacuation and resettlement, the advent of the snowmobile, and the construction of the road: all datable, step-wise events that have constrained and structured local responses. Each parametric step of this kind imposes a division into those for whom new opportunities are opened up for realizing the values they hold, and those who find their opportunities blocked and are forced to compromise. The search for solutions may, in turn, lead to the formulation or adoption of new scales of value.

It seems rather fruitless to be overly concerned that the community should persist as an exclusive reserve of Skolt culture. The implementation of such a view would mean laying down in advance the constituent attributes of culture, investing the available resources to ensure a repetitive, traditional performance. The effect of blocking local but non-traditional alternatives would be to hasten cultural collapse through the emigration of personnel and stagnation among those left at home (Brox 1973). More important is that the groundwork be laid through overall policies of regional development for a sound economy in the community, which would allow opportunities for constructive self-expression and personal fulfilment according to values held by the people themselves. It is up to them either to follow a preconceived image of culture, or to branch out in new directions. Whether or not the people of the future community will be regarded as culturally Skolt, or will consider themselves so, is for our present purposes beside the point. Individuals create, cultural labels can be applied only retrospectively.

Notes

Notes to chapter 1

1 This Lappish word appears in numerous different spellings in the literature, owing to orthographic and dialectical variation. The spelling adopted here is the conventional Finnish form.

Notes to chapter 2

1 Owing to the lack of a suitable English terminology, it has been necessary to substitute bovine terms.
2 The term *separation* (Fin. *erotus*) is used throughout to refer to these events.
3 This term referred originally to the wild deer.

Notes to chapter 3

1 The term 'snowmobile' is adopted to conform with established usage. The machine is known by many other names, for example 'snow-scooter', 'motor-sledge', and the brand-names 'Ski-doo', 'Sno-Tric', etc. Reindeermen have nicknamed it the 'tinplate gelding' (Fin. *peltipailakka*). The snowmobile should not be confused with the larger 'snow-cats' that have been used in the North for post and passenger services and for military purposes.
2 Pelto and his associates have studied the impact of the snowmobile in reindeer management with special reference to the Skolt area. Their material, based on brief field-trips in spring 1967 and summer 1971, gives a useful picture of the state of affairs right in the midst of the transition. Müller-Wille has made a comparable study of the Utsjoki area, based on fieldwork in 1968–9 and 1971–2. Their results appear in a number of publications of more or less similar content (Pelto, Linkola and Sammallahti 1969, Müller-Wille 1971, Müller-Wille and Aikio 1971, Müller-Wille and Pelto 1971, Linkola 1973, Pelto 1973, Pelto and Müller-Wille 1973). Hall (1971) and Smith (1972) have made comparative studies of snowmobile adoption in the Canadian arctic; and Canadian and Lappish materials are compared by Pelto and Müller-Wille (1972).
3 The intensive/extensive distinction is adopted from Paine (1972).

Notes to chapter 4

1 These figures are derived from the official annual association lists of

recorded holdings per owner, filed in the archives of the Reindeer Associations' Union at Rovaniemi.
2 Possession of a reindeer mark is a formal prerequisite for the ownership of deer. A father who hopes that his sons will continue in reindeer management applies for marks for them when they are still small. Traditionally, children's marks were derived from their fathers' by the addition of extra cuts. Nowadays, as marks proliferate, it is not easy to find unique patterns, and a man may have to ask the help of a local expert in devising a new mark, which then has to be submitted to the association meeting and to the Reindeer Associations' Union for approval. Once a child has an earmark of his own, his father can build up for him the nucleus of a herd by putting the mark on a certain number of calves each year. Since a mark, once made, cannot be altered, and since the herd itself is nowadays scattered, appearing only as small random samples in separations, synchronic partition of the herd is impossible. A time-lag is inevitably involved in the system of inheritance, whose length is based on the life-span and reproduction rate of the deer.
3 For a diagrammatic representation of this picture, see Ingold (1974b: 533).

Notes to chapter 5

1 The career of M is examined in greater detail in ch. 18.
2 The remaining 3 per cent are owned by an assortment of non-resident members.
3 Here, I am adopting the distinction made by Paine (1972) between herding as 'the control and nurturance of animals in the terrain' and husbandry as 'the growth of capital and the formation of profit'. A preliminary discussion of these concepts is presented in an earlier paper by the same author (1965b).

Notes to chapter 7

1 My information on cone-gathering is indirect, as my fieldwork was already concluded at the time.

Notes to chapter 8

1 The announcement, in 1974, that the Sevettijärvi Trading and Tourist Centre was to be sold to the owner of the 'general stores' exemplifies the complete reversals of fortune that characterize local commercial histories.
2 A study of the career choices of a sample of Lappish male school-leavers indicated that the frontier patrol ranked second only to the most popular fields of machine engineering (Vaarama 1973).

Notes to chapter 9

1 'Able-bodied' males are defined as those over sixteen years of age not receiving retirement or disablement pensions. There are 102 Skolts in this category. For a comparison of age-distributions of active herders and men on the casual labour and unemployment circuit, see fig. 16. A

realistic percentage figure for other forms of casual labour cannot be given, as they involve only a transitory commitment.

Notes to chapter 10

1 The migrant may be distinguished from the emigrant as one who expects to return to the community at intervals, and finally upon retirement; whereas the emigrant never expects to return except perhaps for occasional holidays to see relatives back at home. In practice, it may only be possible to apply this distinction retrospectively.

Notes to chapter 11

1 The suffix *-järvi* is the Finnish term for 'lake'. In references to the neighbourhood it is commonly omitted, thus: Nitsi, Rautaperä, Sevetti, etc. This abbreviation will be adopted in the following chapters.

Notes to chapter 14

1 See also Pelto's discussion of male and female role behaviour (1962: 140–4, 148–51).
2 A somewhat similar interpretation has been offered by Robbins (1973), in a study of drinking behaviour among urbanized Naskapi in Quebec.

Notes to chapter 15

1 In a study of Skolt schoolchildren, Seitamo (1972) found that 58 per cent of girls enjoyed school, as against 24 per cent of boys. The figures for a comparative group of northern Finnish children were 87 per cent and 65 per cent respectively.

Notes to chapter 16

1 Reindeer information is typically presented in a highly oblique style. For an example, see Pelto (1962: 36–7).
2 A pseudonym. This neighbourhood is analysed in greater detail in Ingold (1975: ch. 16).

Notes to chapter 17

1 The difference between 'middle' and 'civic' school is comparable to that between British 'grammar' and 'secondary modern'. From autumn 1972, the system is changing to a comprehensive form. At present, an approximately equal number of pupils from Lapland as a whole follow each educational career. There are no pupils from the community currently attending 'senior-school'.
2 This kind of transition, from dispersed neighbourhood to concentrated village settlement, has been described in the context of Norwegian coast Lappish society by Paine (1960).

Notes to chapter 18

1 'Headman' is the closest rendering of the Skolt term. In Finnish, the office is most often referred to by the term *luottamusmies*, literally 'trusted man' or representative; sometimes also by the term *kylänvanhin*, 'village elder'.

Notes to chapter 19

1 The report was approved by the government, and its proposed amendments to the law relating to Skolts were passed by Parliament in 1974. Seventy-eight applications for plots in the two resettlement areas were received during the following year.

Notes to chapter 20

1 SMP was split by a leadership crisis in 1973, when the majority of members left to form a new 'People's Unity Party' (SKYP).

Notes to chapter 21

1 The principal sources for this debate are the proceedings of the pan-Lappish conferences held since 1953. The first four are collected in two volumes in English translation (Hill 1960, Hill and Nickul 1969). The proceedings of the fifth and the sixth conferences are published in Nordiska Udredningsserie (1965, 1969).

Notes to chapter 22

1 Thus, the 1971 State Commission on Lapp Affairs speaks of the 'historical and structural position of Lappish Culture in the societal power hierarchy.' (KM 1973, 46: 130, trans.)
2 I am drawing here on the discussion of Barth (1969), but my presentation differs in some respects from his.

Bibliography

Aikio, S. 1971. Saamelaisten juomatavoista. *Alkoholipolitiikka* 1971, 2: 61–65. Helsinki.

Alaruikka, Y. 1964. *Suomen porotalous.* Rovaniemi: Lapin maakuntapaino.

Asp, E. 1965. Lappalaiset ja Lappalaisuus. *Turun Yliopiston Julkaisuja* C, 2. Turku/Forssa.

Asp, E. 1966. The Finnicization of the Lapps: a case of acculturation. *Turun Yliopiston Julkaisuja* B, 100. Turku/Forssa.

Asp, E. 1968. Les Lapons finlandais d'aujourd'hui et leur différenciation. *Inter-Nord.* 10: 279–284. Centre d'études arctiques et finno-scandinaves, Sorbonne, Paris.

Asp, E. 1971. Suomen nykylappalaiset ja Lappalaisuuden erittyminen. *Kalevalaseuran Vuosikirja* 51. Helsinki: WSOY.

Barth, F. 1969. Introduction, in Barth, F. (ed.): *Ethnic groups and boundaries,* Bergen–Oslo: Universitetsforlaget, London: Allen & Unwin.

Brox, O. 1972. Sameproblemet som glesbygdsproblem, in *Strukturfascismen och andra essäer.* Uppsala: Verdandi Debatt nr. 65. Bokförlaget Prisma/ Föreningen Verdandi.

Brox, O. 1973. 'Conservation' and 'destruction' of traditional culture. pp. 39–44 in Berg, G. (ed.) *Circumpolar problems.* Oxford: Pergamon.

Dikkanen, S. L. 1965. Sirma. Residence and work organization in a Lappish-speaking community. *Samiske Samlinger* 8, Oslo.

Eidheim, H. 1958. Erverv og kulturkontakt i Polmak. *Samiske Samlinger* 4, 1. Oslo.

Eidheim, H. 1971. *Aspects of the Lappish minority situation.* Oslo: Universitetsforlaget.

Eriksson, A. W., D. Hughes and F. A. Milan (eds.) 1970. Health and biology of circumpolar human populations, Section 1: Proceedings of the IBP Scandinavian Human Adaptability Conference in Hurdal, Norway, 5th June 1969. *Arctic Anthropology* 7, 1. University of Wisconsin.

Espmark, Y. 1970. Poron käyttäytymismuotoja. *Poromies* 1970, 1: 6–9. Rovaniemi.

Forsius, H. 1973. The Finnish Skolt Lapp children: a child psychiatric study. *Acta Paediatrica Scandinavica.* Suppl. 239. Oulu.

Forsius, H. and Seitamo, L. 1970. Mental state of Skolt Lapp children: a preliminary report. *Arctic Anthropology* 7, 1: 6–8. University of Wisconsin.

Gjessing, G. 1954. *Changing Lapps: a study of culture relations in northernmost Norway* (Lond. Sch. Econ. Monogr. social Anthrop. 13). London: Bell.

Goodenough, W. H. 1964. Componential analysis of Könkämä Lapp kinship terminology. pp. 221–238 in Goodenough, W. H. (ed.) *Explorations in*

Bibliography

cultural anthropology. New York: McGraw-Hill.

Hall, E. S. 1971. The 'iron dog' in northern Alaska. *Anthropologica* (N.S.) 13: 237–254. Ottawa.

Hatt, G. 1919. Notes on reindeer nomadism. *Memoirs of the American Anthropological Association* 6, 2: 75–133.

Helle, R. 1966. An investigation of reindeer husbandry in Finland. *Acta Lapponica Fenniae* 5. Rovaniemi.

Higgs, E. S. and M. R. Jarman 1972. The origins of animal and plant husbandry. pp. 2–13 in Higgs (ed.) *Papers in economic prehistory.* Cambridge: University Press.

Hill, R. G. P. (ed.) 1960. *The Lapps today, in Finland, Norway and Sweden.* Bibl. arctique et antarctique 1. École pratique des hautes études, Sorbonne. Paris: Mouton.

Hill, R. G. P. and K. Nickul (eds.) 1969. *The Lapps today, in Finland, Norway and Sweden, Volume II.* Oslo–Bergen–Tromsø: Universitetsforlaget.

Homme, L. R. (ed.) 1969. *Nordisk nykolonialisme: samiske problem i dag.* Oslo: Det norske samlaget (Orion Debatt no. 91).

Ingold, T. 1973. Social and economic problems of Finnish Lapland. *Polar Record* 16, 105: 809–826.

Ingold, T. 1974a. Entrepreneur and protagonist: two faces of a political career. *Journal of Peace Research* XI, 3: 179–188. Oslo: Universitetsforlaget.

Ingold, T. 1974b. On reindeer and men. *Man* (N.S.) 9: 523–538.

Ingold, T. 1975. *The social organization of a Finnish Lapp community: the Skolts of Sevettijärvi.* Unpublished doctoral dissertation: University of Cambridge.

Ingold, T. n.d.a. Statistical husbandry: chance, probability and choice in a reindeer management economy. Paper presented at the session on 'Mathematics and statistics in social anthropology ", Decennial Conference of the A.S.A., Oxford, 1973.

Ingold, T. n.d.b. The rationalization of reindeer management among Finnish Lapps. Paper presented at the SSRC symposium on ' The future of traditional " primitive " societies', Cambridge, December 1974.

Isotalo, A. 1971. Poron luonnonvaraisten rehukasvien ravintoarvosta (The value of the natural fodder plants for reindeer feeding). *Lapin Tutkimusseuran Vuosikirja* XII: 28–45. Kemi.

Itkonen, T. I. 1931. Koltan ja Kuolanlappalaisia Satuja. *Memoires de la Société Finno-Ougrienne* 60. Helsinki.

Itkonen, T. L.1948. *Suomen Lappalaiset vuoteen 1945* (2 vols.). Porvoo: WSOY.

Itkonen, T. I. 1958. *Koltan ja Kuolanlapin sanakirja* (Wörterbuch des Kolta- und Kolalaplischen). 2 vols. Suomalais-Ugrilainen Seura (Soc. Finno-Ougrienne). Helsinki.

Kärenlampi, L. 1973. Suomen poronhoitoalueen jäkälämaiden kunto, jäkälämäärät, ja tuottoarviot vuonna 1972. *Poromies* 1973, 3: 15–19. Rovaniemi.

KM (Komiteanmietintö) 1971. Inarin, Enontekiön ja Utsjoen vesirajatoimikunnan täydennetty ja tarkistettu mietintö. *Komiteanmietintö* 1971: B69. Helsinki.

KM (Komiteanmietintö) 1971. Saamelaisten koulutuksen kehittämistoimikunnan mietintö. *Komiteanmietintö* 1971: B63. Helsinki.

Bibliography

KM (Komiteanmietintö) 1973. Saamelaiskomitean mietintö (2 vols.). *Komiteanmietintö* 1973: 46. Helsinki.

KM (Komiteanmietintö) 1973. Kolttatoimikunnan mietintö. *Komiteanmietintö* 1973: 69. Helsinki.

Koutonen, J. 1972. Kolttasaamelaisten sosiaalisten olojen kehitykseen vaikuttavia tekijöitä. *Sairaanhoidon Vuosikirja* 1972: 261–294. Helsinki.

Küng, A. 1970. *Samemakt!* Stockholm: Raben & Sjögren.

Lee, R. B. 1968. What hunters do for a living, or, how to make out on scarce resources. Ch. 4 in Lee, R. B. and DeVore, I. (eds.): *Man the hunter*. Chicago: Aldine.

Lewin, T. (ed.) 1971. Introduction to the biological characteristics of the Skolt Lapps. *Suomen hammaslääkäriseuran toimituksia* 67, suppl. 1. Helsinki.

Lewin, T. and A. W. Eriksson 1970. Scandinavian IBP/HA investigations in 1967–1969. *Arctic Anthropology* 7, 1: 63–69. University of Wisconsin.

Linkola, M. 1973. The snowmobile in Lapland – its economic and social effects. pp. 127–134 in Berg, G. (ed.): *Circumpolar problems*. Oxford: Pergamon.

Mikkola, J. J. 1941. Kolttakylän arkisto. *Lapin Sivistysseuran Julkaisuja*, 8. Helsinki: WSOY.

Müller-Wille, L. 1971. Snowmobiles among Lapps. *Nord-Nytt* 4: 271–287. Lyngby.

Müller-Wille, L. and O. Aikio 1971. Die Auswirkungen der Mechanisierung der Rentierwirtschaft in der lappischen Gemeinde Utsjoki/Ohcijohka (Finnish Lapland). *Terra* 83, 3: 179–185. Helsinki.

Müller-Wille, L. and P. J. Pelto 1971. Technological change and its impact in arctic regions: Lapps introducing snowmobiles into reindeer herding (Utsjoki and Inari, northern Finland). *Polarforschung* VII, 41: 142–148. Münster.

Naukkarinen, A. 1969. Population development in northern Finland 1950–65 with particular reference to regional age and sex composition features as explaining migration and natural population changes and as providing a basis for classification by demographic development. *Oulun Yliopiston Maantieteen Laitoksen Julkaisuja* 26. Oulu.

Nickul, E. 1968. Suomen saamelaiset vuonna 1962 (the Finnish Lapps in 1962). *Tilastokatsauksia* (Finnish Bulletin of Statistics) 1968, 7: 59–63. Helsinki.

Nickul, K. 1948. The Skolt Lapp community Suenjelsijd during the year 1938. *Acta Lapponica* V. Nordiska Museet, Stockholm.

Nickul, K. 1950. The Finnish Lapps in wartime and after. *Man* 50: 57–60.

Nickul, K. 1953. Huomioita poronhoidosta Suonikylässä 1800–luvulla. *Virittäjä* 57: 76–81. Helsinki.

Nickul, K. 1956. Changes in a Lappish Community: a reflection of political events and state attitude. *Studia Ethnographica Upsaliensia* XI: 88–95. Uppsala.

Nickul, K. 1970. *Saamelaiset kansana ja kansalaisina*. Suomalaisen kirjallisuuden seuran toimituksia 297. Helsinki.

Nickul, K. 1973. Suenjelin kolttayhdyskunnan elämästä. *Memoires de la Société Finno-Ougrienne* 150: 238–244. Helsinki.

Nordiska Udredningsserie 1965. Femte nordiska samekonferensen i Tana, 1965. *Nordiska Udredningsserie* 1965, 13. Stockholm.

Bibliography

Nordiska Udredningsserie 1969. Sjätte nordiska samekonferensen i Hetta, 1968. *Nordiska Udredningsserie* 1969, 6. Stockholm.

Otnes, P. 1970. *Den samiske nasjon. Interesseorganisasjoner i samenes politiske historie.* Maxipax 12. Oslo.

Paine, R. 1957. Coast Lapp society I. *Tromsø Museums Skrifter* IV. Tromsø.

Paine, R. 1960. Emergence of the village as a social unit in a coast Lappish fjord. *American Anthropologist* 62: 1004–1017.

Paine, R. 1965a. Coast Lapp society II. *Tromsø Museums Skifter* IV, 2. Tromsø.

Paine, R. 1965b. Herding and husbandry. Two basic distinctions in the analysis of reindeer management (Lapps of Kautokeino). *Folk* 6, 1: 83–88. Copenhagen.

Paine, R. 1970. Lappish decisions, partnerships, information management, and sanctions – a nomadic pastoral adaptation. *Ethnology* 9: 52–67.

Paine, R. 1971a. Animals as capital: comparisons among northern nomadic herders and hunters. *Anthropalogical Quarterly*, 44: 157–172.

Paine, R. 1971b. A theory of patronage and brokerage. Chapter 2 in Paine, R. (ed.): *Patrons and brokers in the east Arctic.* Newfoundland Social and Economic Papers No. 2. Memorial University of Newfoundland.

Paine, R. 1972. The herd management of Lapp reindeer pastoralists. *Journal of Asian and African Studies* VII: 76–87.

Paltto, K. 1973. *Saamelaiset.* Helsinki: Tammi.

Pehrson, R. N. 1954. The Lappish herding leader: a structural analysis. *American Anthropologist* 56: 1076–1080.

Pehrson, R. N. 1957. *The bilateral network of social relations in Könkämä Lapp district.* Indiana University Research Centre in Anthropology, Folklore and Linguistics, Publication III. Bloomington.

Pelto P. J. 1962. *Individualism in Skolt Lapp society.* Kansatieteellinen Arkisto 16, Suomen Muinaismuistoyhdistys. Helsinki.

Pelto, P. J. 1973. *The snowmobile revolution: technology and social change in the Arctic.* Cummings Publishing Company inc. Menlo Park, Calif.

Pelto, P. J., M. Linkola and P. Sammallahti 1969. The snowmobile revolution in Lapland. *Journal de la Société Finno-ougrienne* 69, 3. Helsinki.

Pelto, P. J. and L. Müller-Wille 1972. Snowmobiles: technological revolution in the Arctic. pp. 165–199 in Bernard, R. H. and Pelto, P. J. (eds): *Technology and social change.* New York: Macmillan.

Pelto, P. J. and L. Müller-Wille 1973. Reindeer herding and snowmobiles: aspects of a technological revolution (Utsjoki and Sevettijärvi, Finnish Lapland). *Folk* 14/15: 119–144. Copenhagen.

Piirola, J. 1972. The Inari region of Finnish Lapland. *Fennia* 111 Helsinki.

Robbins, R. H. 1973. Alcohol and the identity struggle: some effects of economic change on interpersonal relations. *American Anthropologist* 75: 99–122.

Rudie, I. 1969. Household organization: adaptive process and restrictive form. A viewpoint on economic change. *Folk* 11/12: 185–200. Copenhagen.

S A (Suomen Asetuskokoelma) 1955. Laki eräiden kolttien asuttamisesta. *Suomen Asetuskokoelma*: 273. Helsinki. 20.5.1955.

S A (Suomen Asetuskokoelma) 1969. Porotilalaki. *Suomen Asetuskokoelma*: 590. Helsinki 19.9.1969. Laki eräiden kolttien asuttamisesta annetun lain muuttamisesta. *Suomen Asetuskokoelma*: 592. Helsinki 19.9.1969.

Bibliography

Kolttien maanjärjestelylaki. *Suomen Asetuskokoelma*: 593. Helsinki 19. 9.1969.

Sahlins, M. 1972. *Stone age economics.* London: Tavistock.

Seitamo, L. 1972. Intellectual functions in Skolt and northern Finnish children with special reference to cultural factors. *Inter-Nord,* 12: 338–343. Centre d'études arctiques. Paris: Mouton.

Smith, L. 1972. The mechanical dog team: a study of the Skidoo in the Canadian Arctic. *Arctic Anthropology,* IX, 1: 1–9. University of Wisconsin.

Solem, E. 1933. *Lappiske rettsstudier.* Inst. for sammenlignende kulturforskning. Serie B, skrifter XXIV. Oslo.

Sturdy, D. A. 1975. Some reindeer economies in prehistoric Europe. pp. 55–95 in Higgs, E. S. (ed.): *Palaeoeconomy.* Cambridge: University Press.

Tanner, V. 1929. Antropogeografiska studier inom Petsamo-området I: Skolt Lapparna. *Fennia* 49. Helsinki.

United Nations 1945. *Charter of the United Nations.* U.S. Department of State Publications no. 2353. Conference Series 74.

Vaarama, P. 1973. Saamelaisnuorten ammatintoiveet, koulutussuunitelmat ja työelämään sijoittuminen. *Turun Yliopiston Sosiologian Laitos Monisteita* 59. Turku.

Valkeapää, N. A. 1971. *Terveisiä Lapista.* Helsinki: Otava.

Varo, M. 1969. Poronjalostuksen ongelmia. *Poromies* 1969, 5: 14–19. Rovaniemi.

Vorren, Ø. 1965. Researches on wild reindeer catching constructions in the Norwegian Lapp area. pp. 513–536 in Hvarfner, H. (ed.): *Hunting and fishing.* Luleå: Norbottens museum.

Vorren, Ø. 1973. Some trends of the transition from hunting to nomadic economy in Finnmark. pp. 185–194 in Berg, G. (ed.): *Circumpolar problems.* Oxford: Pergamon.

Vorren, Ø. and Manker, E. 1962. *Lapp life and customs.* Oxford: University Press.

Whitaker, I. 1955. Social relations in a nomadic Lappish community. *Samiske Samlinger* 2. Oslo.

Whitaker, I. 1956. Declining transhumance as an index of culture change. *Studia Ethnographica Upsaliensia* XI (Arctica). Uppsala.

Wynne-Edwards, V. C. 1965. Social organization as a population regulator. *Zoological Society of London Symposia* 14: 173–78.

Guide to further reading

Major historical sources on the Lapps:

Bosworth, J. *A description of Europe, and the voyages of Othere and Wulfstan* (from original by Alfred the Great). London 1853.

Leem, K. An account of the Laplanders of Finnmark. In J. Pinkerton (ed.) *Voyages and travels,* vol. I. London 1808.

Magnus, O. *Historia de gentibus septentrionalibus.* Rome 1555.

Schefferus, J. *Lapponia.* Latin orig. Frankfurt 1673, English trans. Oxford 1674. Republished as *Acta Lapponica* VIII Uppsala 1956.

General works on the Lapps available in English include:

Collinder, B. *The Lapps.* New York 1949.

Gjessing, G. Changing Lapps (see main bibliography).

Manker, E. *Lapland and the Lapps.* Stockholm 1953.

Manker, E. *The nomadism of the Swedish Mountain Lapps.* Acta Lapponica VII. Stockholm 1953.

Nesheim, A. *Introducing the Lapps.* Oslo 1963.

Ruong, I. *The Lapps in Sweden.* Stockholm 1967.

Vorren, Ø. and E. Manker *Lapp life and customs* (see main bibliography). For specific monographs on Lappish societies, see references in main bibliography to Dikkanen (1965), Nickul (1948), Paine (1957, 1965a), Pehrson (1957), Pelto (1962) and Whitaker (1955),

Symposia dealing wholly or in part with problems in relation to Lappish ethnography:

Berg, G. (ed.). *Circumpolar problems.* Oxford: Pergamon 1973.

Instituttet for sammenlignende kulturforskning: *Lapps and Norsemen in olden times.* Oslo: Universitetsforlaget. 1967.

Hvarfner, H. (ed.). *Hunting and fishing.* Norbottens Museum, Luleå. 1965.

Studia Ethnographica Upsaliensia, vol. XI (Arctica). Uppsala 1956.

Studia Ethnographica Upsaliensia, vol. XXI (Lapponica). Lund 1964.

Vorren, Ø. (ed.). *Norway north of 65.* London: Allen & Unwin 1960.

General and review articles on Lappish ethnography:

Anderson, R. T. Acculturation and indigenous economy as factors in Lapp culture change. *Anthropological papers of the University of Alaska,* 7, 1: 1–22. 1958.

264

Guide to further reading

Bergsland, K. Norwegian research on the language and folklore of the Lapps. Part I, language. *J.R.A.I.* 80: 79–85. 1950.

Christiansen, R. Th. Norwegian research on the language and folklore of the Lapps. Part II. mythology and folklore. *J.R.A.I.* 80: 89–95. 1950.

Gjessing, G. Norwegian contributions to Lapp ethnology. *J.R.A.I.* 77: 47–60. 1947.

Gjessing, G. Prehistoric social groups in North Norway. *Proc. Prehist. Soc.* 21: 84–91. 1955.

Hultkrants, A. Swedish research on the religion and folklore of the Lapps. *J.R.A.I.* 85: 81–99. 1955.

Itkonen, T. I. The Lapps of Finland. *Southwest. Jnl. of Anthrop.* 7: 32–68. 1951.

Lowie, R. H. A note on Lapp culture history. *Southwest. Jnl. of Anthrop.* 1: 447–454. 1945.

Manker, E. Swedish contributions to Lapp ethnography. *J.R.A.I.* 82: 39–54. 1953.

Contemporary Lappish problems and the minority issue:

Eidheim, H. *Aspects of the Lappish minority situation* (see main bibliography).

Ingold, T. Social and economic problems of Finnish Lapland. *Polar Record* 16, 105. 1973 (see main bibliography).

The Lapps Today in Finland, Norway and Sweden, vol. I (R. G. P. Hill, ed.) and vol. II (R. G. P. Hill and K. Nickul, eds.) (see main bibliography). Vol. II contains a bibliography of works on the Lapps published in the decade 1950–60.

Nickul, K. Report on Lapp affairs (abridged translation of original Finnish State Commission report). *Fennia* 76, 3. Helsinki 1952.

Snell, H. G. and T. Snell. Samish responses to processes of national integration. pp. 165–184 in J. Boissevain and J. Friedl (eds.). *Beyond the community: social processes in Europe.* University of Amsterdam: Dept. of educational science of the Netherlands.

Monographs and articles on other reindeer/caribou herding or hunting peoples:

Chukchi (Siberia):

Bogoras, W. The Chukchee Jesup North Pacific Expedition, vol. 7 (3 parts). *Am. Mus. Nat. Hist., Mem* 11, Brill, Leiden, Netherlands. 1904–1909.

Leeds, A. Reindeer herding and Chukchi social institutions. pp. 87–128 in A. Leeds and A. P. Vayda (eds.): *Man, Culture and Animals.* Am. Assoc. for the Advancement of Science Pub. 78. Washington D.C. 1965.

Tungus (Siberia):

Shirokogoroff, S. M. *Social organization of the northern Tungus.* Shanghai: Commercial Press. 1933.

Shirokogoroff, S. M. *Psychomental complex of the Tungus.* London: Kegan Paul. 1935.

Guide to further reading

North American Indians and Eskimo:

Balikci, A. *The Netsilik Eskimo.* Garden City, New York: Natural History Press. 1967.

Gubser, N. J. The Nunamiut Eskimos: hunters of Caribou. New Haven: Yale University Press. 1965.

Henriksen, G. *Hunters in the barrens: the Naskapi on the edge of the white man's world.* Newfoundland social and economic studies no. 12 Memorial University of Newfoundland. 1973.

Mowat, F. *People of the Deer.* London: Michael Joseph 1952.

Spencer, R. F. *The North Alaskan Eskimo: a study in ecology and society.* Smithsonian Institution, Bureau of American Ethnology Bulletin 171. Washington: Government Printing Office. 1959.

Index

administration, 7–8, 9–10, 227–8, 252
  Communal, 231, 233, 243; of build-
    ing, 142, 149; of education, 207;
    of planning, 209, 224–5; of wel-
    fare, 122
  provincial, 76–7, 83–4, 222, 225
  recognition of Skolt assembly by,
    213, 220
  see also: Forestry Authority; roads,
    Department of
alcoholic drinks
  consumption of, see under drinking
  sale of, 117, 170
Asp, E., 12
assembly of householders
  meetings of, 216–18, 227, 233–4,
    241–2; compared with paliskunta
    meetings, 217–18
  in Sevettijärvi resettlement area, 76,
    148, 200, 213–14, 220–1
  in Suenjel, 15, 98, 147, 213
  see also: headman
avoidance relationships, see under neigh-
    bourhood

band organization, see under siidat
banks
  at Ivalo, 117, 166, 170
  payment by instalments through,
    162, 164
  representatives of, present at separa-
    tions, 42, 55–7, 163, 166, 170
  as sources of cash, 117, 162, 166, 170
bars
  drinking in, 112, 170–1, 184
  employment of Skolts in, see under
    casual labour
  establishment of, 111–12, 184
  as settings for youth activities, 177,
    182, 183, 184
berries
  consumption of, 106–7, 160–1
  species of, 106
  trading of, 106–7, 161
  see also: gathering

big-men, of reindeer management, 69–73
  association positions of, 70–1, 80
  consumption of meat by, 64, 160
  domination of summer separations by,
    71, 73, 79
  hunting of peurat by, 64, 71
  investment in peurat by, 38, 66–7,
    69, 72–3
  rivalry between, 71, 78, 84, 87
  see also: herding; hunting; paliskunnat;
    peurat
brokerage, see under headman; merchants

calves
  attachment to mothers of, 21
  birth and survival rates of, 30, 36,
    64–6
  generation of peurat from, see under
    peurat
  loss of, 27, 57, 75, 83, 87
  numbering of, 50
  recorded numbers of, 30, 65–6
  summer-marking of, 57–9, 79, 83
  see also: reindeer
cars
  as indicators of household status, 207
  operated by youths, 178, 180
  see also: driving
cash in the pocket
  expenditure of, 159, 163–6, 169–72;
    at separations, 55, 166; by youths,
    171, 174
  represents irregular component of
    money income, 165, 167
  sources of, see under banks; post-
    office
  see also: drinking; driving; gambling
casual labour, 114–21
  allocation of income from, 159, 163–
    7; to snowmobile payments, 164,
    168–9
  fathers and sons together in, 69, 70,
    154
  hired through patronage of Forest
    Warden, 114, 205

Index

electrification *(cont.)*
  and settlement planning, 209
  also, 241
emigration, *see under* migration
entrepreneurship, constraints on, for
  Skolts, 110–11
estates (defined, 136):
  'colonist estates', 99–101, 226;
    association of holders of, 100,
    214
  'reindeer estates', 224–5
  'Skolt estates', 6, 102, 223–4, 225;
    inheritance of, 150
  see also: legislation
ethnicity
  in associational reindeer politics, 76,
    78–9, 80, 85, 87, 222–3, 241,
    248, 249
  and cultural identity, 249–50
  as a political asset, 218–19
  and social boundaries, 247–8
  Skolt *v.* Lapp, 241–2
  see also: culture; Lappish movement
ethnographic present, xi
evacuations, of Skolts during the Second
  World War, 5, 7, 27, 253
exchange trade
  with the Norwegian merchant, 9, 27–
    8, 39, 106, 158–60, 161; in cloud-
    berries, 106–7; in ptarmigan, 104;
    in reindeer, 27–8, 39, 41, 42, 86
  with Russian *pomores*, 4

family areas, in Suenjel, *see under* Suenjel
  siita
fighting
  abhorrence of, 189
  in the dwelling, 192, 196
  by Norwegians, 184
Finnish colonists
  as landowners, *see under* estates
  reindeer management by, 21, 25, 85
  settlement of, 4, 6, 25, 85
  see also: 'old inhabitants'
fish
  as food, 90, 160
  population dynamics of, 90–1
  species and habits of, 92
  see also: fishing; fishing waters
fishing, 90–102
  boats for, 94; with outboard motors,
    98, 157
  for salmon, 96, 97
  seasons for, 92–4
  for sport, 96, 176
  stigma attached to, 91, 94, 160

in Suenjel, 24, 96, 98
  techniques of: angling, 96, 176; gill-
    netting, 92–4, 95; seine-sweeping,
    91, 94, 95
  under ice, 92–3, 95, 96
  see also: fish; fishing cabins; fishing
    waters
fishing cabins, 96–7
  design of, 96
  establishment of, 96, 135
  location of, in the resettlement area,
    92, 93, 96
  rights to waters beside, 98, 103
  in Suenjel, 4, 96
  use of, 97; in berry-picking season,
    97, 106; to escape from neigh-
    bourhood, 193; as permanent
    dwellings, 149; in relation to
    settlement planning, 208–9; as
    'summer cottages', 97, 100, 249
fishing waters
  allocation of rights over, 98–102,
    103
  stocking of, 91, 98, 102
  quality of, 90
  see also: fish, fishing
flaglines, 48–9, 58, 82–3
  see also: herding, in summer;
    separation fences
footpaths, to fishing cabins, 96–7
Forest Warden
  accommodation of, 144, 201
  as patron, 114, 204–5
  position of, 10, 114; in connection
    with the 'Trading and Tourist
    Centre', 111, 114, 203
  selection of logging sites by, 103,
    107–8
  see also: Forestry Authority; logging
Forestry Authority
  as employer of casual labour, 107, 117
  management of land and water
    resources by, 10, 100, 107–8, 213
  position of Forest Warden in, 10,
    204–5
  see also: Forest Warden; logging
frontier patrol station, 113, 124, 150,
  181

gambling
  competitive display in, 172
  redistribution of hard cash in, 162,
    165–6, 170
  at separations, 55, 57
gathering, 106–7
  apportionment of grounds for, 103

Index